With My Best Wishes,

John J. Nowell.

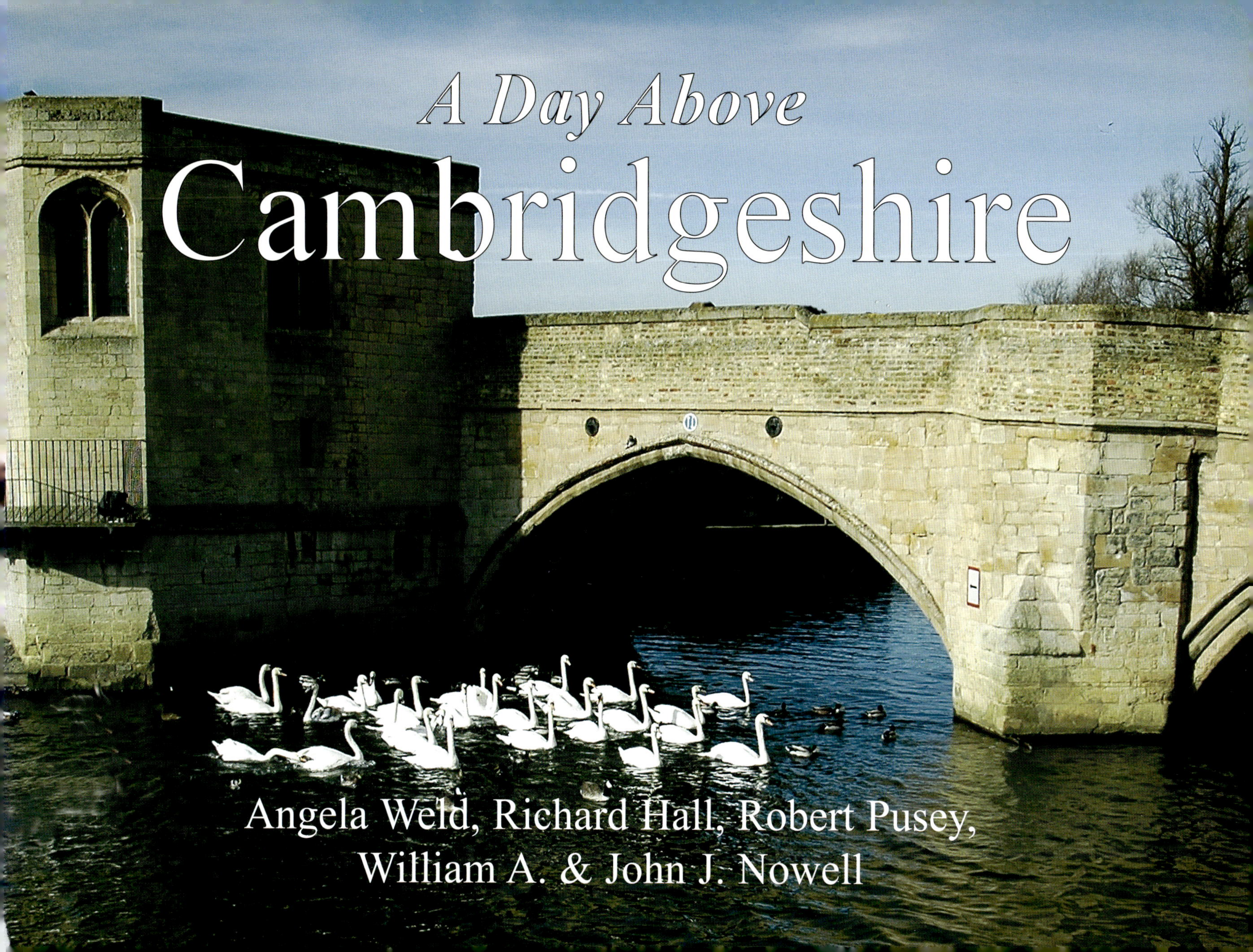

A Day Above
Cambridgeshire

Angela Weld, Richard Hall, Robert Pusey,
William A. & John J. Nowell

Foreword.

The natural beauty of Cambridgeshire is renowned. Perhaps because of the vast changes that occur in the colours and shapes during the year. The vibrant yellows of the rape crops vying with the varied greens of newly grown cereal crops are complimented by the soft hues of browns and purples neatly carved with ditches, lanes and byways. This timeless scene comes to life as the warmth of spring arrives to be followed by the summer haze softening the horizon and deepening the colours to a ripened state. Autumn creeps in often unnoticed other than the bustle of harvesting machines quickly followed by ploughing new lines into the fields to prepare for the quiet calm of winter, which increases with intensity as the temperature drops and the rain falls to potentially shroud the countryside in cloud and mist. All this I view from the cockpit of the Grace Spitfire as I navigate over the Cambridgeshire countryside soaking up all that my eyes can take in. It is a joy to to have this experience re-created in this superb book of photographs depicting all that one has seen during the year for all to see.

Carolyn Grace,
The Grace Spitfire,
www.ml407.co.uk
Photographed by Darren Harbar.

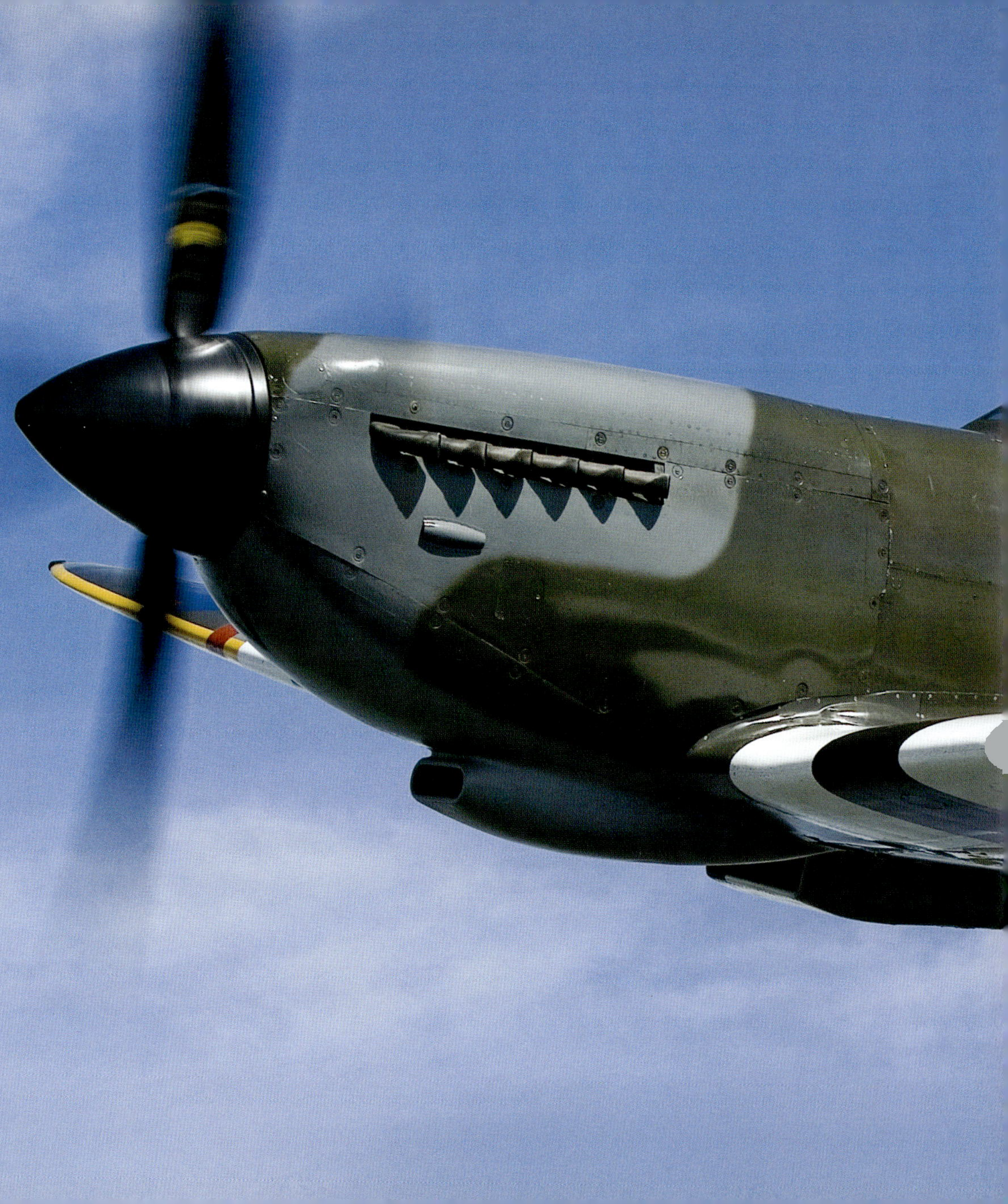

A Day Above
Cambridgeshire

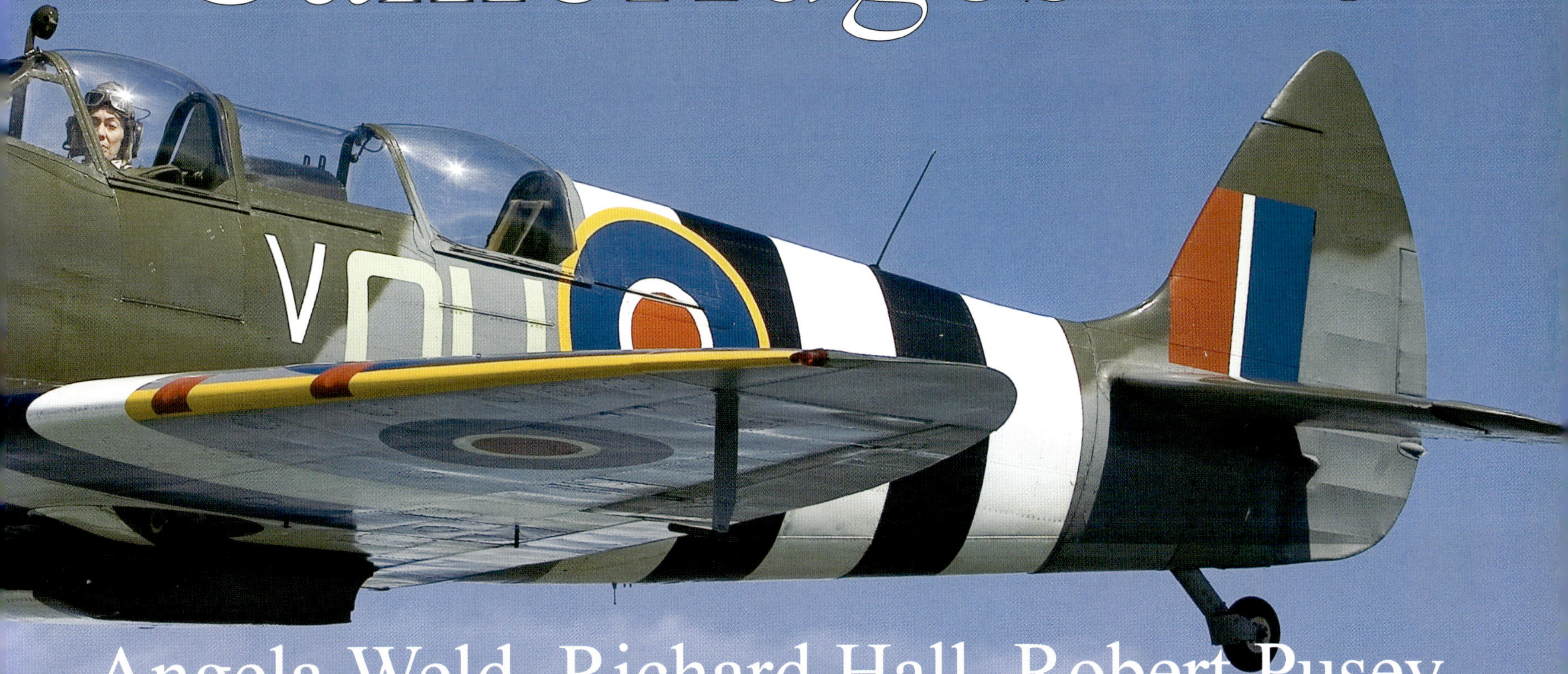

Angela Weld, Richard Hall, Robert Pusey,
William A. & John J. Nowell.

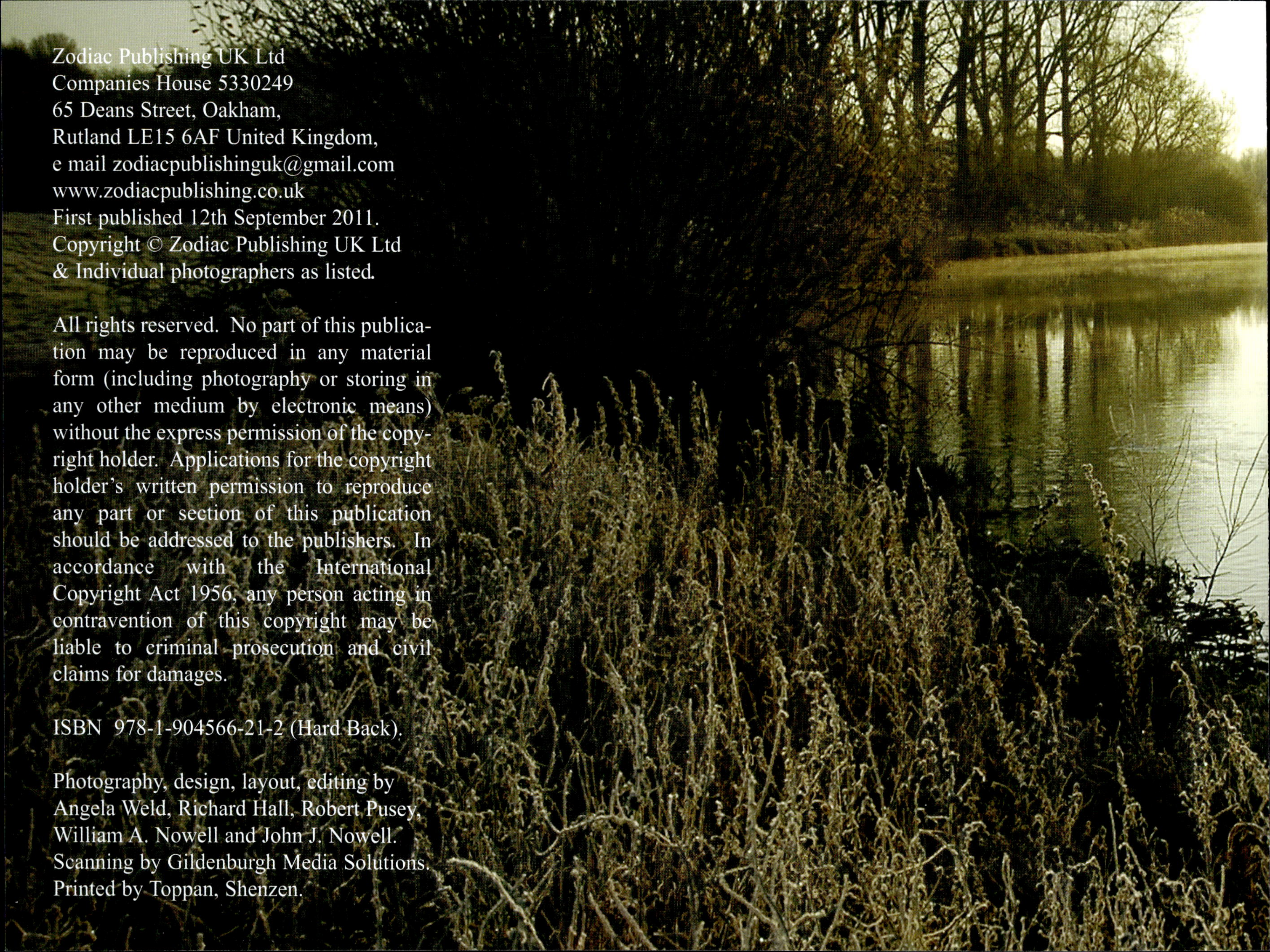

Zodiac Publishing UK Ltd
Companies House 5330249
65 Deans Street, Oakham,
Rutland LE15 6AF United Kingdom,
e mail zodiacpublishinguk@gmail.com
www.zodiacpublishing.co.uk
First published 12th September 2011.

ISBN 978-1-904566-21-2 (Hard Back).

Photography, design, layout, editing by
Angela Weld, Richard Hall, Robert Pusey,
William A. Nowell and John J. Nowell.
Scanning by Gildenburgh Media Solutions.
Printed by Toppan, Shenzen.

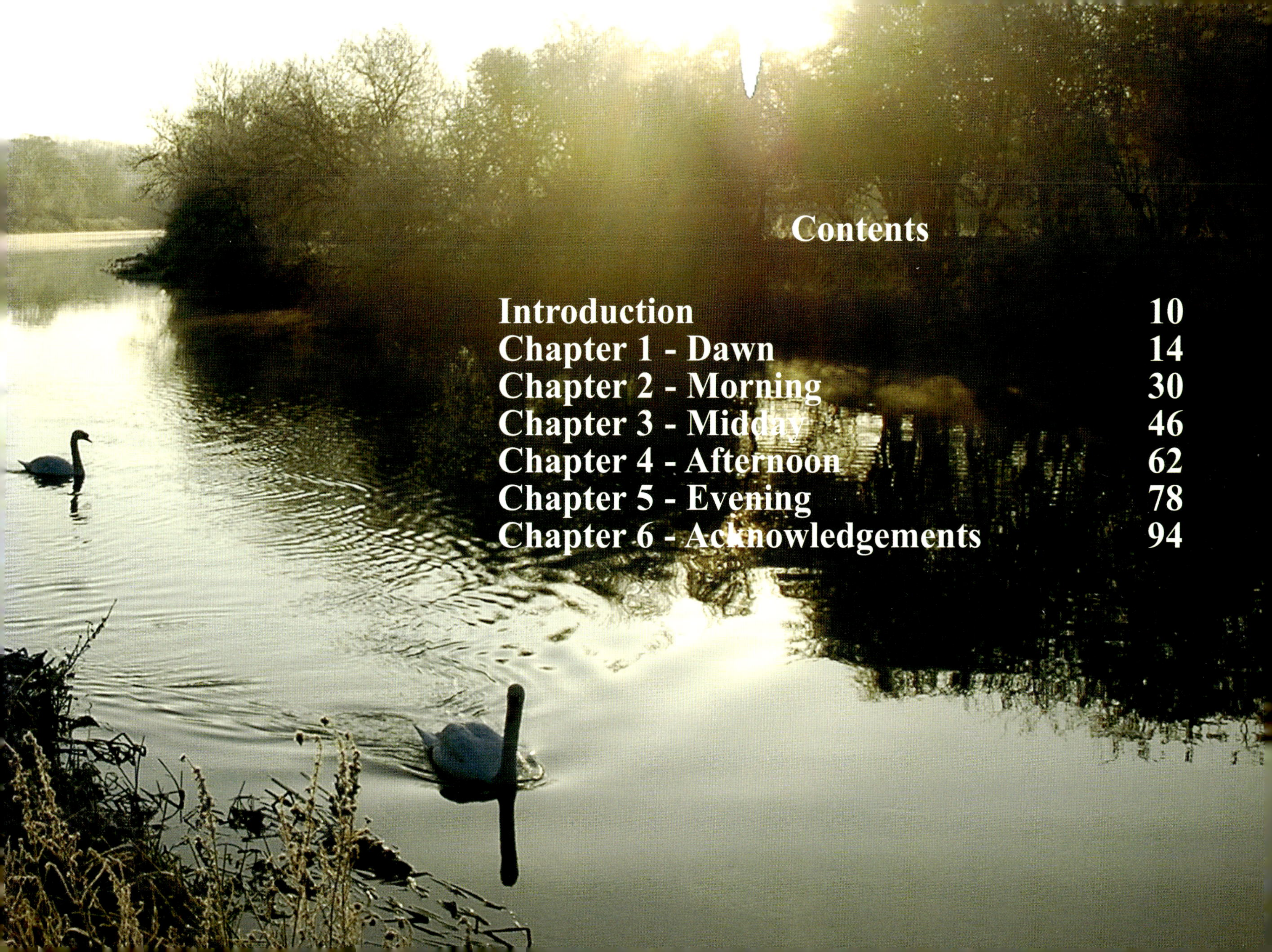

Contents

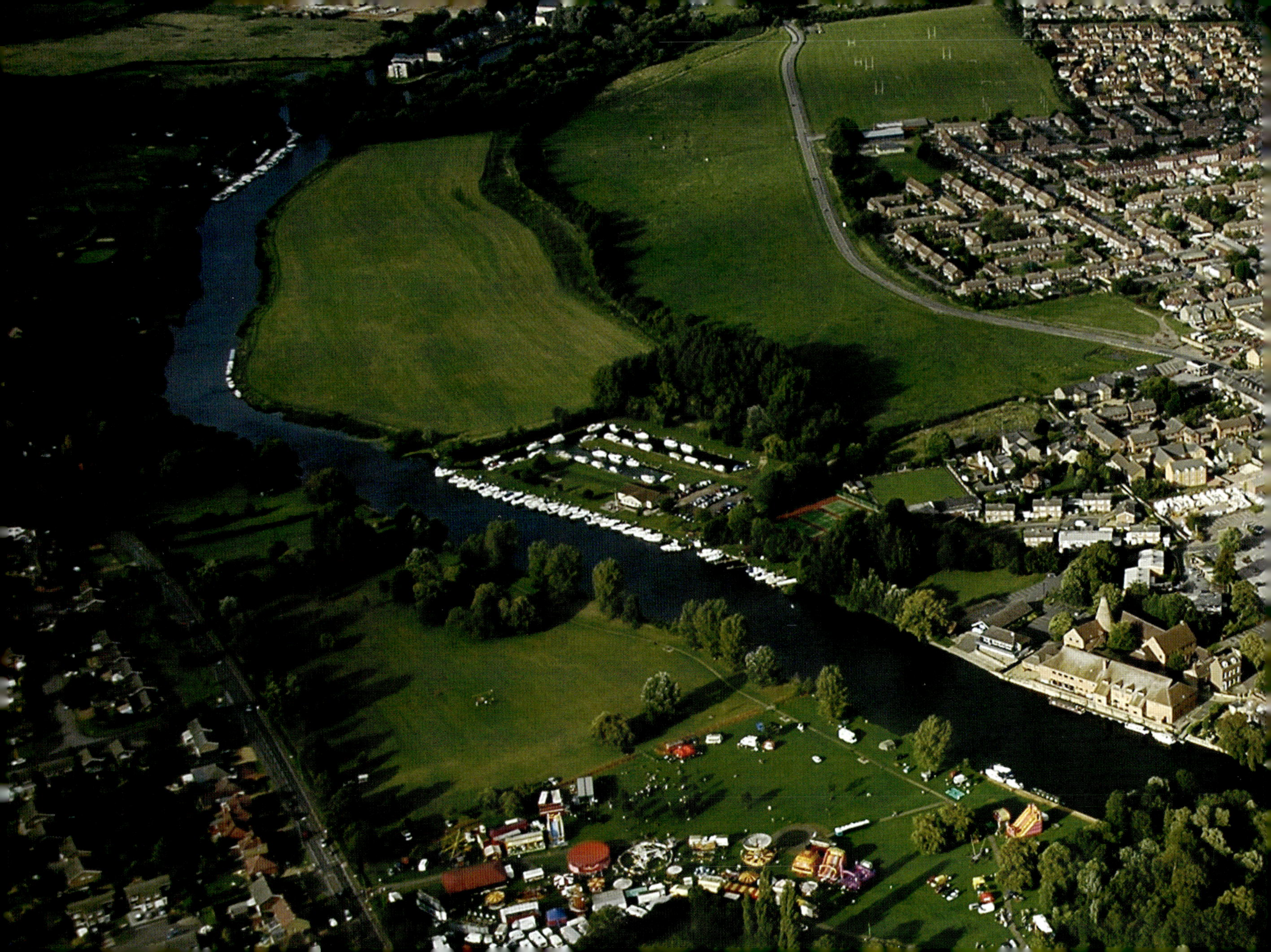

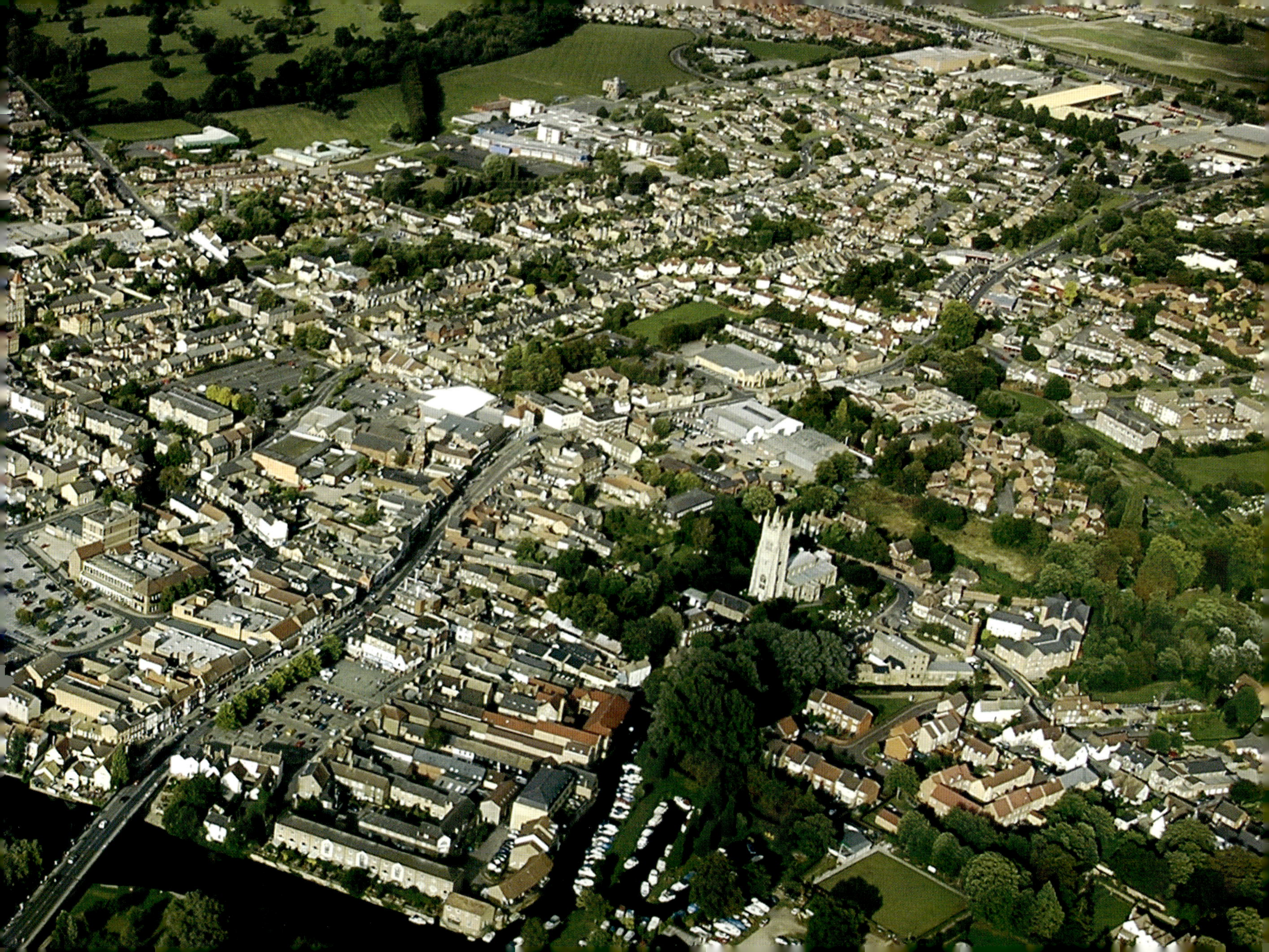

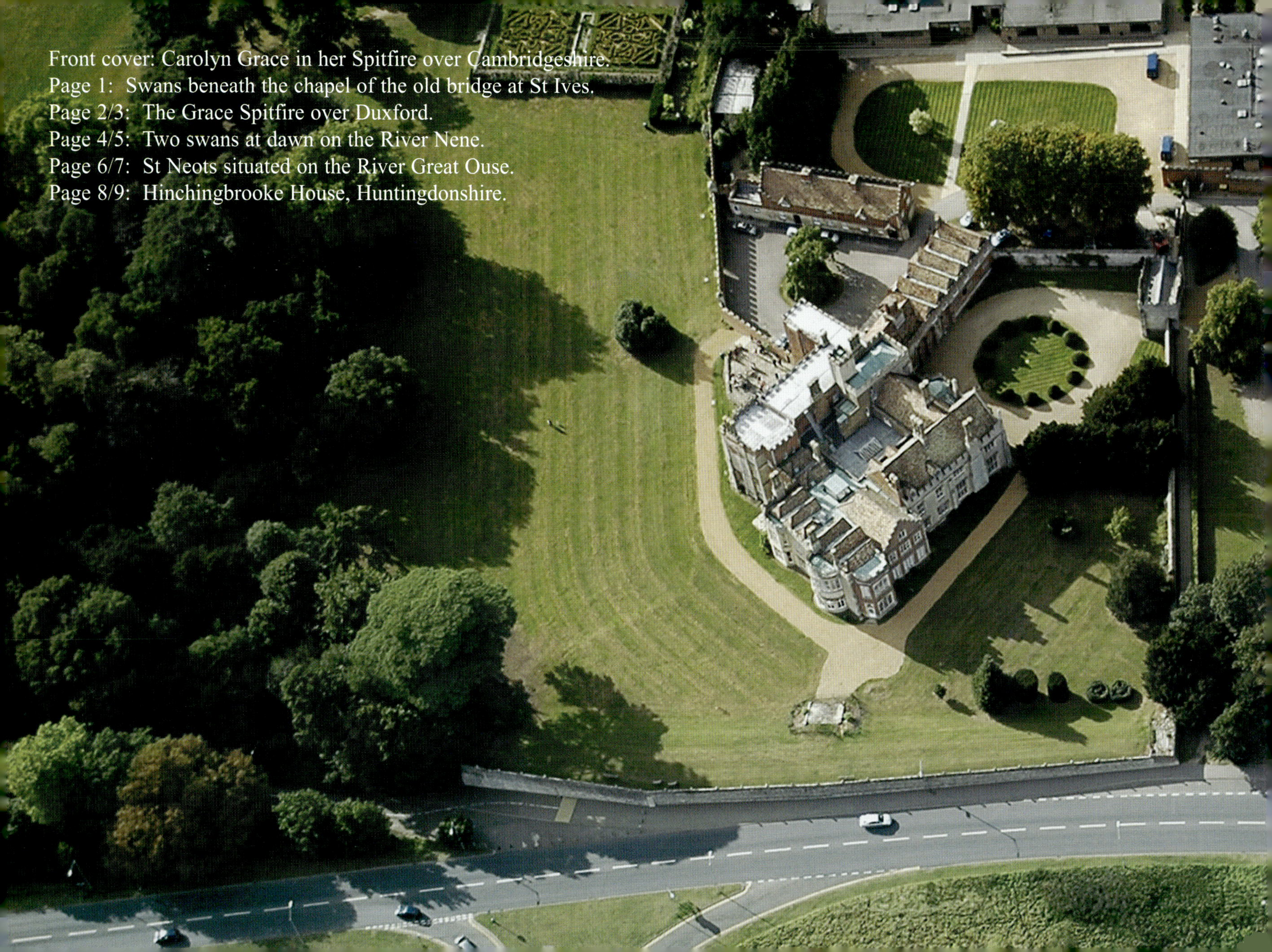

Front cover: Carolyn Grace in her Spitfire over Cambridgeshire.
Page 1: Swans beneath the chapel of the old bridge at St Ives.
Page 2/3: The Grace Spitfire over Duxford.
Page 4/5: Two swans at dawn on the River Nene.
Page 6/7: St Neots situated on the River Great Ouse.
Page 8/9: Hinchingbrooke House, Huntingdonshire.

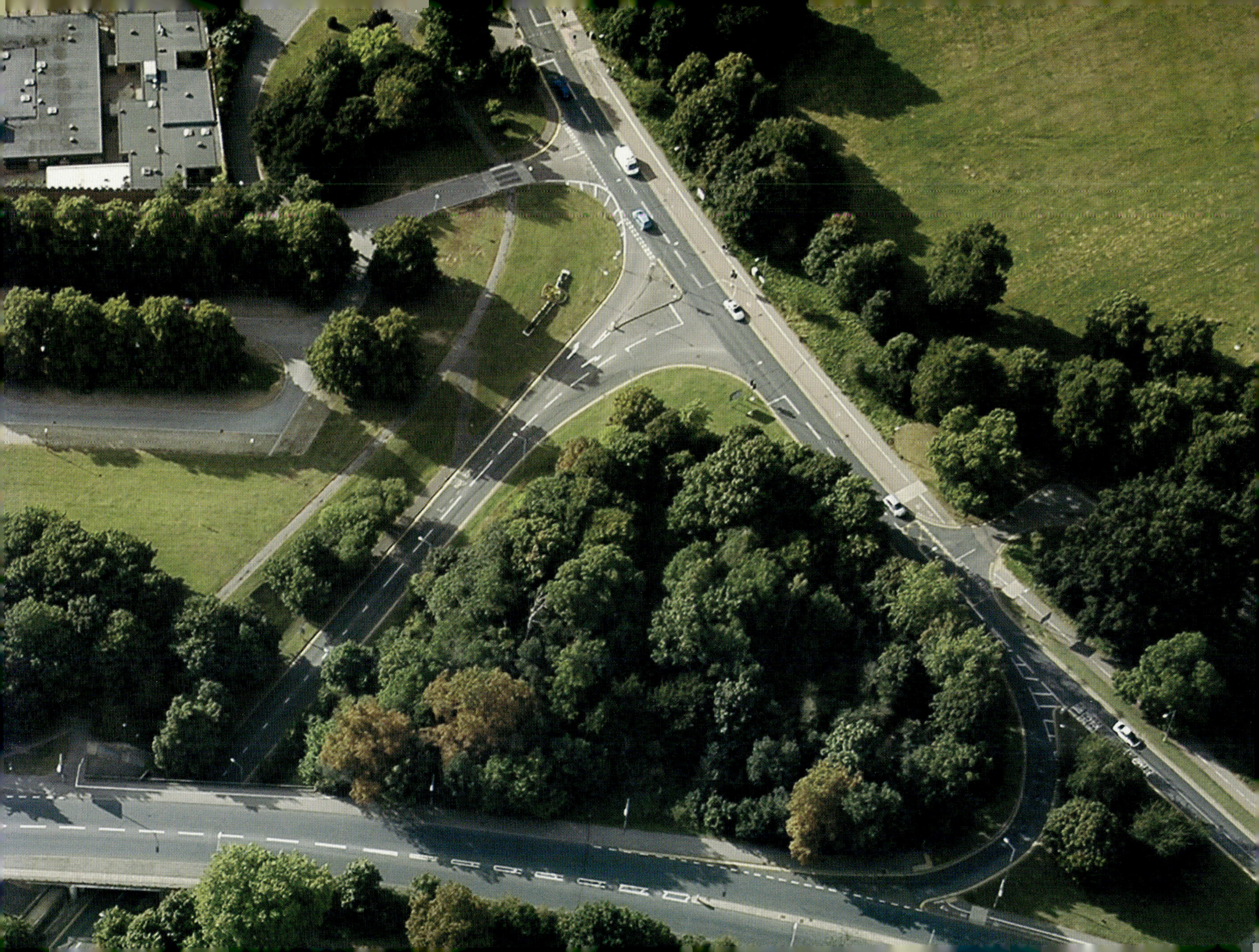

Introduction.

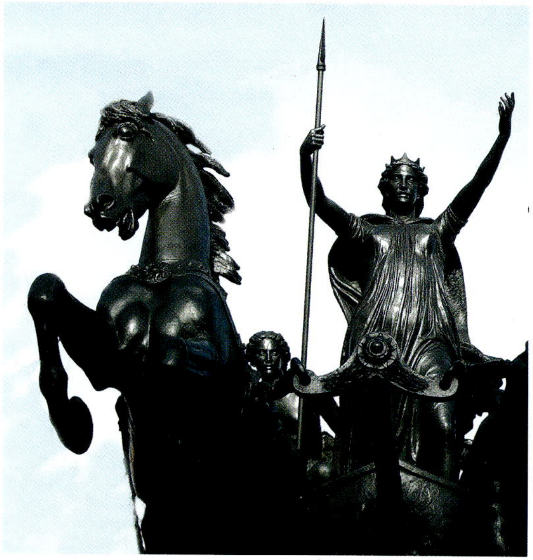

The modern County of Cambridgeshire is a fascinating blend of three original counties, traditional Cambridgeshire itself, the former county of Huntingdonshire and the Soke of Peterborough, formerly part of Northamptonshire. Cambridgeshire is a young landscape, once a collection of island settlements amongst the water-filled Fens and only visible since the start of serious drainage schemes begun during the Roman period. It was only after the last Ice Age, 10,000 years ago that men and women returned to the area again to occupy the 'islands' of Jurassic boulder clay and slowly transformed it into the landscape we see today. Excavations at Flag Fen near modern day Peterborough revealed a prehistoric wooden platform, built around 800 BC, to stand in shallow water. A visit to Wicken Fen, near Cambridge, visually shows how the landscape of reeds, grasses and trees would have looked 2,000 years ago when a very few people lived in the Fens. These people became skilled at fishing for eels, catching wildfowl, making reed dwellings, constructing well-built boats and were also able to grow some crops on the rich peat deposits. To the southeast were the graceful Gog Magog hills while further west of the Fens, the higher upland areas of what became Huntingdonshire were more widely populated, but there were no major towns of any size. The only evidence of a settlement in Cambridge that remains is the fortification now known as Castle Hill.

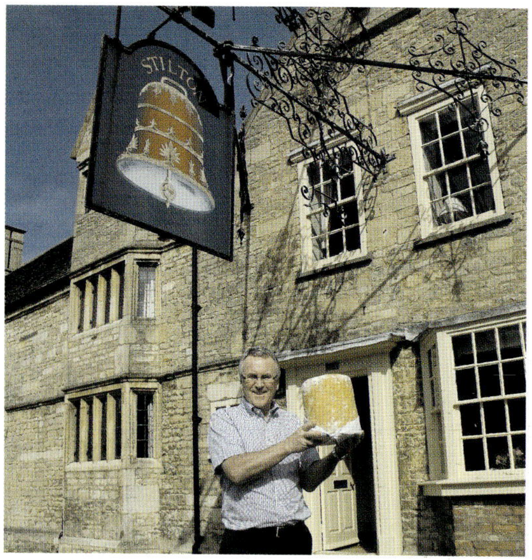

By the 1st century AD, the Trinovantes, Iceni and Catuvellauni Celtic tribes had established themselves in this region. After the Roman invasion in 43 AD, the tribes swore allegiance to Rome but in 60 AD, Prasutagas, Chieftain of the Iceni died and local centurions flogged his widow, Boudicca, and raped her daughters. The response was a bloody revolt with Boudicca leading the tribes in pursuit of the Roman 9th Legion across the Welland near Stamford to annihilate the entire Legion and going on to destroy Camulodunum, Verulamium and Londinium. 70,000 people died before the revolt was put down at Mancetter. With peace, the Romans commenced building their arrow straight roads and recognised the potential of Fens to be drained to become fertile land. The Via Devana linking Colchester with Lincoln crossed the River Granta where Castle Hill was enlarged as a Roman Fort named Duroliponte. Car Dyke, near present day Waterbeach, was a typical Roman dyke, but it was not until the 17th century that serious drainage was possible. The Romans had left in 400 AD to be replaced by the Saxons and Cambridge is named in the Anglo-Saxon Chronicle as 'Gratebrycge'. Vikings displaced the Saxons in 875 AD and Cambridge began to expand as a river-based trading station.

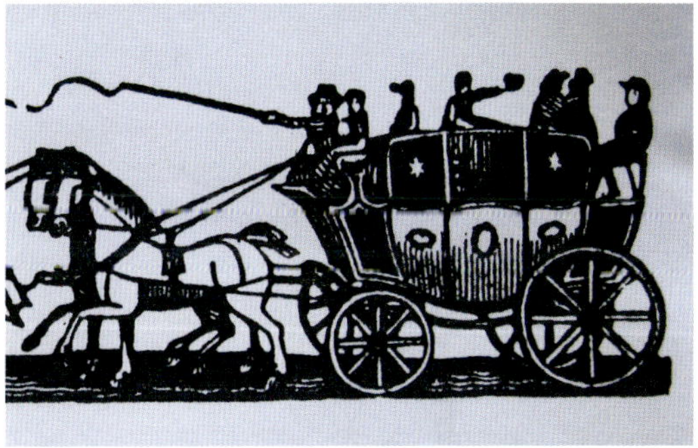

The development that became the counties of Cambridgeshire and Huntingdonshire began around 1000 AD when, in a gradual process, all England began to be divided into shires until there were forty shires. This process occurred after the re-conquest of the Danelaw by King Alfred the Great, who also established the navy and the first standard of English prose in the form of the Anglo-Saxon Chronicle – King Alfred's copy of the Chronicle is now in the library of Corpus Christi. The first capital of England, as a whole, was Winchester and it is here that the modern-day statue of King Alfred stands. Some historic shires were former independent kingdoms such as Sussex or Cornwall but Cambridgeshire and Huntingdonshire were formed based on groups of 'hundreds' centered on the principal towns – Cambridge and Huntingdon - which gave their names to the counties. In 1265, Simon de Montfort summoned representatives from each shire to form the first national parliament, which became the basis of our modern parliament.

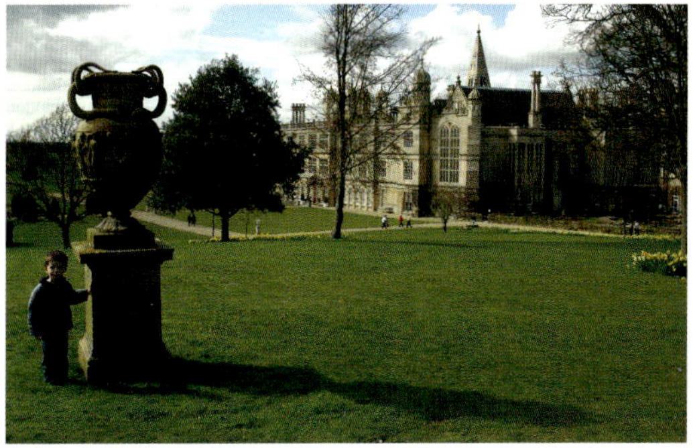

Cambridge University was founded in 1209 when a group of students left Oxford and settled in Cambridge. The oldest surviving college, Peterhouse, was founded in 1284. After the disruption of the Wars of the Roses, the Tudor age in particular revolved around the character of our kings and queens; King Henry VII, King Henry VIII and his daughter, Queen Elizabeth I. King Henry VIII ordered the expansion of the Royal Navy, begun by his father and this expansion set in train a series of events that became the industrial revolution. The Tudors age was a thrilling time of expansion, gallant failures but spectacular successes. When Drake set sail for the Strait of Magellan in 1577, circumnavigating the world and returning to England, the booty was sufficient to enable Elizabeth to pay off the entire national debt of England. Drake was given £10,000 – an enormous sum in those days and equivalent to £20 million today.

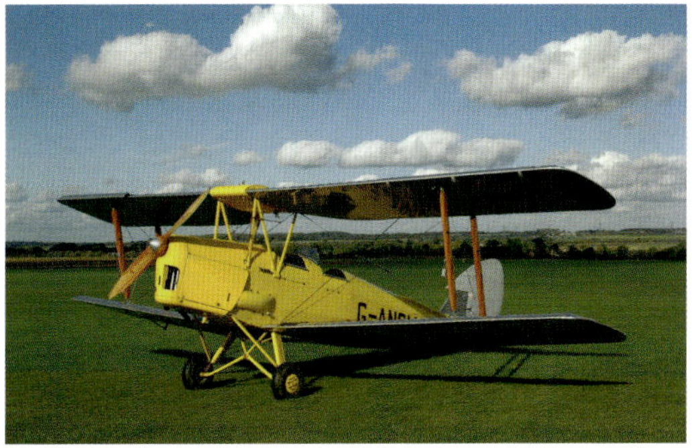

King's College Chapel was begun in 1446 on the orders of King Henry VII and was completed by his son, King Henry VIII in 1515. The College Chapel, now one of the most memorable vistas in the world, was built in the 'Perpendicular' style. King Henry

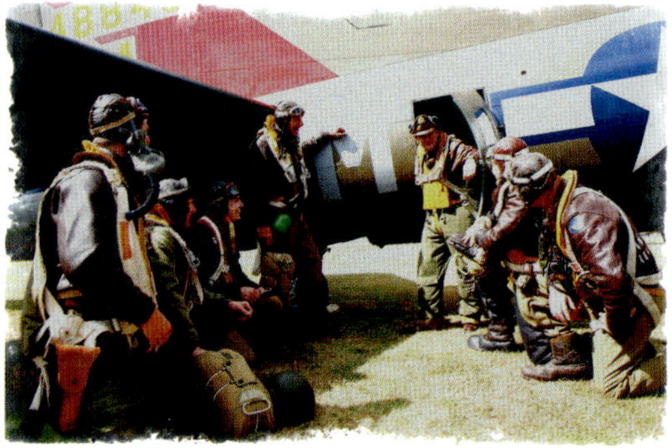

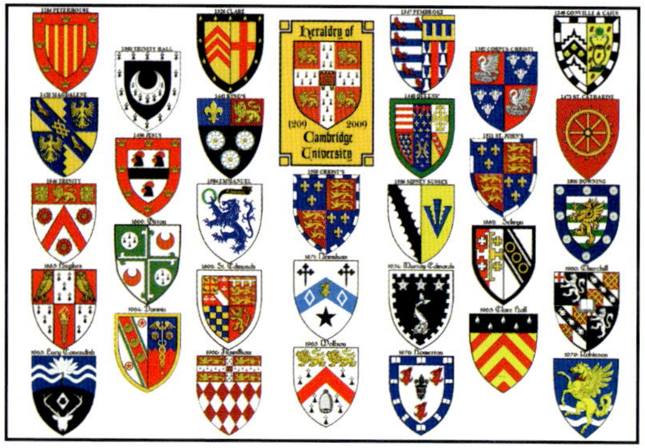

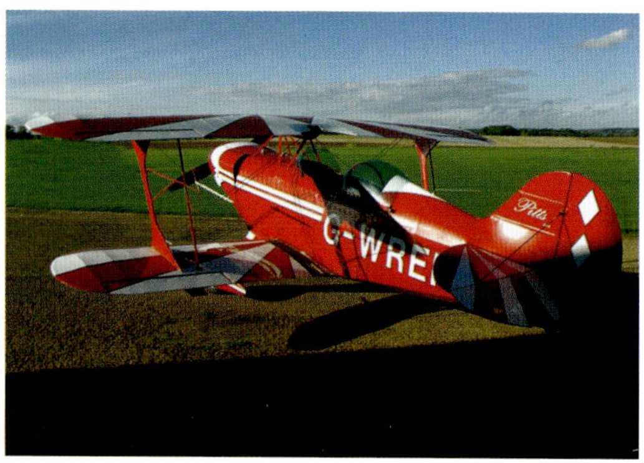

VIII was also responsible for the building of the grandest college in Cambridge – Trinity, using funds from the dissolution of the monasteries. Sir Issac Newton was to become one of the students at Trinity. Queen Elizabeth I continued the work and when she died in 1603, the population of England was a mere five million but by 1750, the population had expanded dramatically to six and a half million and England was ready for the Industrial Revolution.

Within the Industrial Revolution, the era of 'aviation' began which became a vital industry in Cambridgeshire. On the 21st November 1783, the Montgolfier Brothers flew their manned balloon over Paris. Sir George Cayley, a Yorkshireman, experimented with flying machines and his coachman flew a short distance down a slope in 1853. In 1897, the Scots engineer Percy Pilcher built a glider called the Hawk and broke the world distance record when he flew 250 m (820 ft) at the grounds of Stanford Hall in Leicestershire. His attempt to make a powered flight resulted in a crash and his death two days later. Six years later, the Wright Brothers claimed the honour of the first powered flight in 1903. Aviation in England was still in its infancy and much of the enabling technology for successful powered flight was emerging through developments that started in automotive engineering. The first involvement by Marshalls of Cambridge occurred in 1912 when its mechanics helped repair the engine of a British Army airship, the Beta II, which had made an emergency landing in Jesus Green, Cambridge, just behind Marshall's garage. Marshalls went on to open Fen Ditton airfield in 1929 and by 1938, the Marshall Flying School played a major part for the RAF Volunteer Reserve by training over 600 new RAF pilots before the Battle of Britain commenced. By the end of WWII, the school had trained over 20,000 aircrew, including pilots, observers and flying instructors. The Marshall training scheme was universally adopted by the Royal Air Force in 1941 and continues to this day. Marshall also modified or repaired over 5,000 aircraft, from Spitfires to B-17s done by a 3,000 strong workforce, both male and female. This continued after WWII including the production of 65 de Havilland Venoms and eventually the design and production of the Concorde droop nose and visor in 1967. Cambridge Airport had a new concrete runway in 1953, extended in 1971 to be able to handle large aircraft such as the Valiant, Britannia, Belfast, VC-10 and the Hercules.

In 1947, the Bristol Sycamore helicopter first flew, a completely new type of flying machine, used by the Royal Air Force not only for search and rescue but also for the very successful covert insertion and extraction of Royal Marines during the Malayan Emergency. By 1948, the British European Airways Helicopter Unit was established at Westwood Airfield, Peterborough using three Sikorsky S-58s and two Bell 47 helicopters. The first regular mail service commenced on 1st June 1948, the first night mail service on the 17th October 1949 and the world's first scheduled passenger helicopter service on 1st June 1950. Sixty years later, the modern helicopters of the East Anglia Air Ambulance (EAAA) commenced operational service and cover Cambridgeshire plus the counties of Bedfordshire, Norfolk & Suffolk.

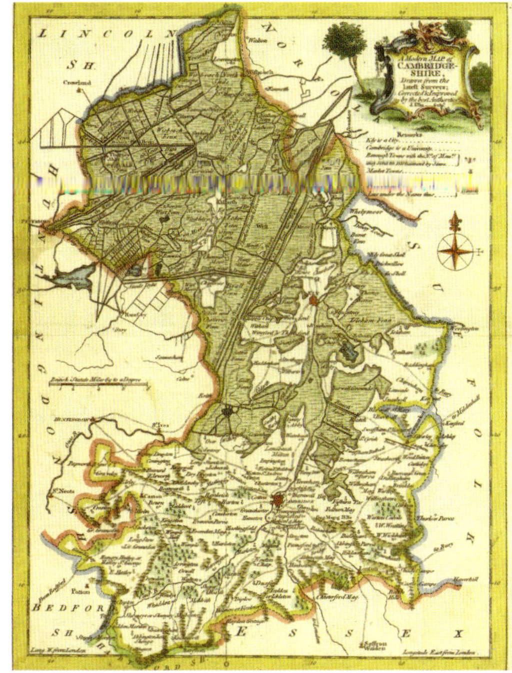

From above, the historic cathedrals of Ely and Peterborugh and the long-established colleges of Cambridge are clearly visible to the aviator and there are still possibilities to experience such a flight by Tiger Moth biplanes or helicopters. Once airborne, it becomes obvious that the towns and cities of Cambridgeshire occupy a relatively small area of the county of Cambridgeshire and one does not have to travel far to be in wide-open, big-sky countryside. Considering that there are no majestic mountains or broad lakes, the impact of the Fens is everywhere. These modern, drained Fens contain almost 50% of the grade one agricultural land in the whole of England; an area of 1500 square miles spread over three counties. It is clear that the black land, though sinking, is incredibly fertile and has been wrested by the ingenuity and perseverance of men and women to change this landscape over only a few hundred years from a salty marsh wasteland into the breadbasket of England. There always seems to be a fresh breeze across the land and the straight roads increase the perspective beneath clear skies. The contrast between the agricultural landscape and the visual heritage within the towns and cities is dramatic, and these environments continue to draw admiration and wonderment from both visitor and resident alike.

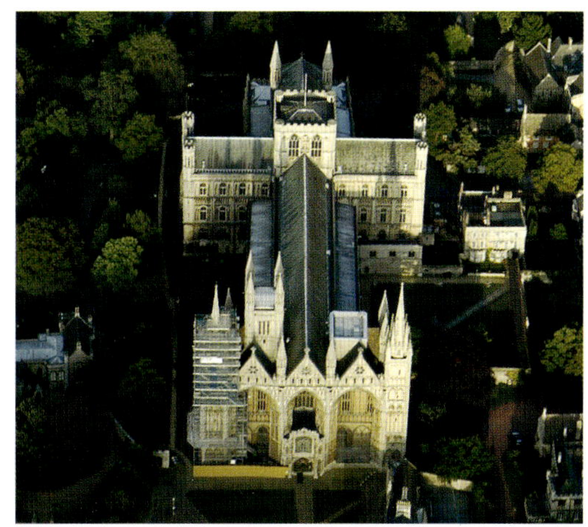

William A. Nowell,
University Centre Peterborough.

Chapter 1

Dawn

6 am

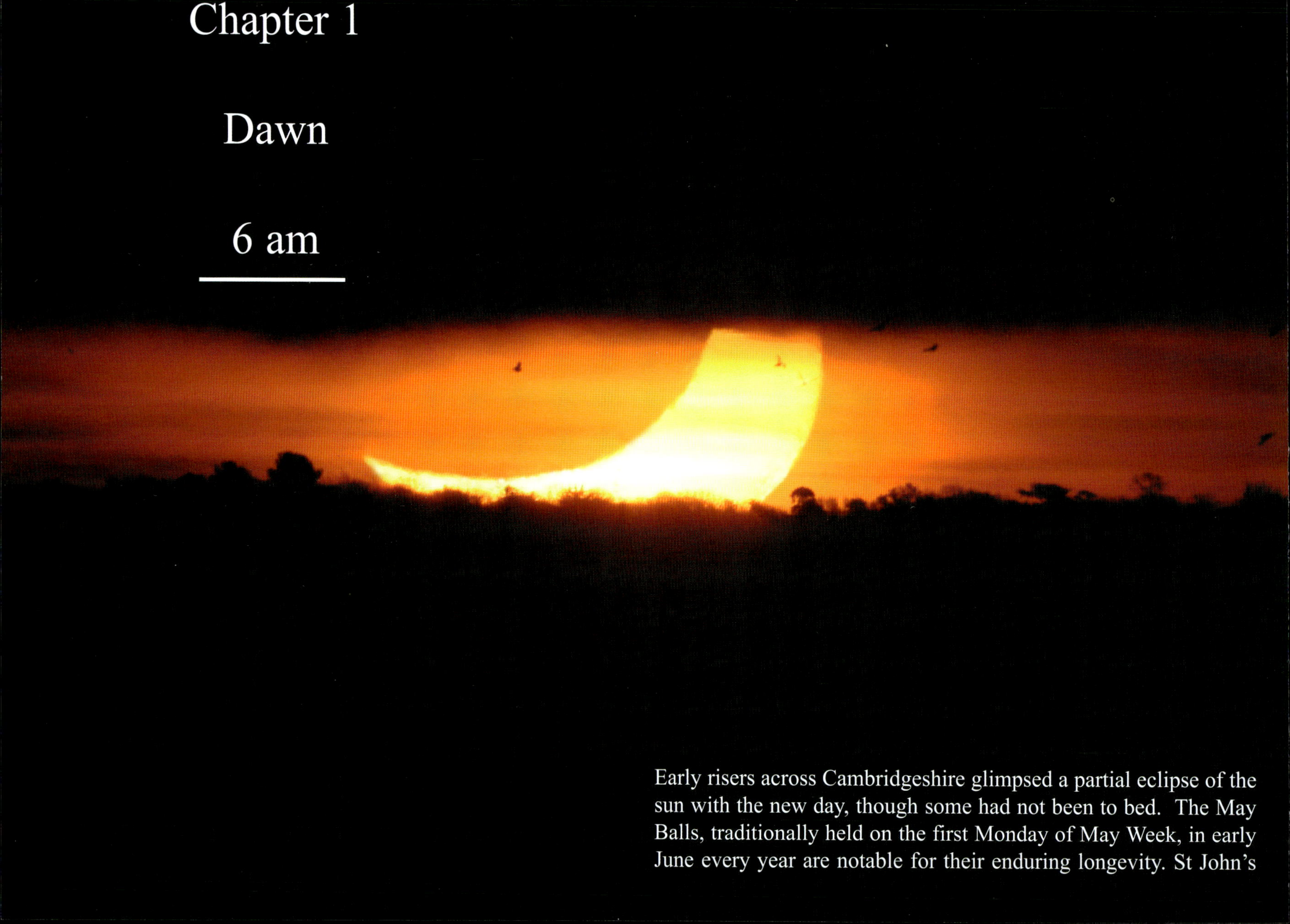

Early risers across Cambridgeshire glimpsed a partial eclipse of the sun with the new day, though some had not been to bed. The May Balls, traditionally held on the first Monday of May Week, in early June every year are notable for their enduring longevity. St John's

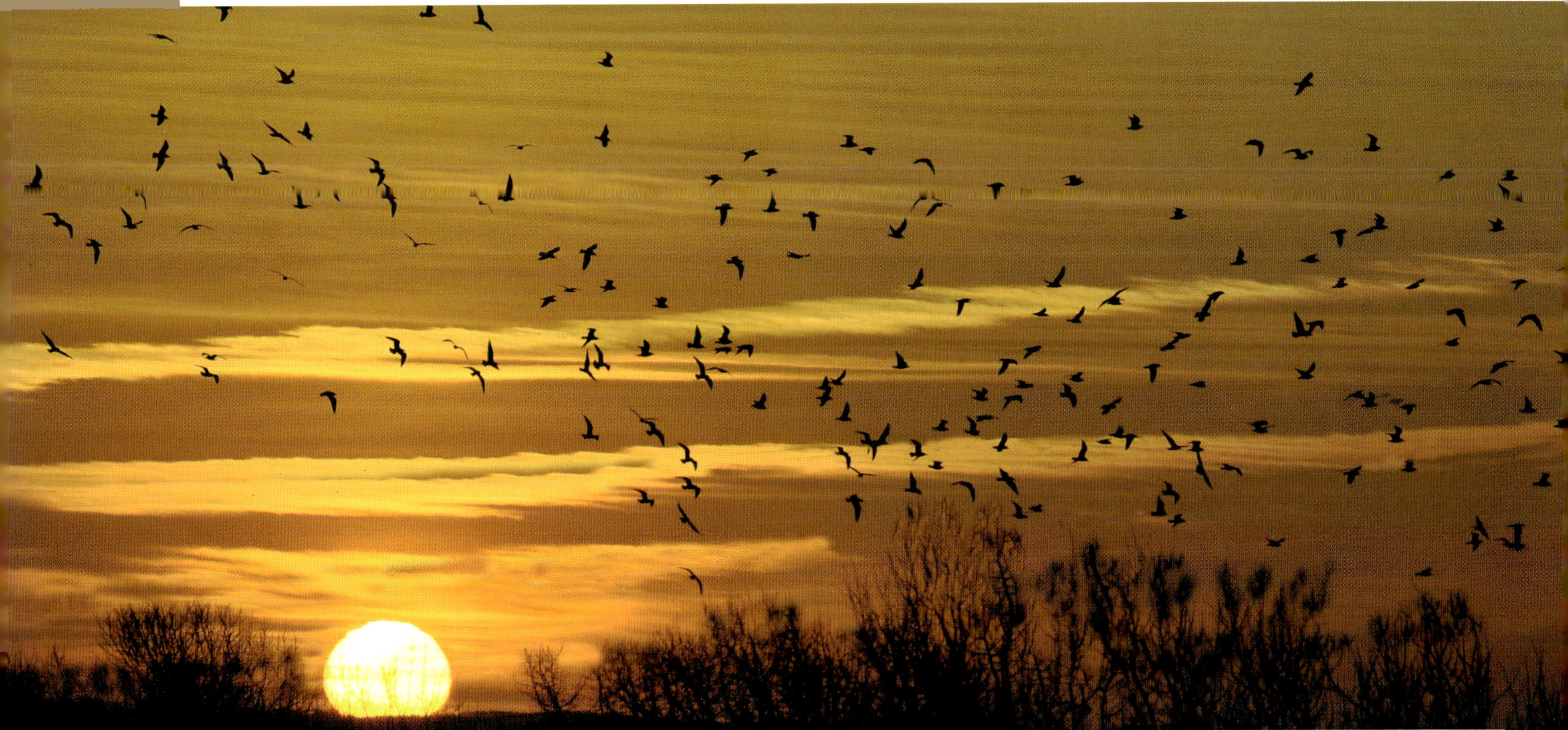

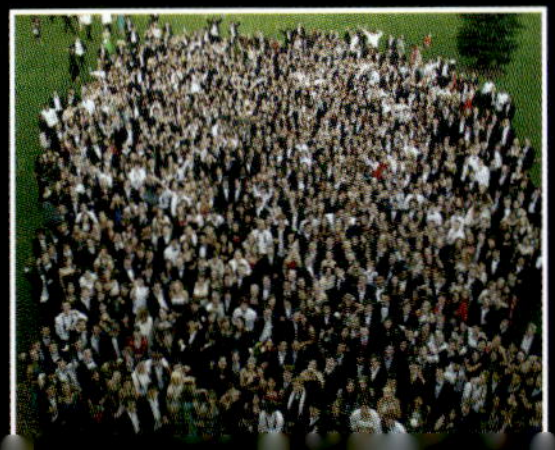

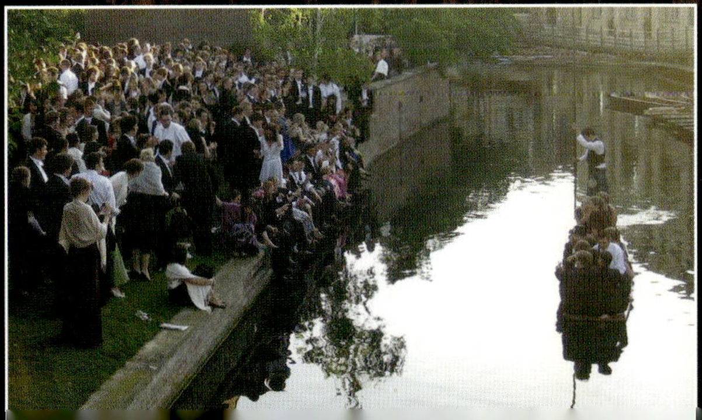

College is celebrating with a 'Quincentenary Ball' in 2011 and its webpage quotes Time Magazine as saying that the ball is the '7th Greatest Party in the World'. The Survivors pose or punt for a photograph with the dawn.

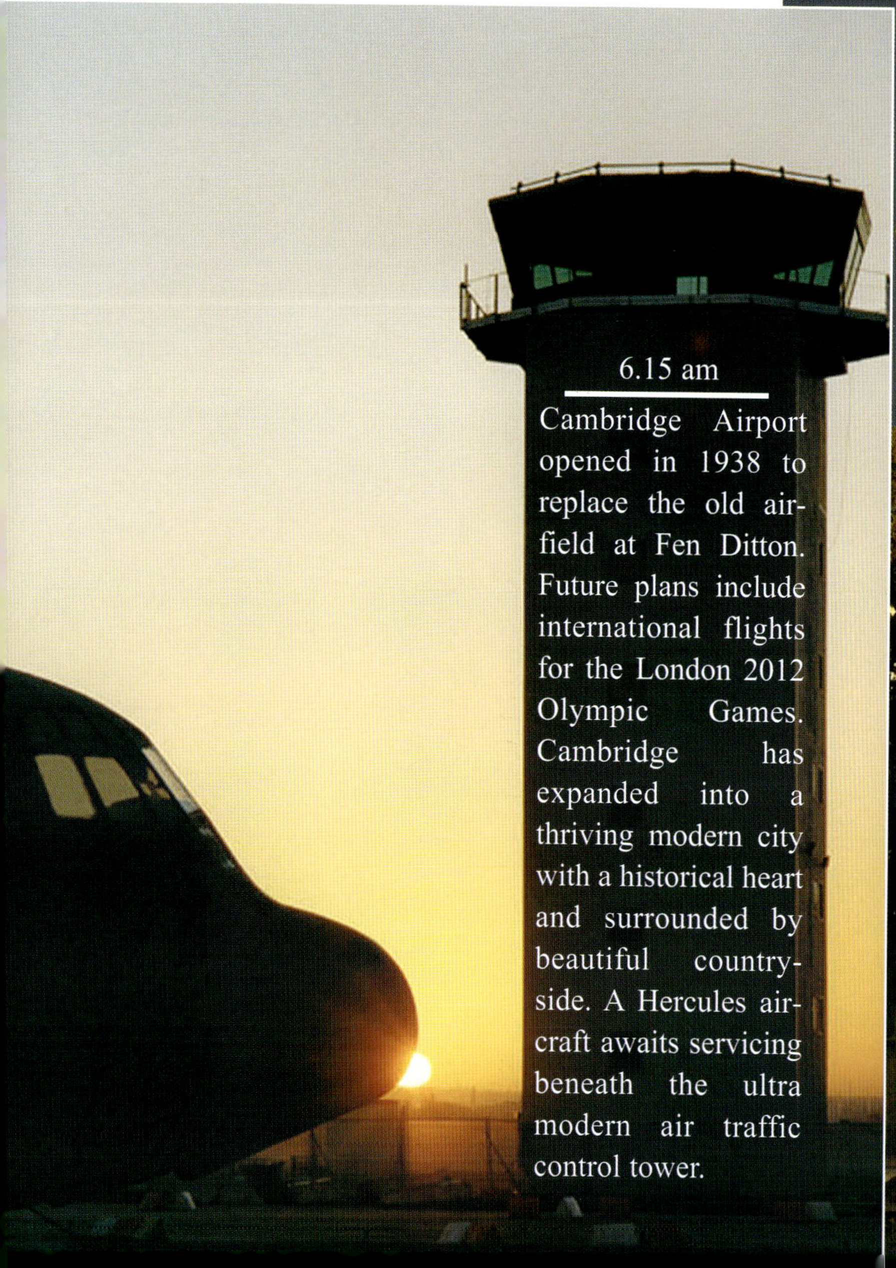

6.15 am

Cambridge Airport opened in 1938 to replace the old airfield at Fen Ditton. Future plans include international flights for the London 2012 Olympic Games. Cambridge has expanded into a thriving modern city with a historical heart and surrounded by beautiful countryside. A Hercules aircraft awaits servicing beneath the ultra modern air traffic control tower.

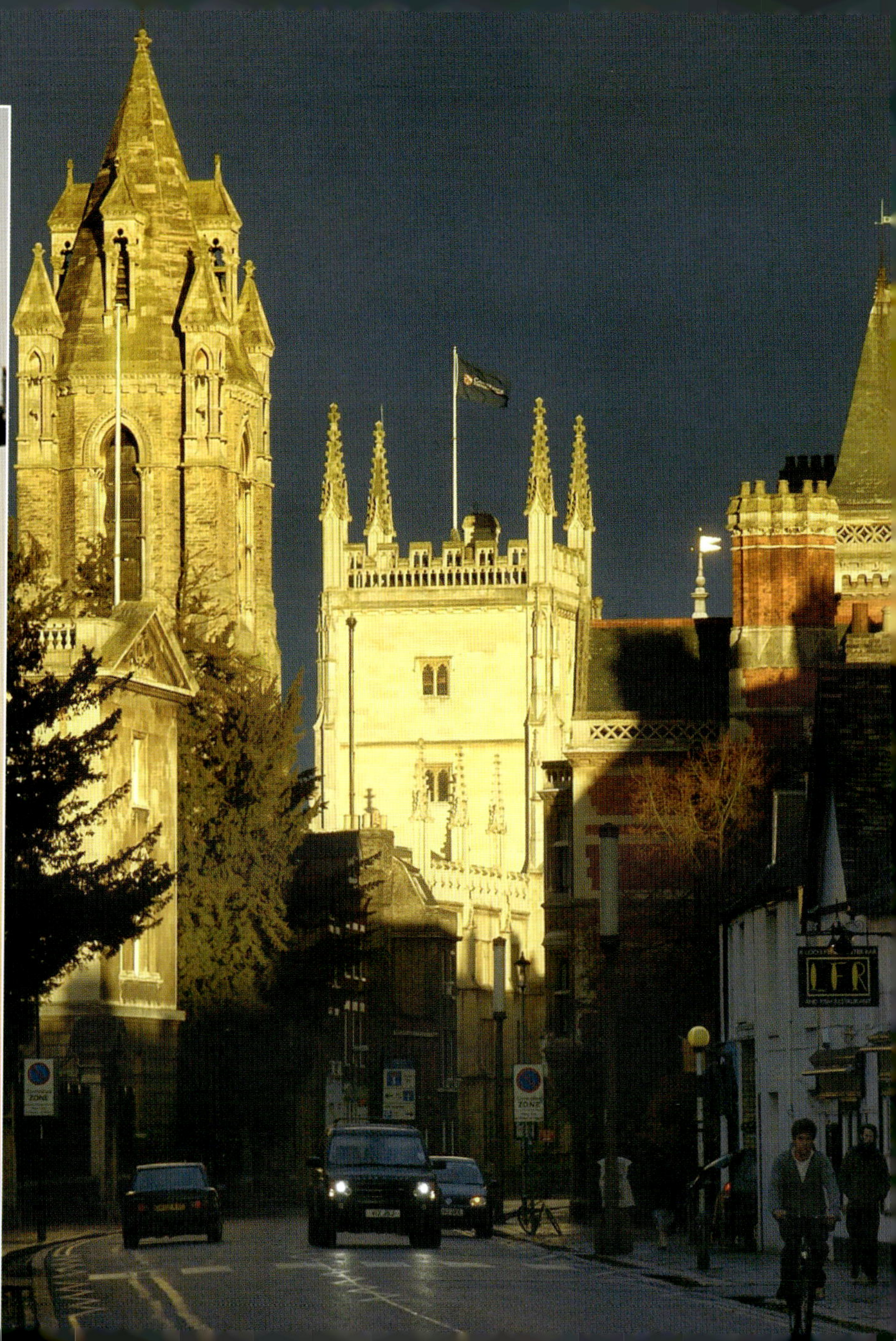

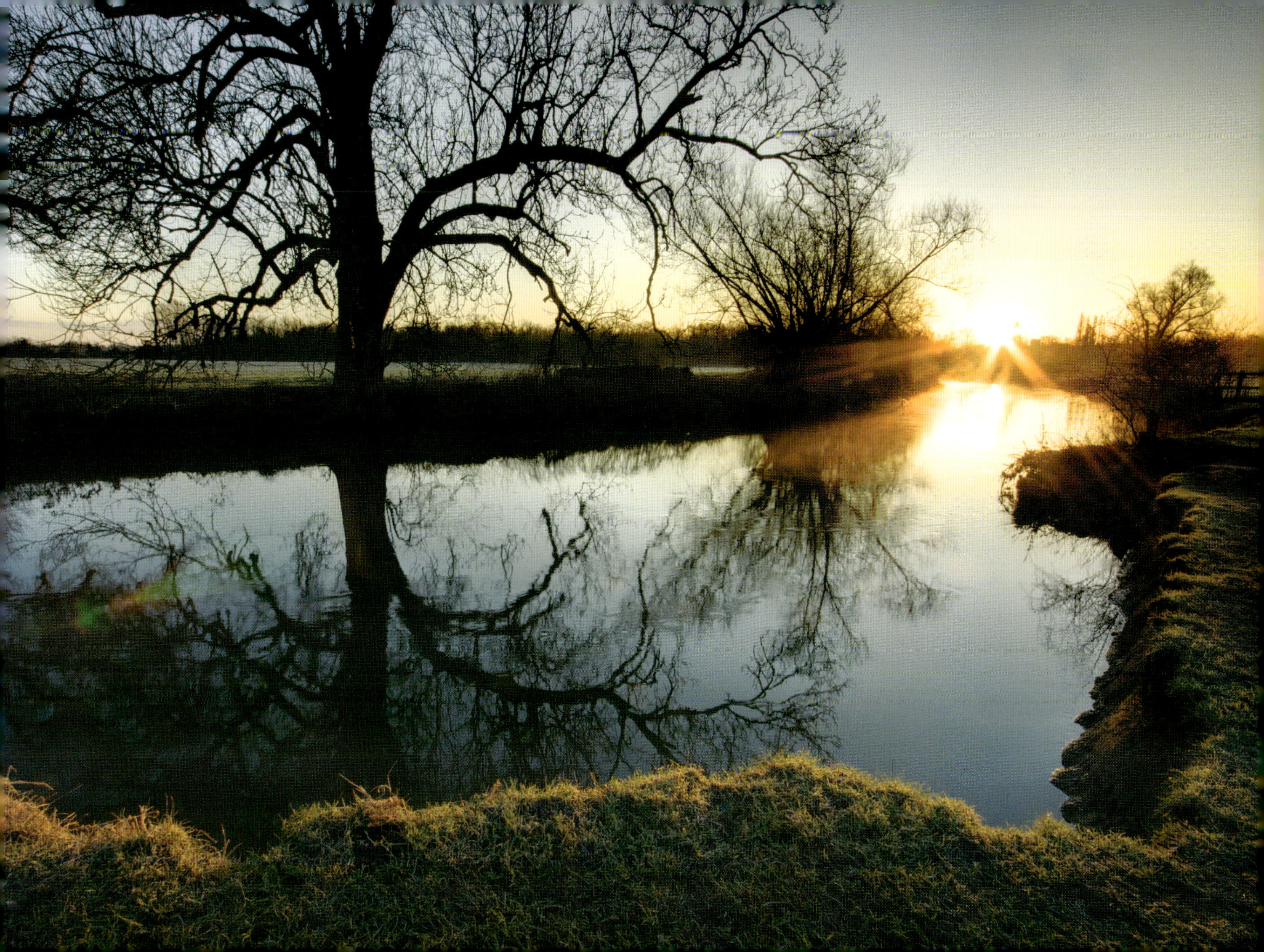

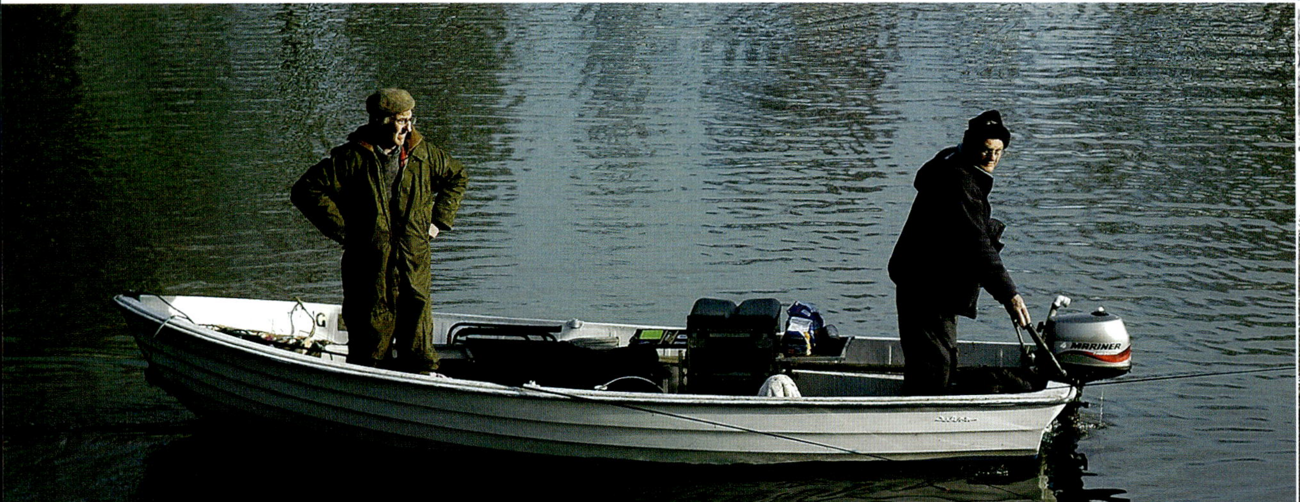

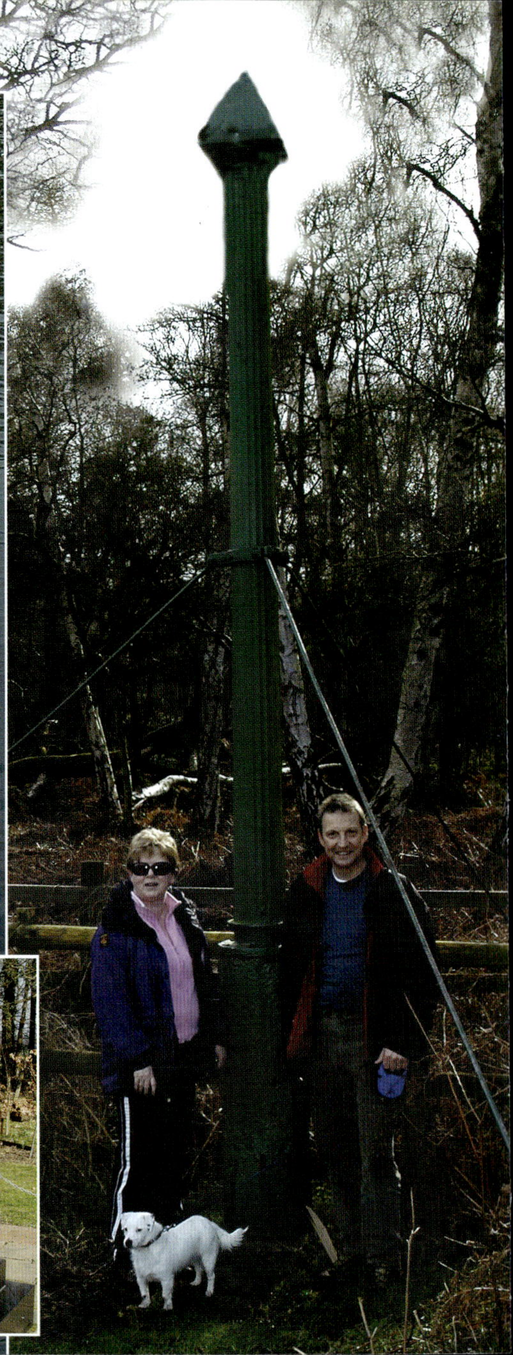

6.30 am

Fishermen, walkers and crews make an early start. The crew, opposite, of a B-17 Flying Fortress WWII bomber wait to board their aircraft. The airfield was US Station Glatton, now known as Peterborough Business Airfield, Conington. Only the memorials remain to remind us of the time when the 457th Bombardment Group of the 8th Air Force operated from this base. Only 2 km away stands a cast-iron post, shown right, at Holme Fen Reserve, situated on the south-west shore of the former Whittlesey Mere. The Mere was drained in 1851to become expansive fields of wheat. In 1852, the post was buried by William Wells at the edge of Holme Lode covert. The top of the post was set at ground level and the rest buried and fixed to timber piles driven into the underlying clay. Since this time the peat has dried out and wasted away due to increased drainage. The top

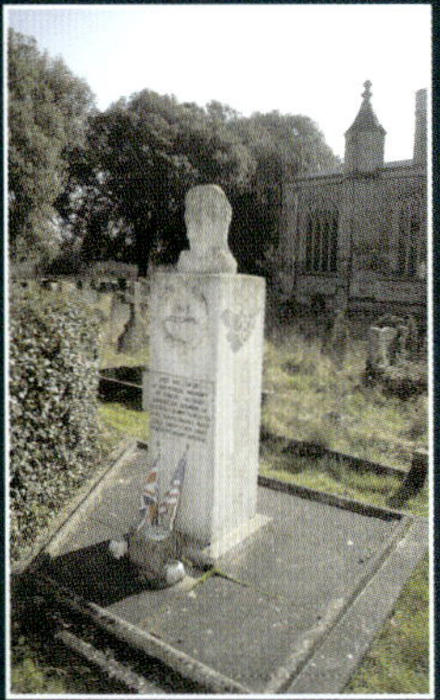

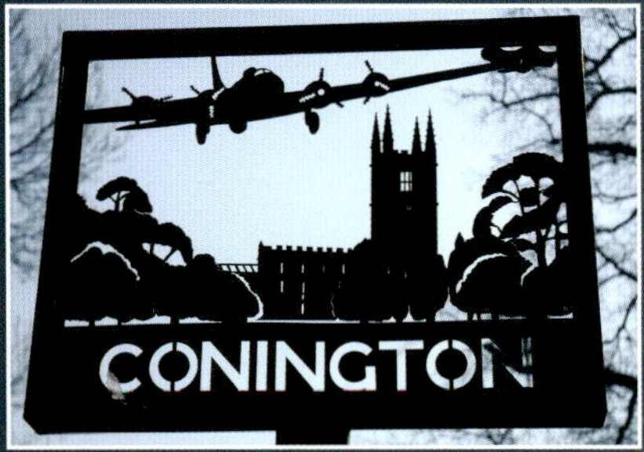

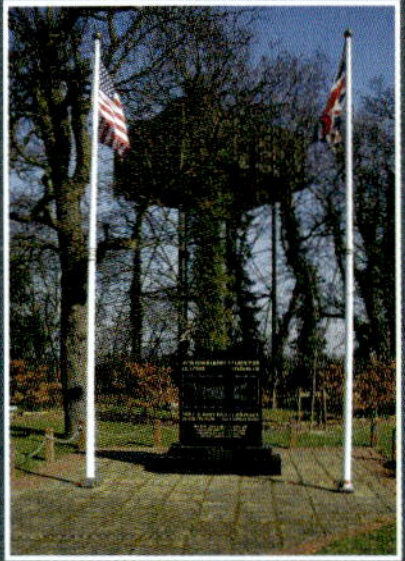

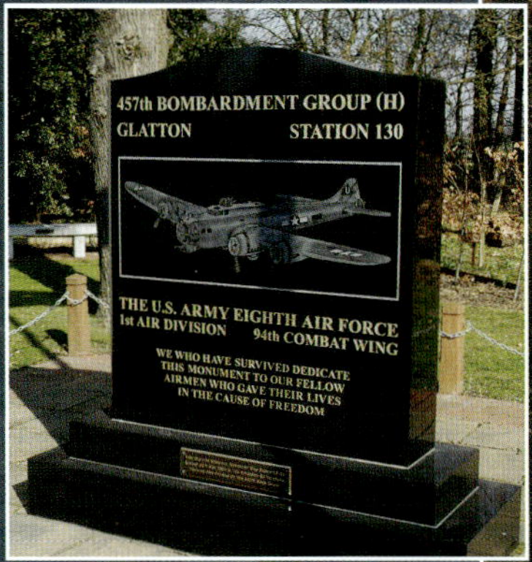

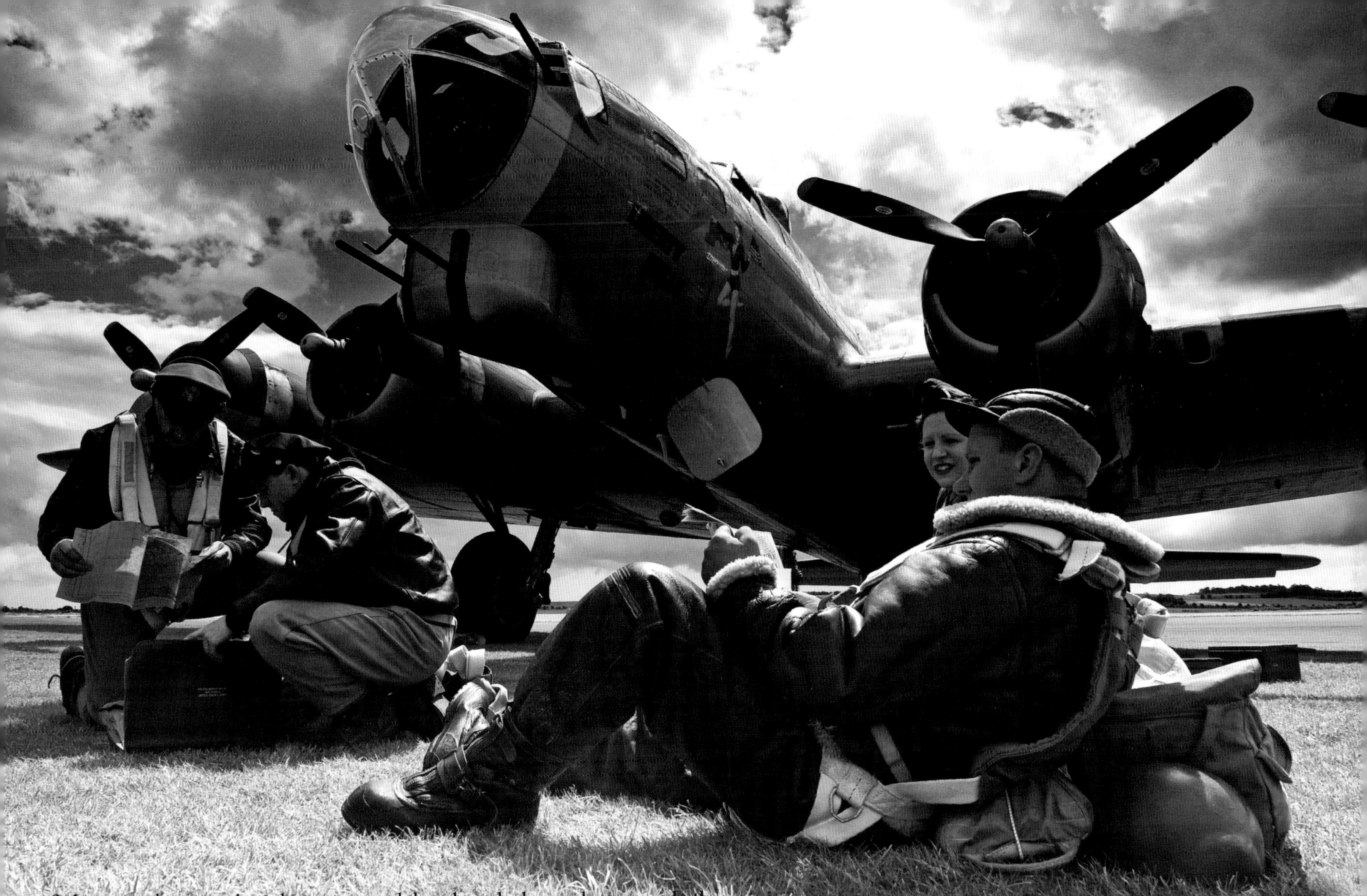

of the post is now 4m above ground level and shows how much the ground has shrunk in the last 150 years. The farmland adjoining the reserve is now the lowest place in England.

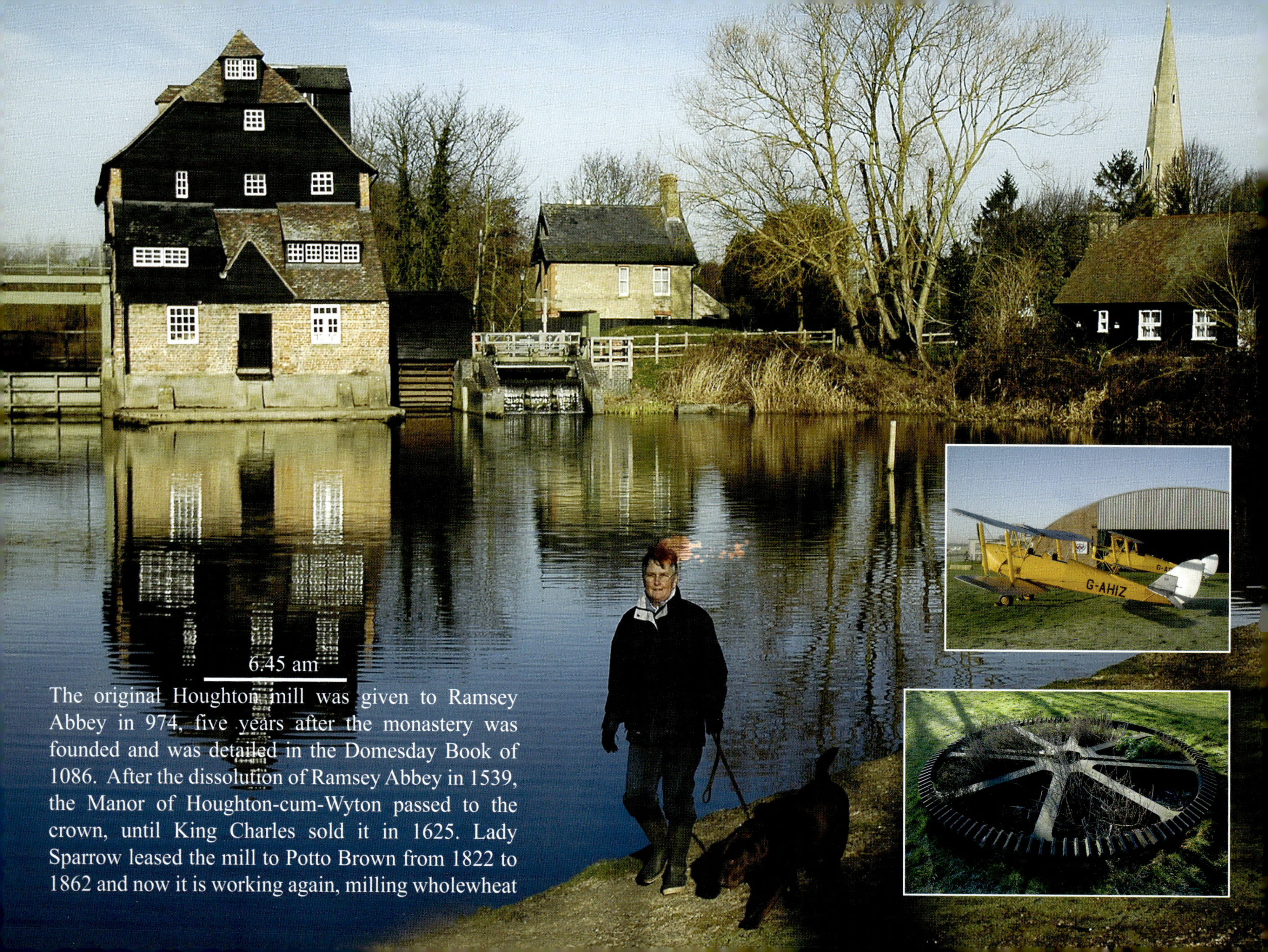

6.45 am

The original Houghton mill was given to Ramsey Abbey in 974, five years after the monastery was founded and was detailed in the Domesday Book of 1086. After the dissolution of Ramsey Abbey in 1539, the Manor of Houghton-cum-Wyton passed to the crown, until King Charles sold it in 1625. Lady Sparrow leased the mill to Potto Brown from 1822 to 1862 and now it is working again, milling wholewheat

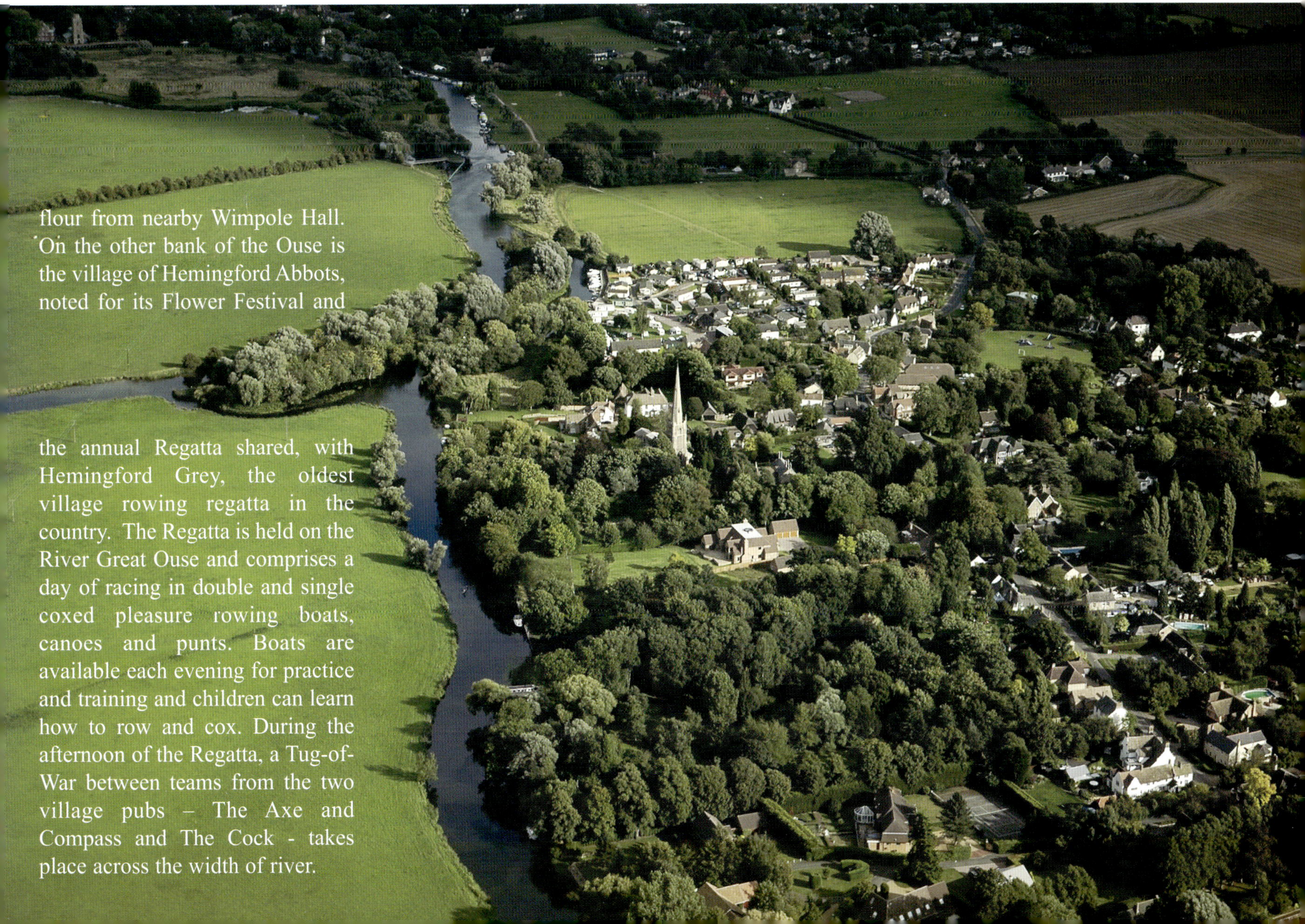

flour from nearby Wimpole Hall. On the other bank of the Ouse is the village of Hemingford Abbots, noted for its Flower Festival and the annual Regatta shared, with Hemingford Grey, the oldest village rowing regatta in the country. The Regatta is held on the River Great Ouse and comprises a day of racing in double and single coxed pleasure rowing boats, canoes and punts. Boats are available each evening for practice and training and children can learn how to row and cox. During the afternoon of the Regatta, a Tug-of-War between teams from the two village pubs – The Axe and Compass and The Cock - takes place across the width of river.

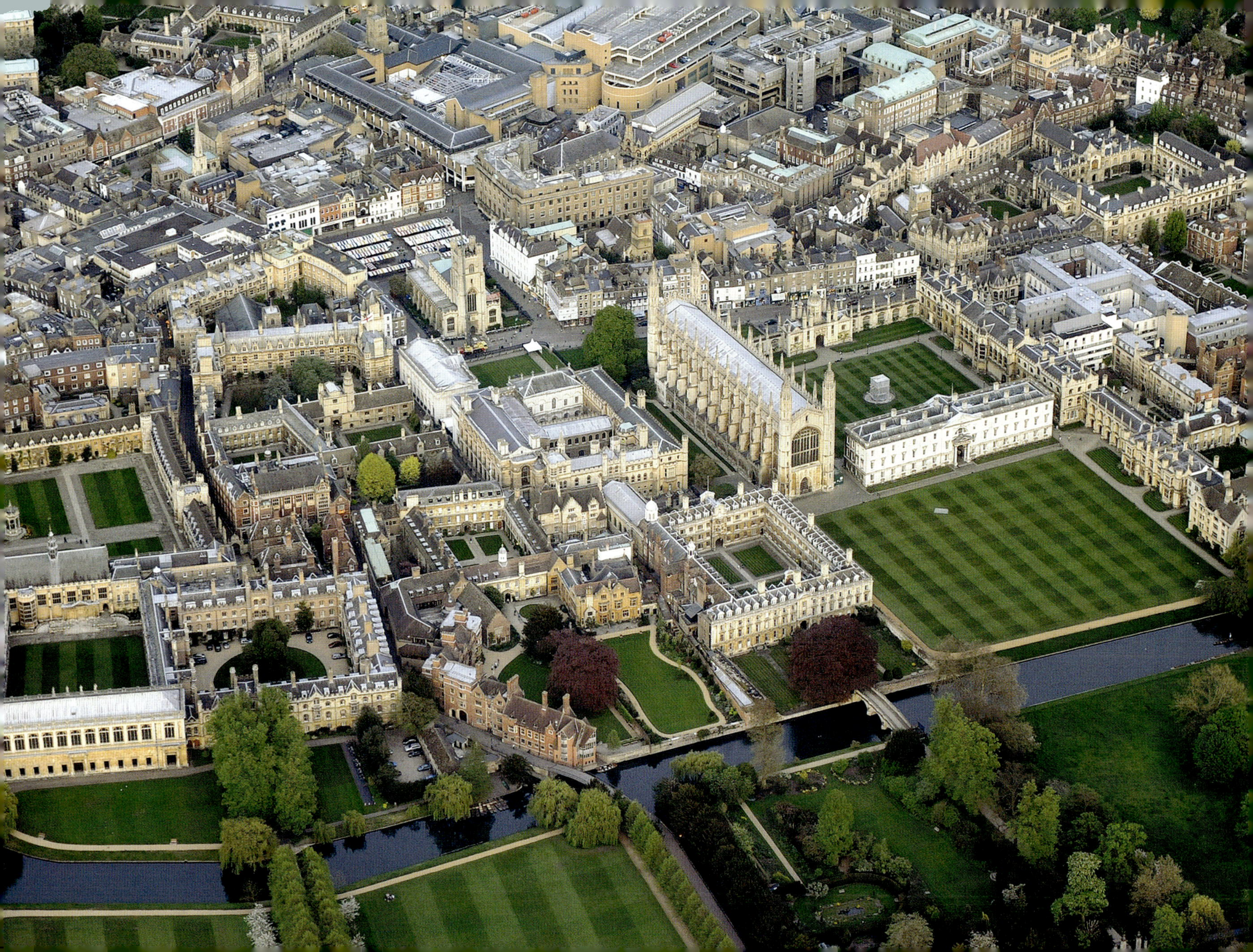

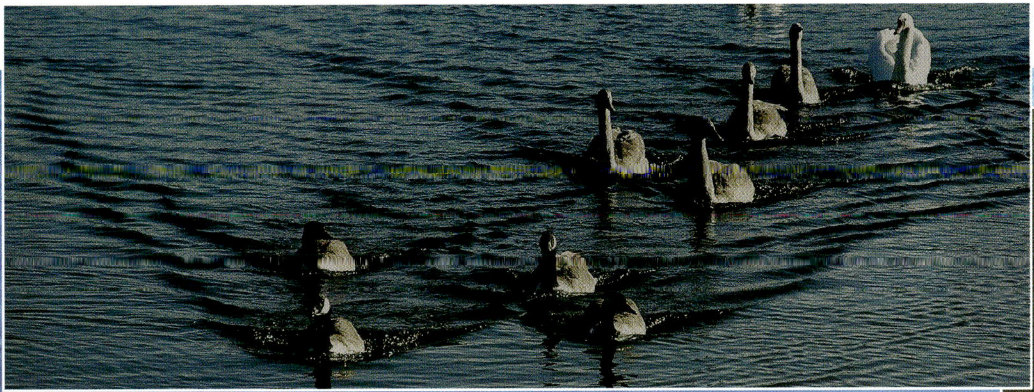

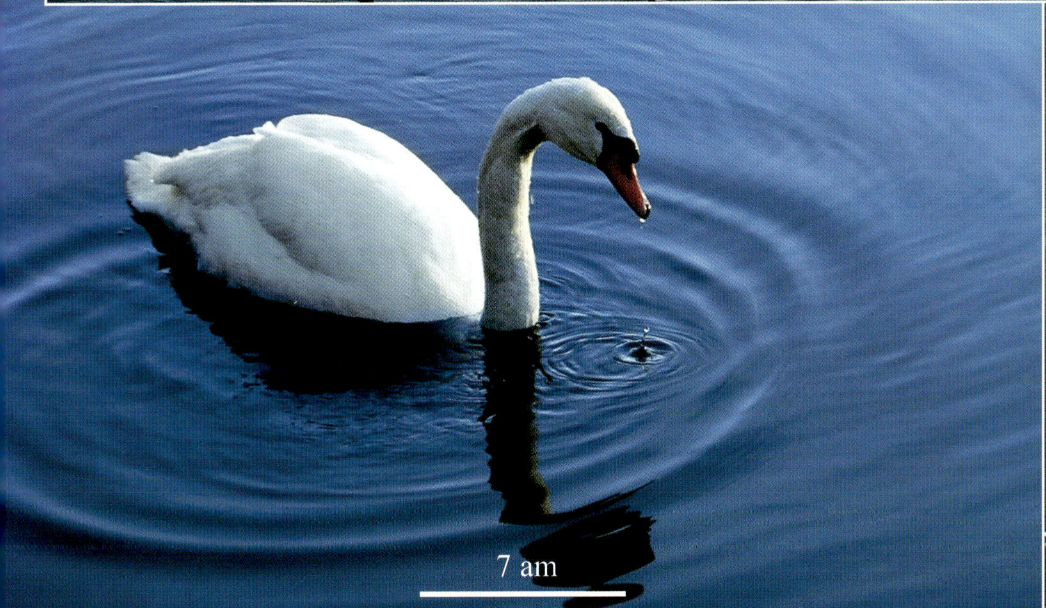

7 am

It's early morning in Cambridge and the river is coming to life. The Cam is home to many types of wildlife including swans and geese. It was the River Cam which attracted settlers who made their homes here giving rise over the years to what we now know as Cambridge. The Cam was originally known as the River Granta. However, when the nearby Anglo-Saxon town of Grantebrycge was renamed as Cambridge, the River Granta became called the River Cam. A tributary is still known as the Granta.

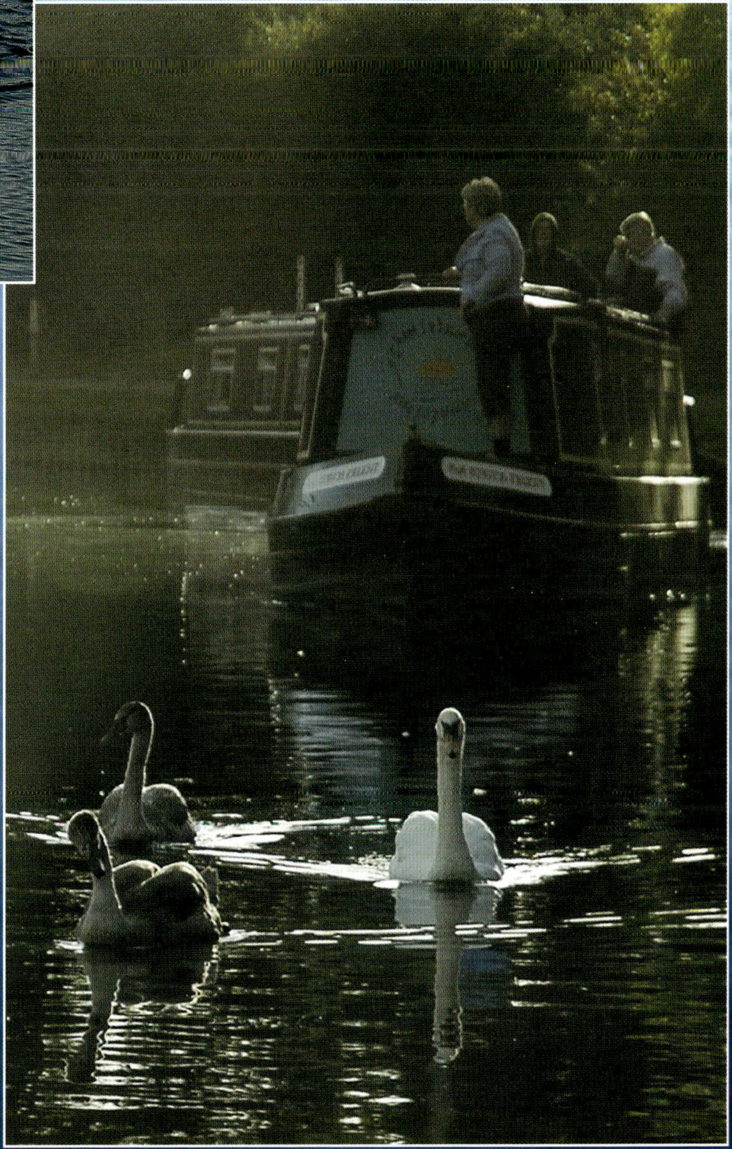

7.30 am

The view from a WWII vintage B-17 bomber, taken from the waist gunner position, looks down on the birthplace of the famous poet, John Clare. Clare was the son of a farm labourer who came to be known for his celebratory representations of the English countryside and he is now considered to be one of the most important 19th century poets. His biographer, Jonathan Bate, said that Clare was 'the greatest labouring-class poet that England has ever produced. No one has ever written more powerfully of nature'. His poem, 'Death', was especially poignant to the bomber crews in WWII.

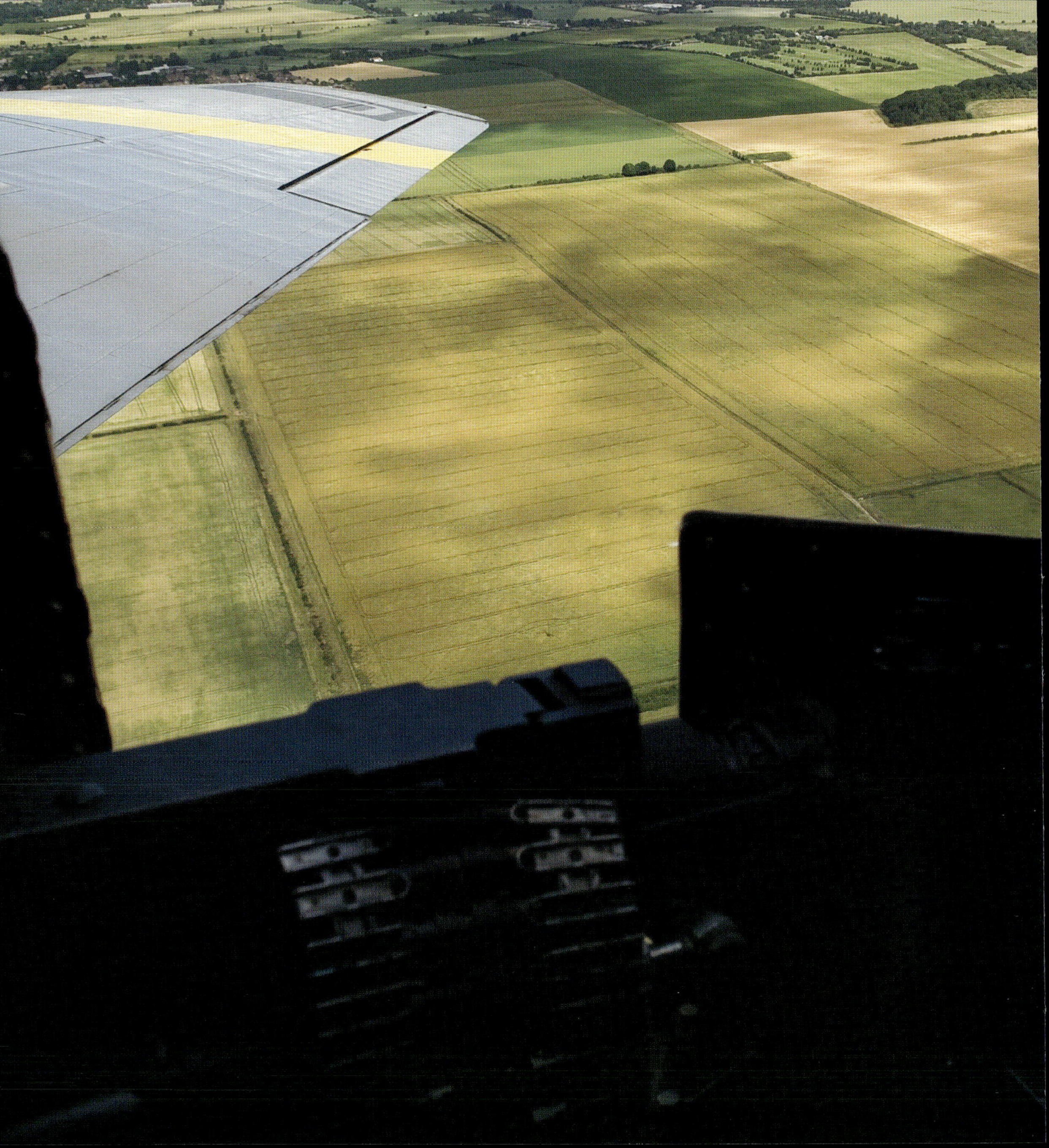

'Why should man's high aspiring mind,
Burn in him with so proud a breath,
When all his haughty views can find,
In this world yields to death?
The fair, the brave, the vain, the wise,
The rich, the poor, the great, and small,
Are each but worm's anatomies,
To strew his quiet hall'.

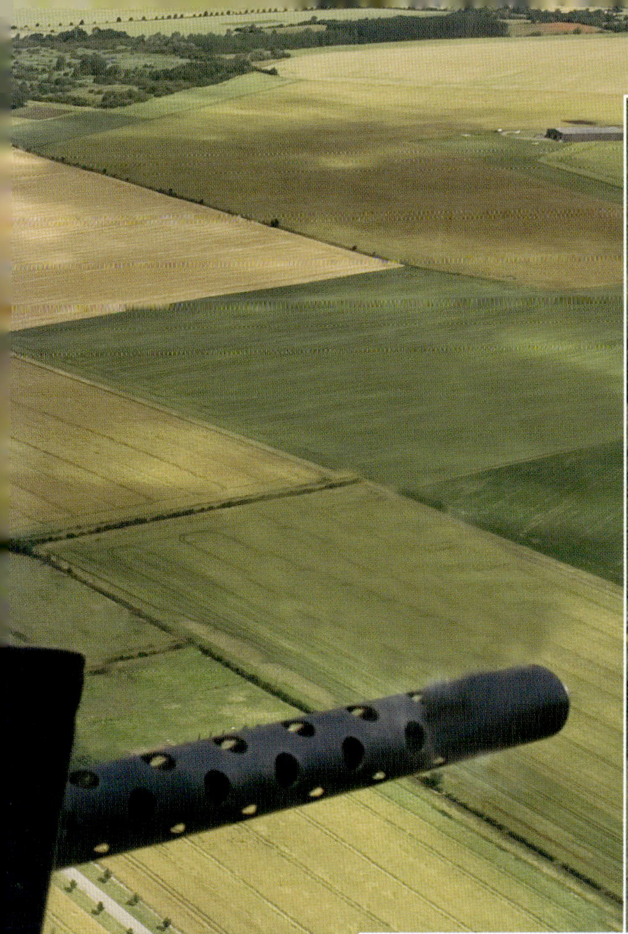

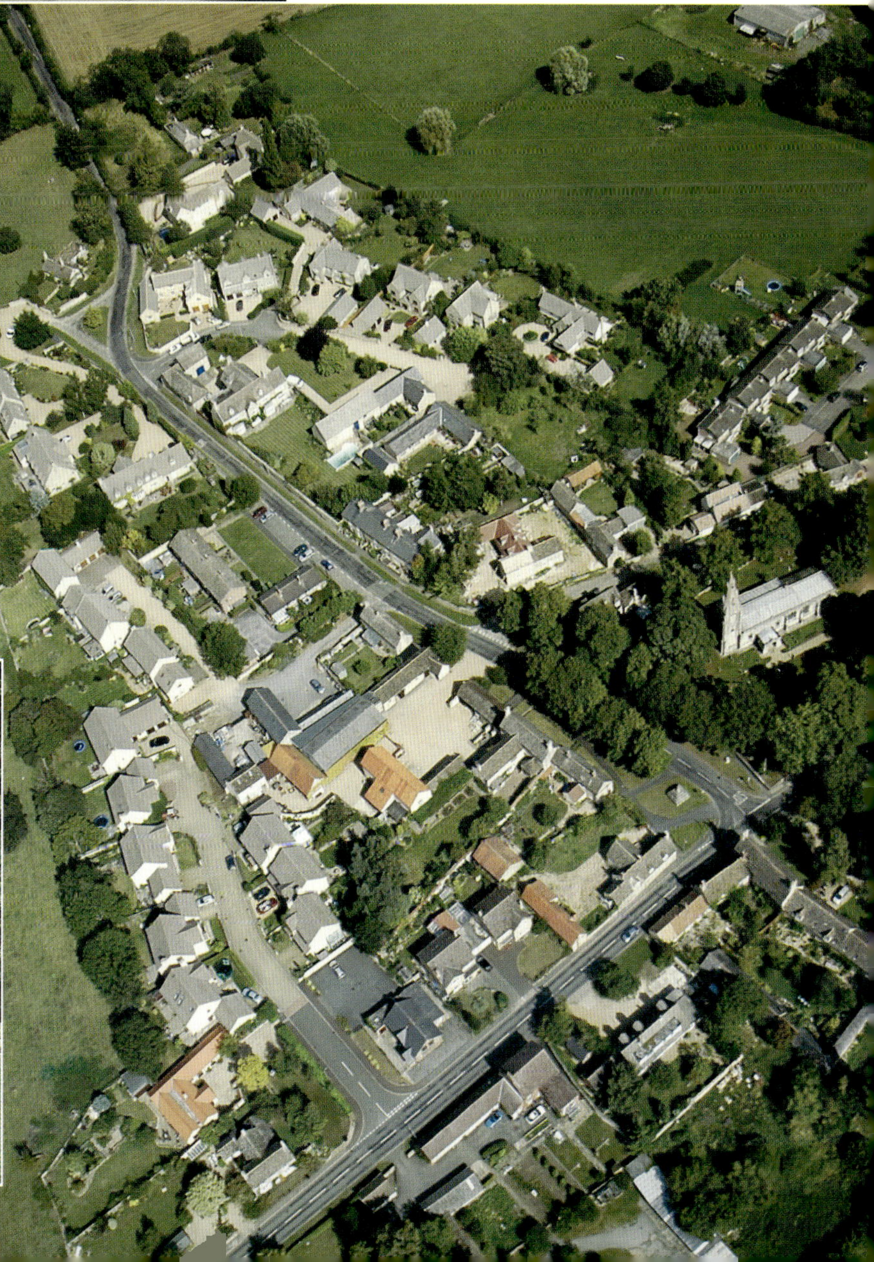

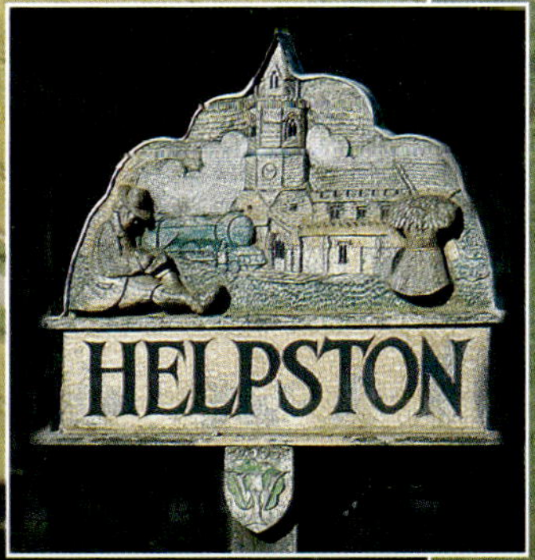
HELPSTON

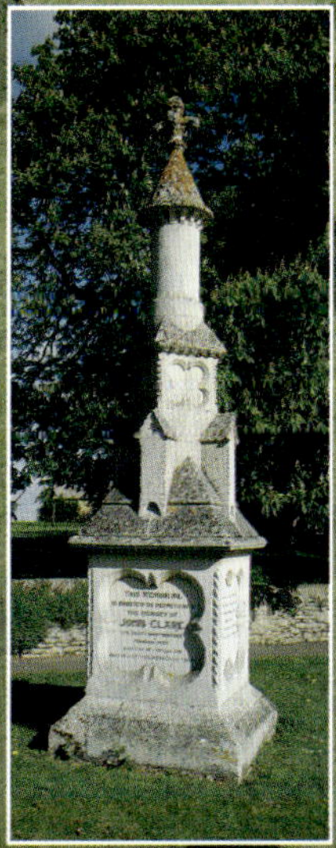

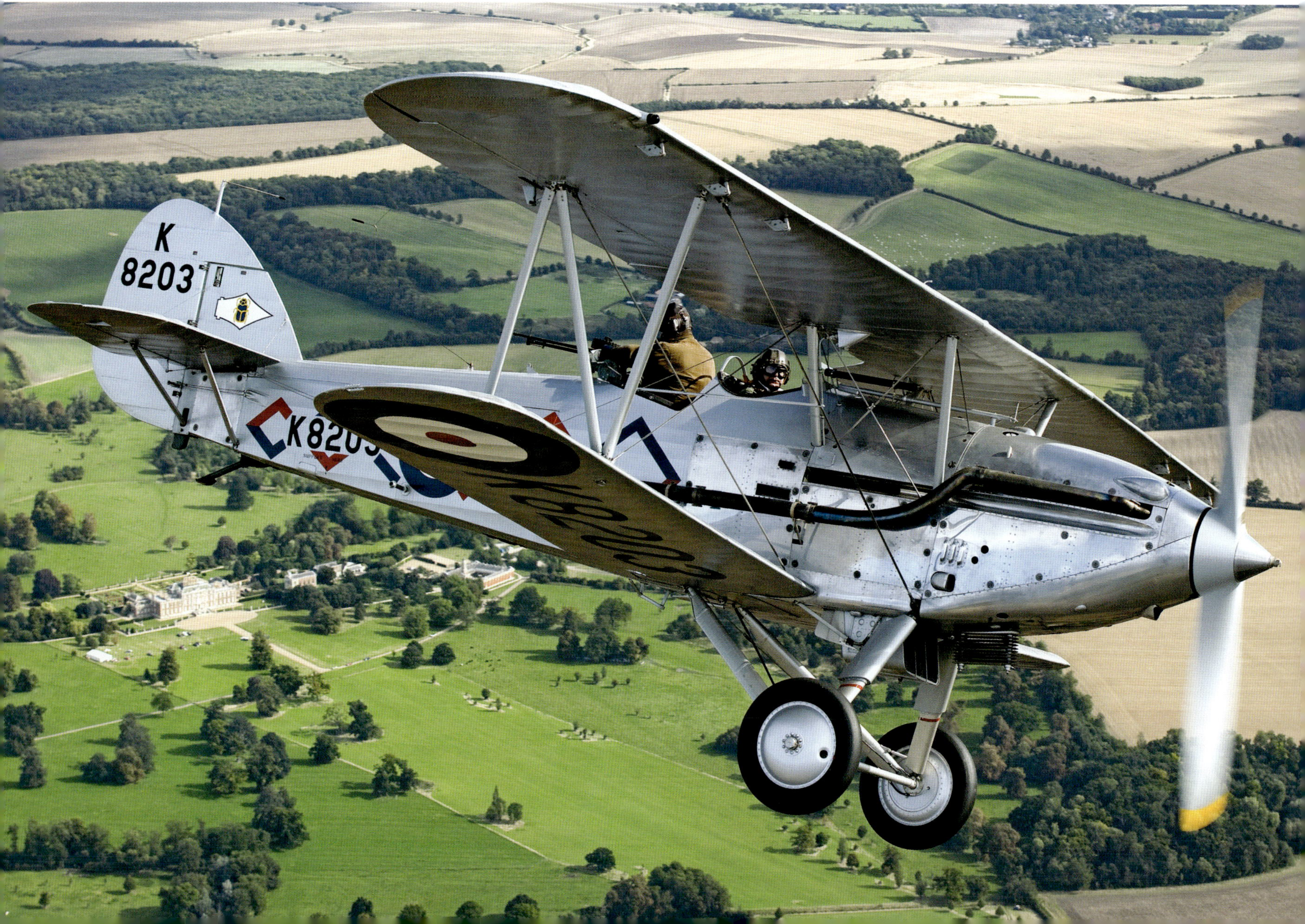
K
8203
K8203

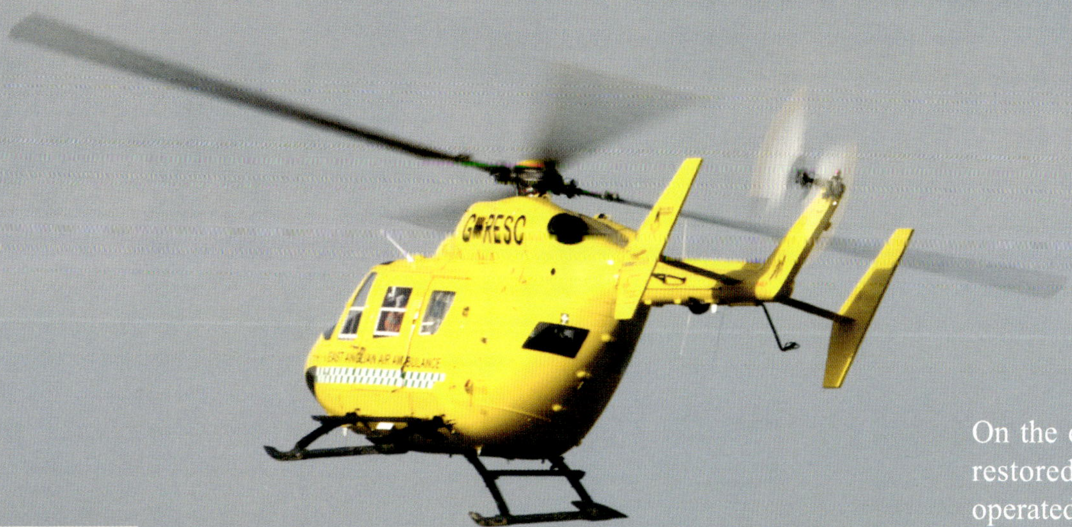

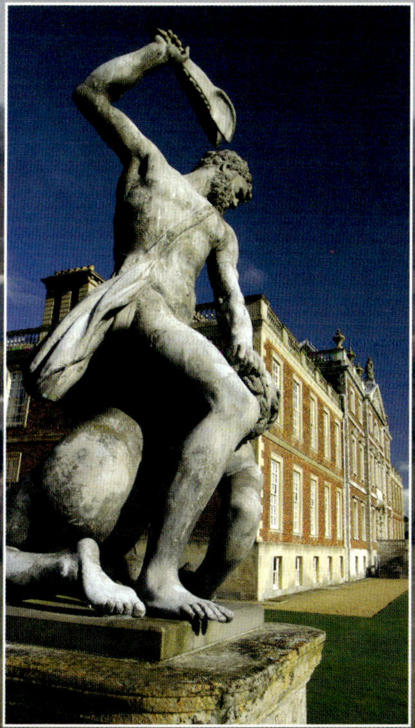

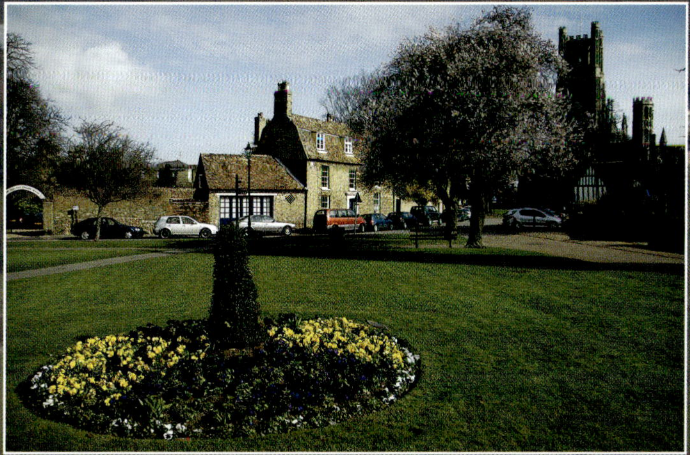

8 am

On the opposite page, a beautifully restored Hawker Demon, once operated from RAF Duxford, flies gracefully over Wimpole Hall, the largest country house in Cambridgeshire. Another warrior statue, the biblical Samson, stands over his enemy beneath a blue sky. During WWII, the hall was used as a hospital by the American forces. The Hall was renovated by Captain & Mrs Bambridge, daughter of Rudyard Kipling, and given to the National Trust in 1976 for everyone to enjoy. Bright yellow flowers bloom on the green in front of Ely Cathedral while above all, the East Anglia Air Ambulance gets airborne in response to a ‘shout’. This helicopter is now based at Cambridge Airport and can reach anywhere in Cambridgeshire within 10 minutes.

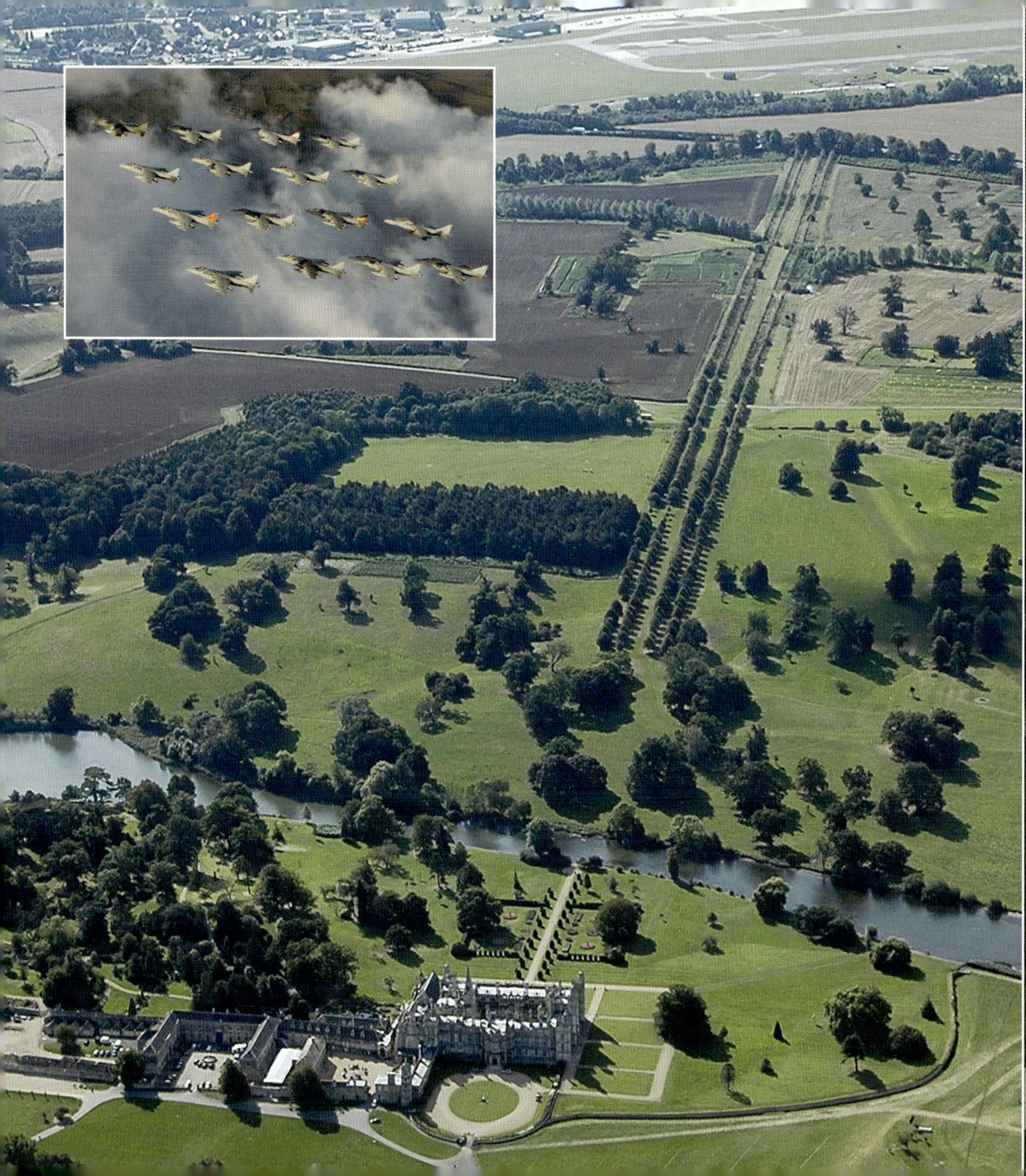

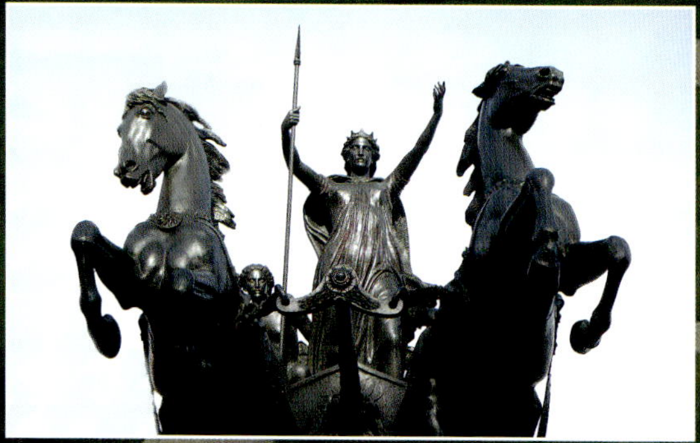

8.30 am

Burghley House was built by William Cecil, Lord High Treasurer to Elizabeth I. Building work began in 1555 and was completed in 1587 - 32 years! Capability Brown designed the parkland, now home to many fallow deer. Modern restoration work began in 1983 to the present day. As a spectacular building with beautiful grounds, Burghley House has been a filming location for *Elizabeth the Golden Age*, *The Da Vinci Code* and *Pride and Prejudice*. In contrast, Boudicca was the Queen of the Icini of Eastern England who led an uprising against the occupying Romans, chasing the legion across the River Welland nearby. Roman forces conquered the south of England in 43 AD and Prasutagus, husband of Boudicca, King of the Icini was allowed to maintain his rule over the East. When Prasutagus died the Romans decided it was time to

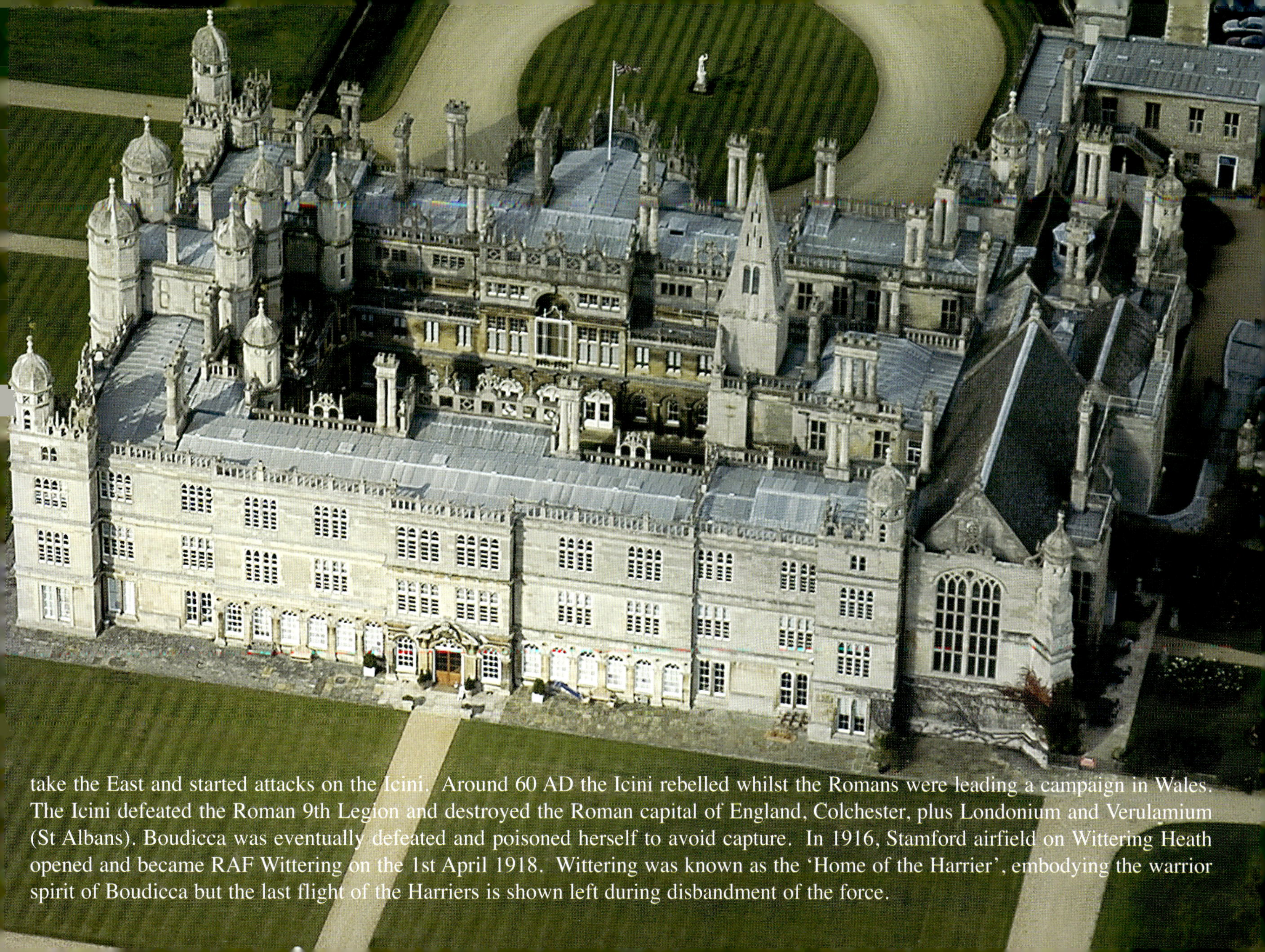

take the East and started attacks on the Icini. Around 60 AD the Icini rebelled whilst the Romans were leading a campaign in Wales. The Icini defeated the Roman 9th Legion and destroyed the Roman capital of England, Colchester, plus Londonium and Verulamium (St Albans). Boudicca was eventually defeated and poisoned herself to avoid capture. In 1916, Stamford airfield on Wittering Heath opened and became RAF Wittering on the 1st April 1918. Wittering was known as the 'Home of the Harrier', embodying the warrior spirit of Boudicca but the last flight of the Harriers is shown left during disbandment of the force.

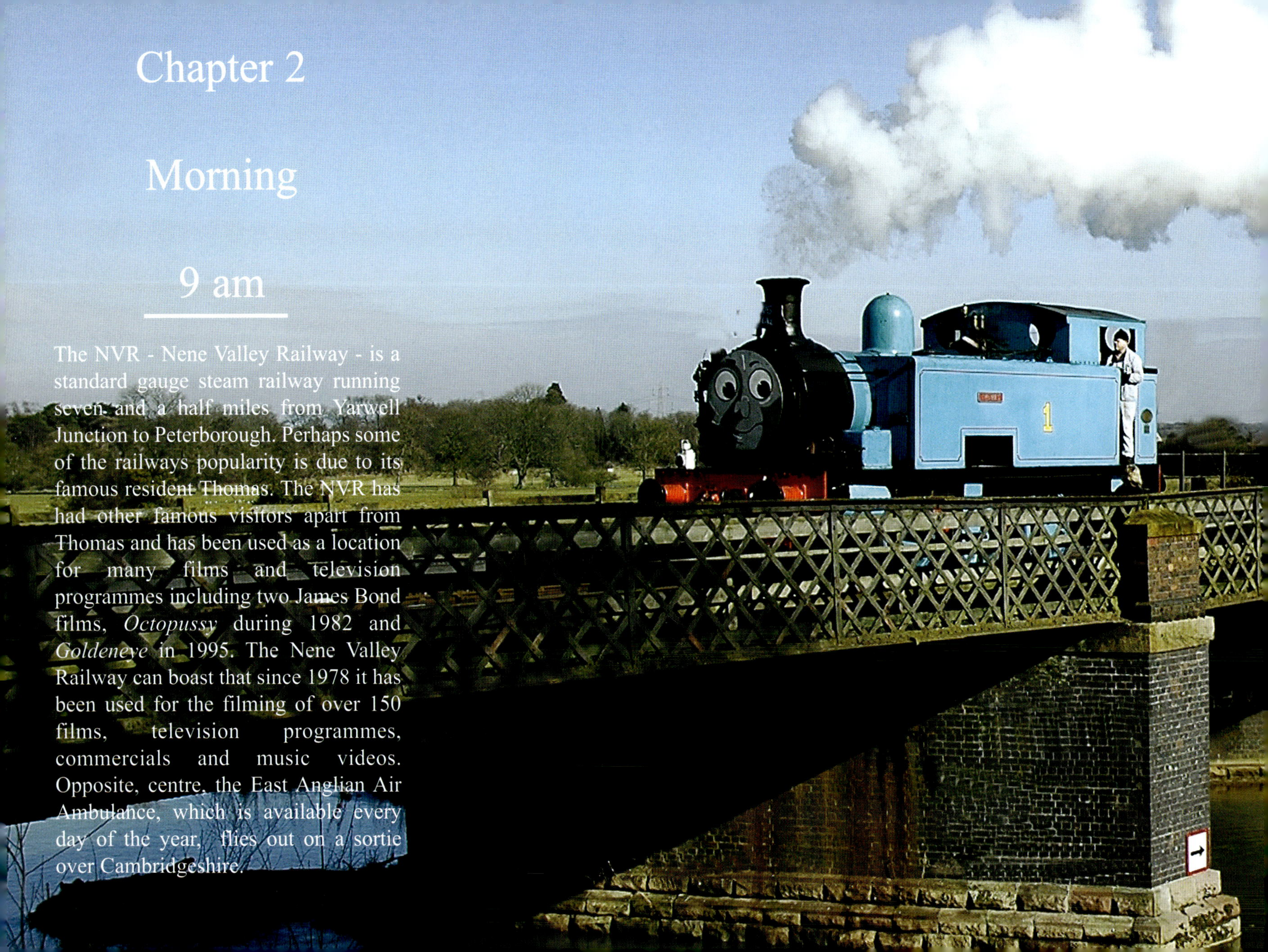

Chapter 2

Morning

9 am

The NVR - Nene Valley Railway - is a standard gauge steam railway running seven and a half miles from Yarwell Junction to Peterborough. Perhaps some of the railways popularity is due to its famous resident Thomas. The NVR has had other famous visitors apart from Thomas and has been used as a location for many films and television programmes including two James Bond films, *Octopussy* during 1982 and *Goldeneye* in 1995. The Nene Valley Railway can boast that since 1978 it has been used for the filming of over 150 films, television programmes, commercials and music videos. Opposite, centre, the East Anglian Air Ambulance, which is available every day of the year, flies out on a sortie over Cambridgeshire.

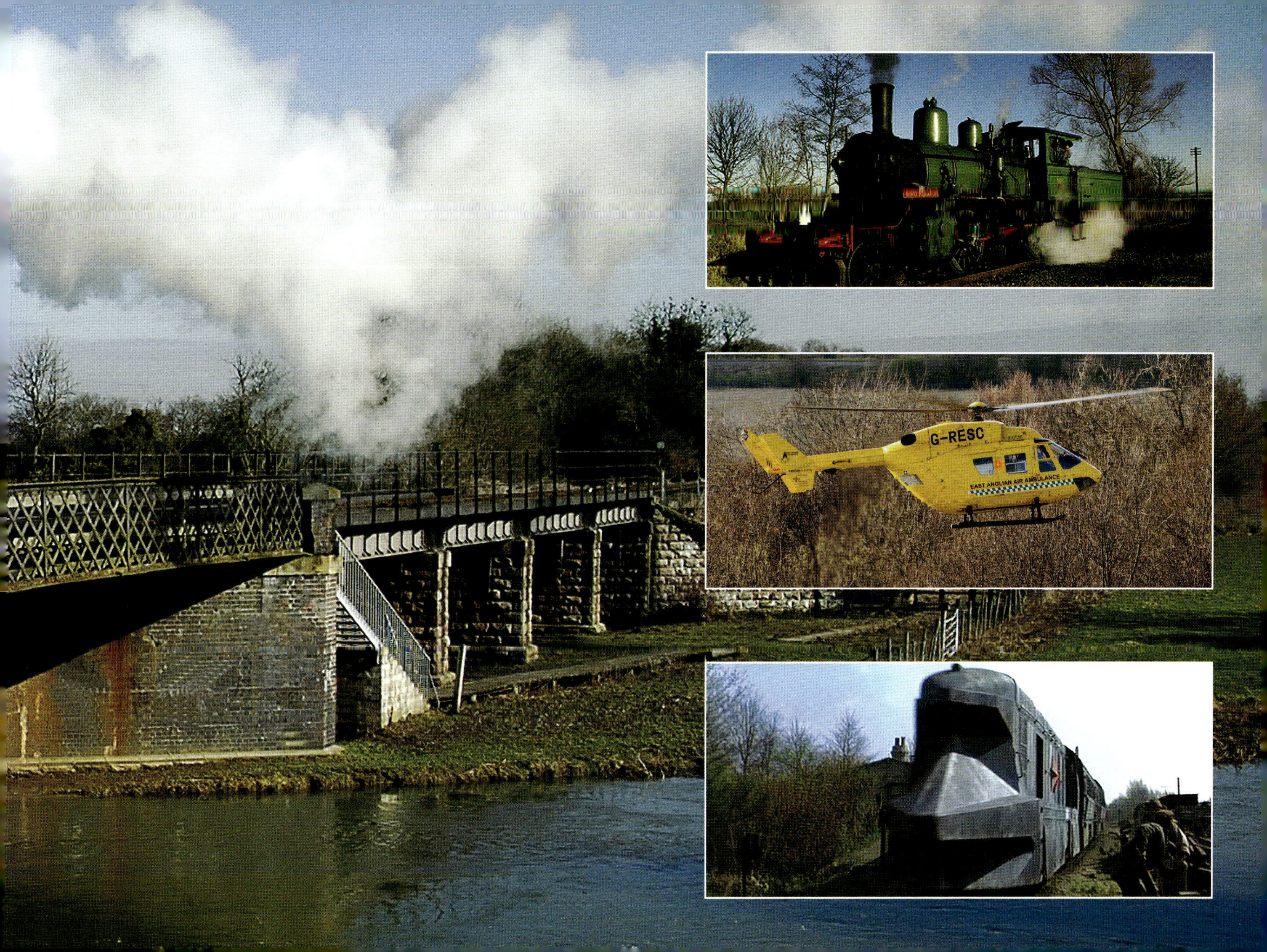
G-RESC
EAST ANGLIAN AIR AMBULANCE

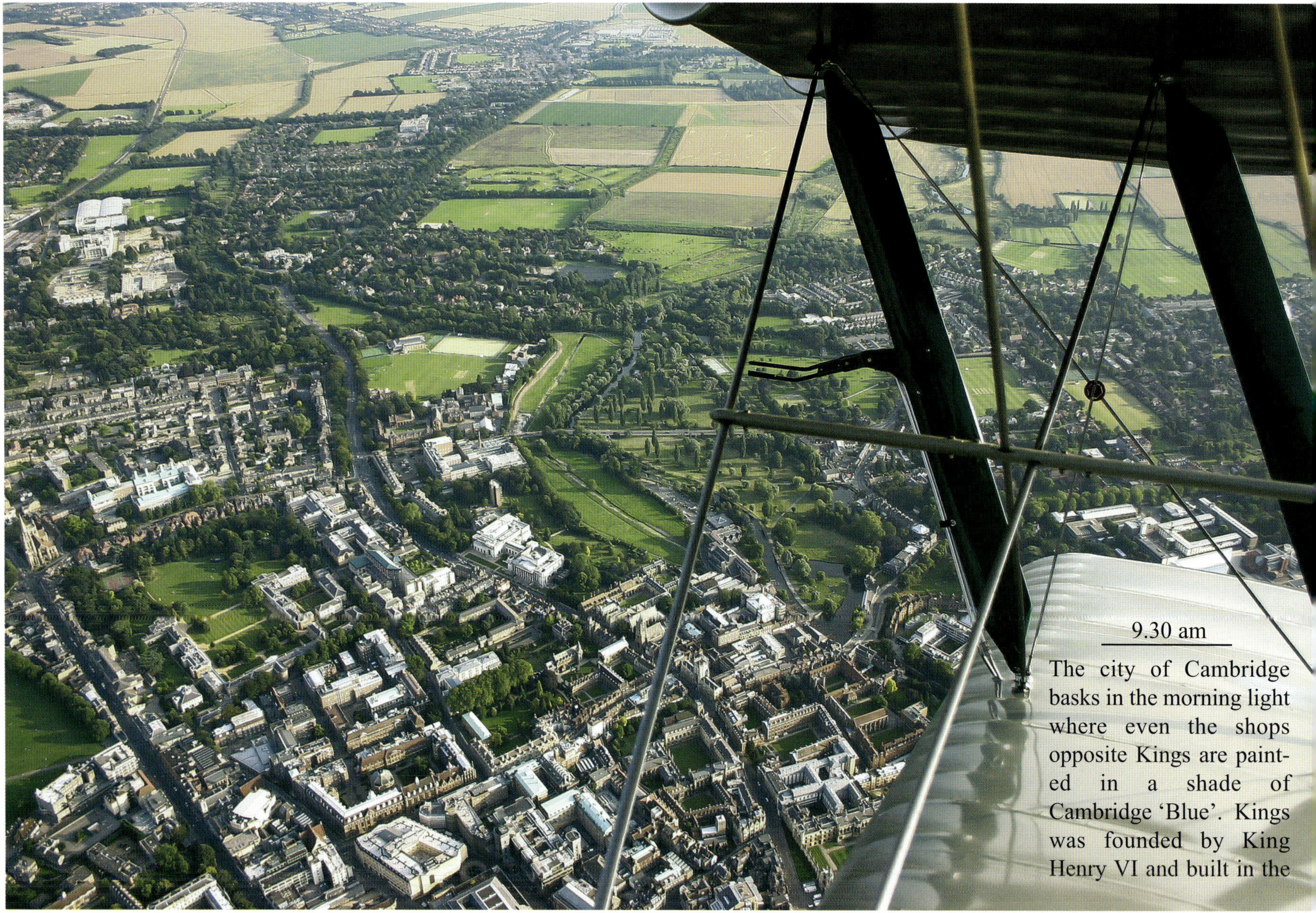

9.30 am

The city of Cambridge basks in the morning light where even the shops opposite Kings are painted in a shade of Cambridge 'Blue'. Kings was founded by King Henry VI and built in the

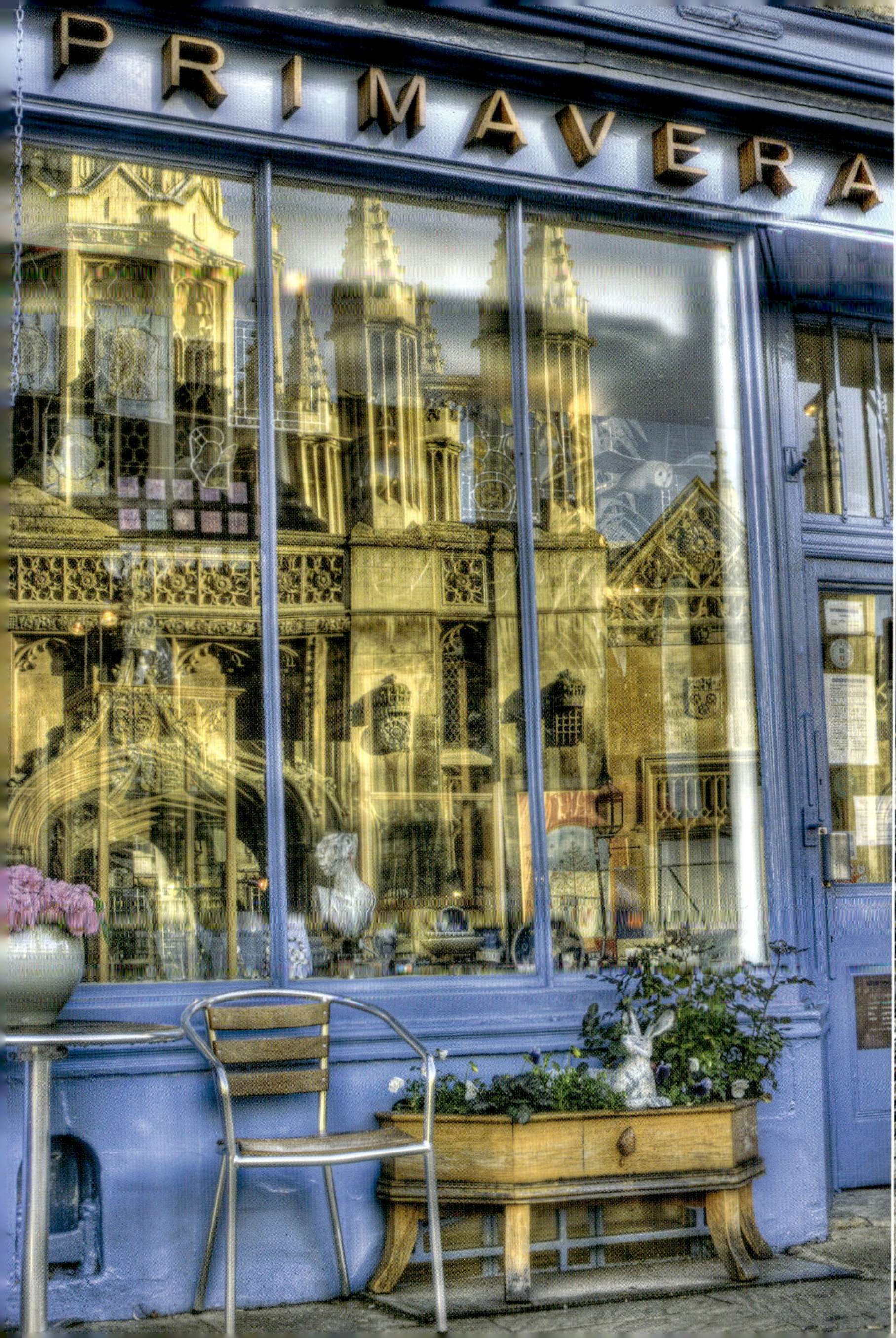

dramatic 'perpendicular' style, long before the invention of the modern bicycle, now a social and cultural feature in every corner of Cambridge.

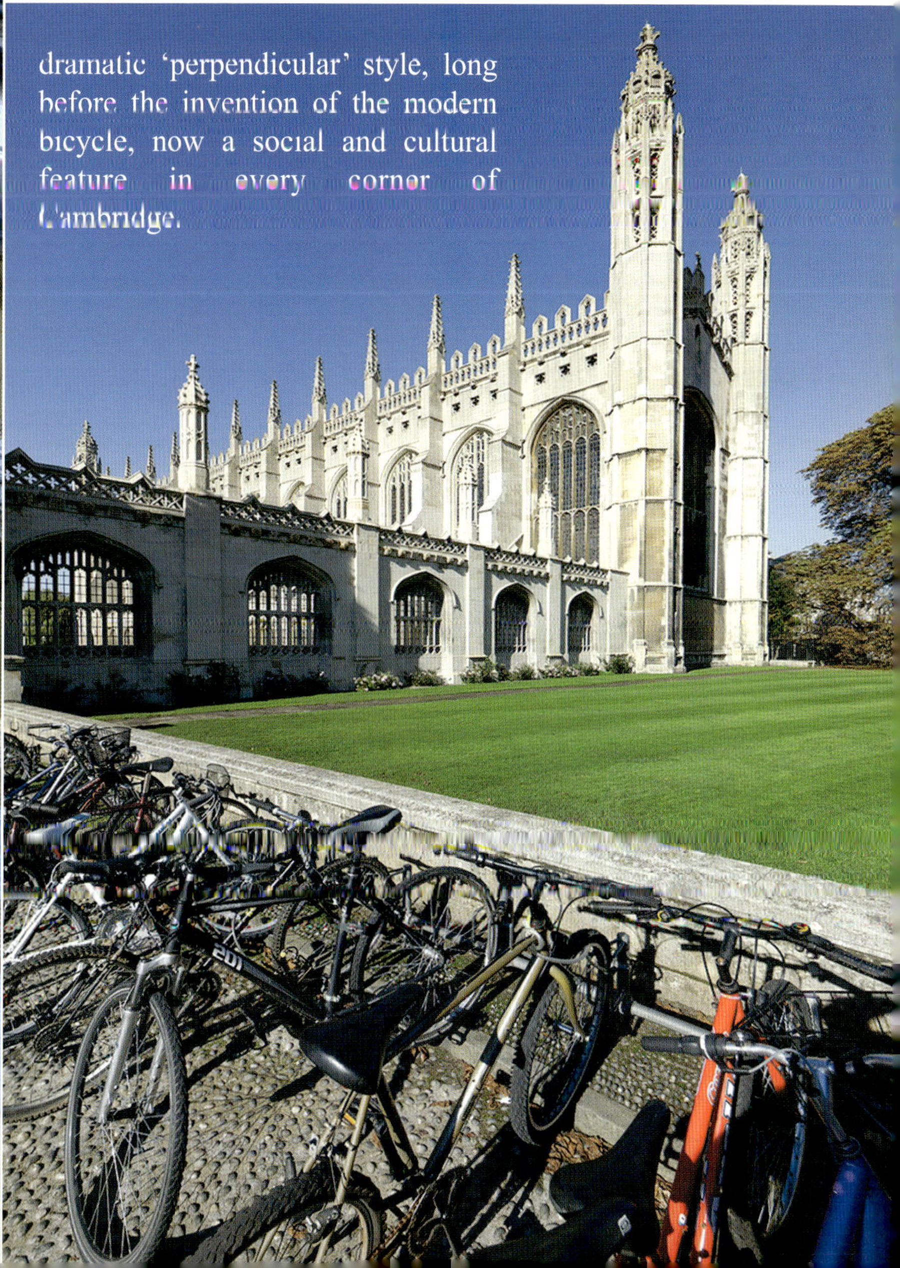

9.30 am

After the dissolution of Ramsey Abbey in 1539, the Manor of Houghton-cum-Wyton passed to the crown. A mill has stood on the present site for over a 1,000 years. In 1625, King Charles sold it and it eventually became the property of Lady Sparrow in the 19th century. She leased the mill to Potto Brown from 1822 to 1862 and then to his son, Bateman, for 14 more years. The mill had three water-wheels which were removed in 1930. With a grant from the Lottery, a new wheel has been fitted and Houghton Mill has now become a working mill once more.

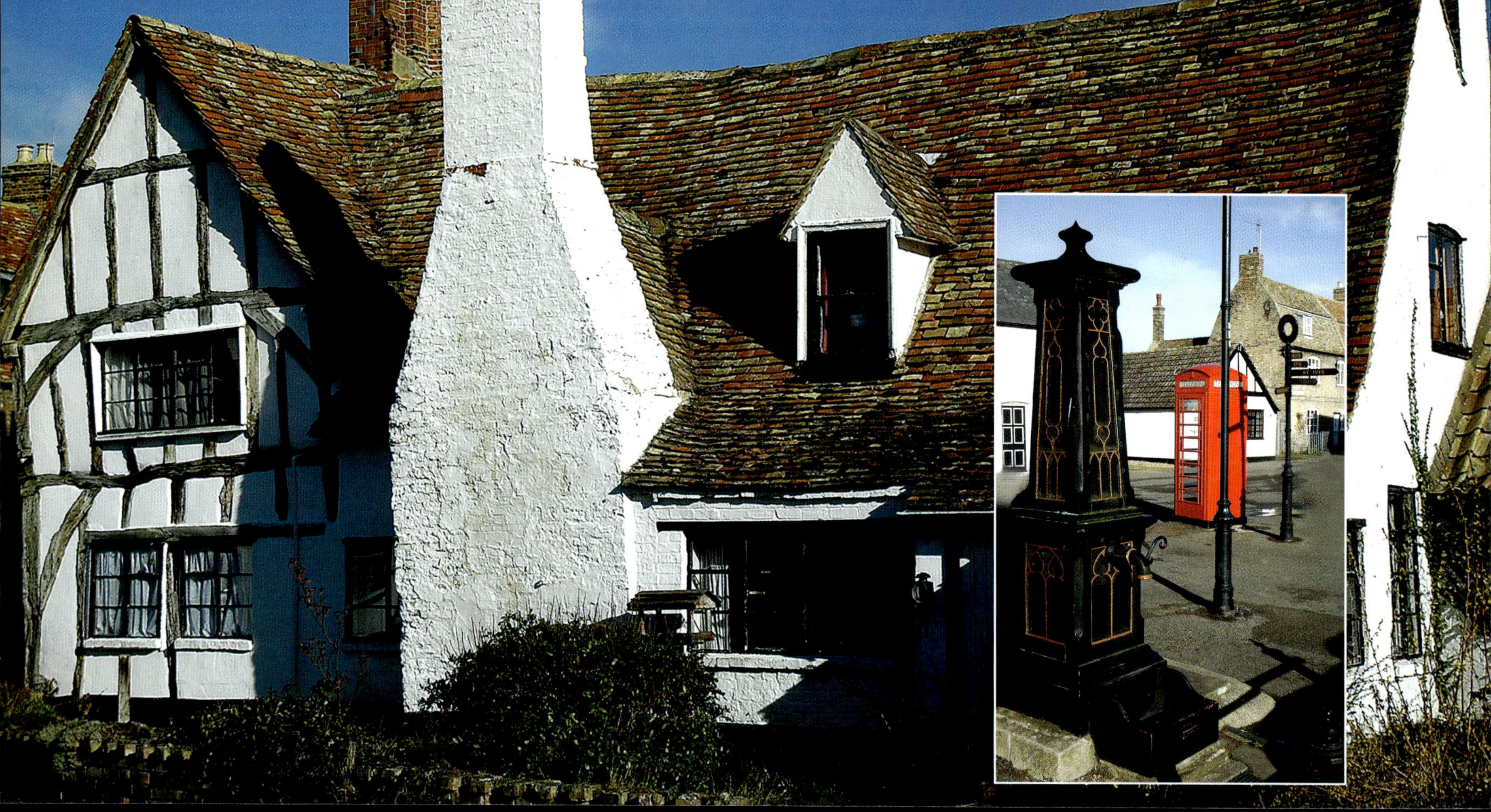

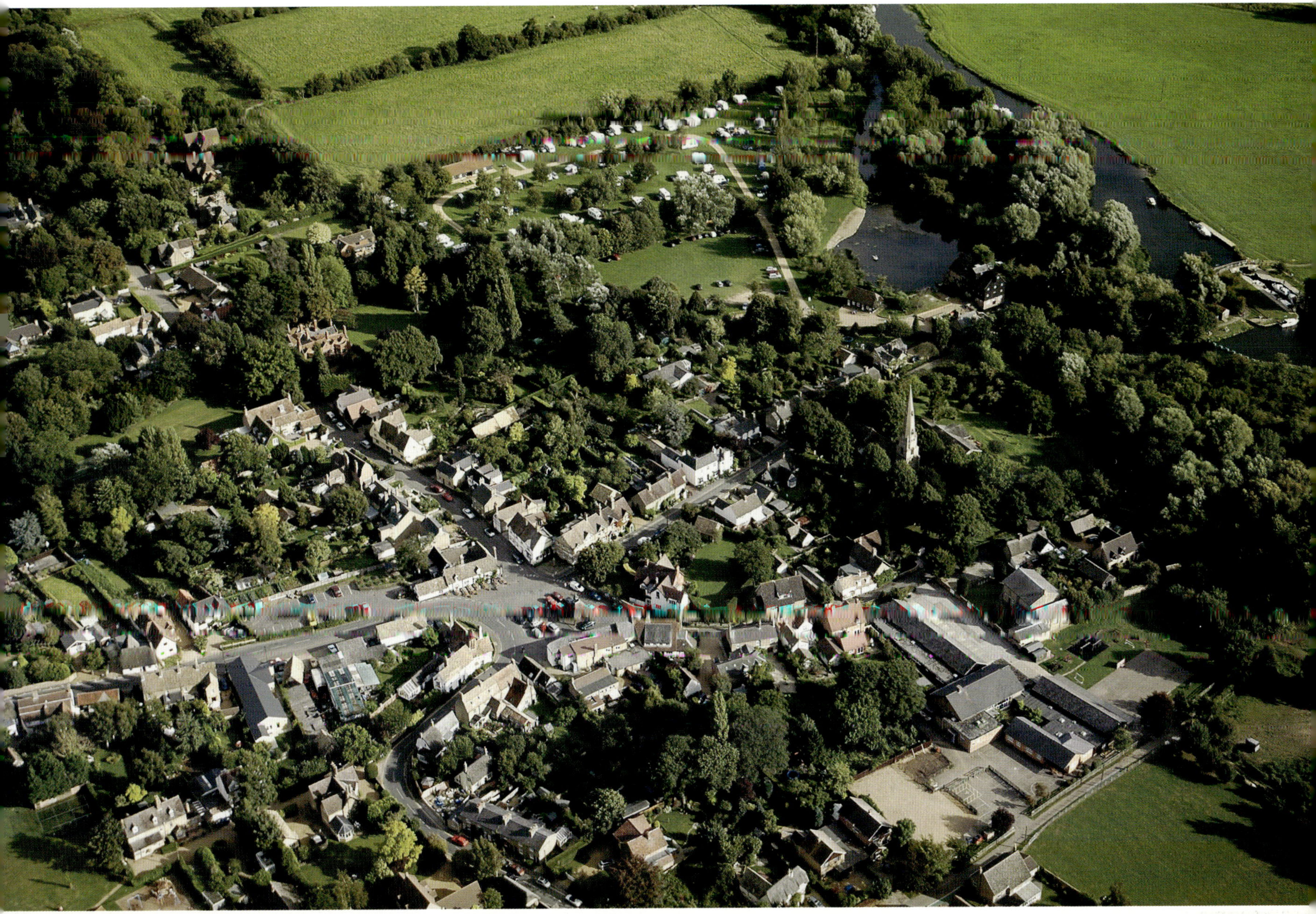

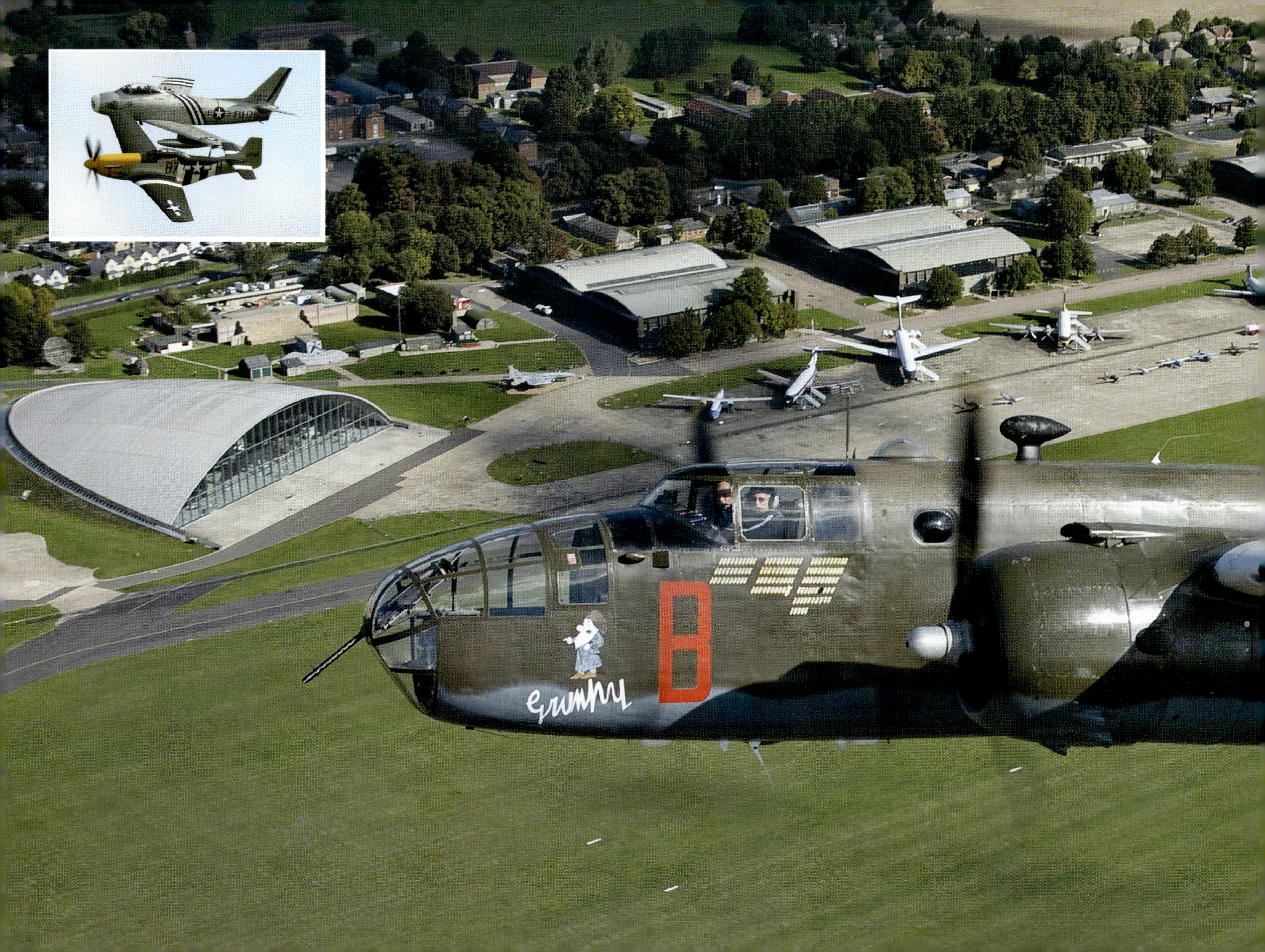
FU-178
B7
B
Grumpy

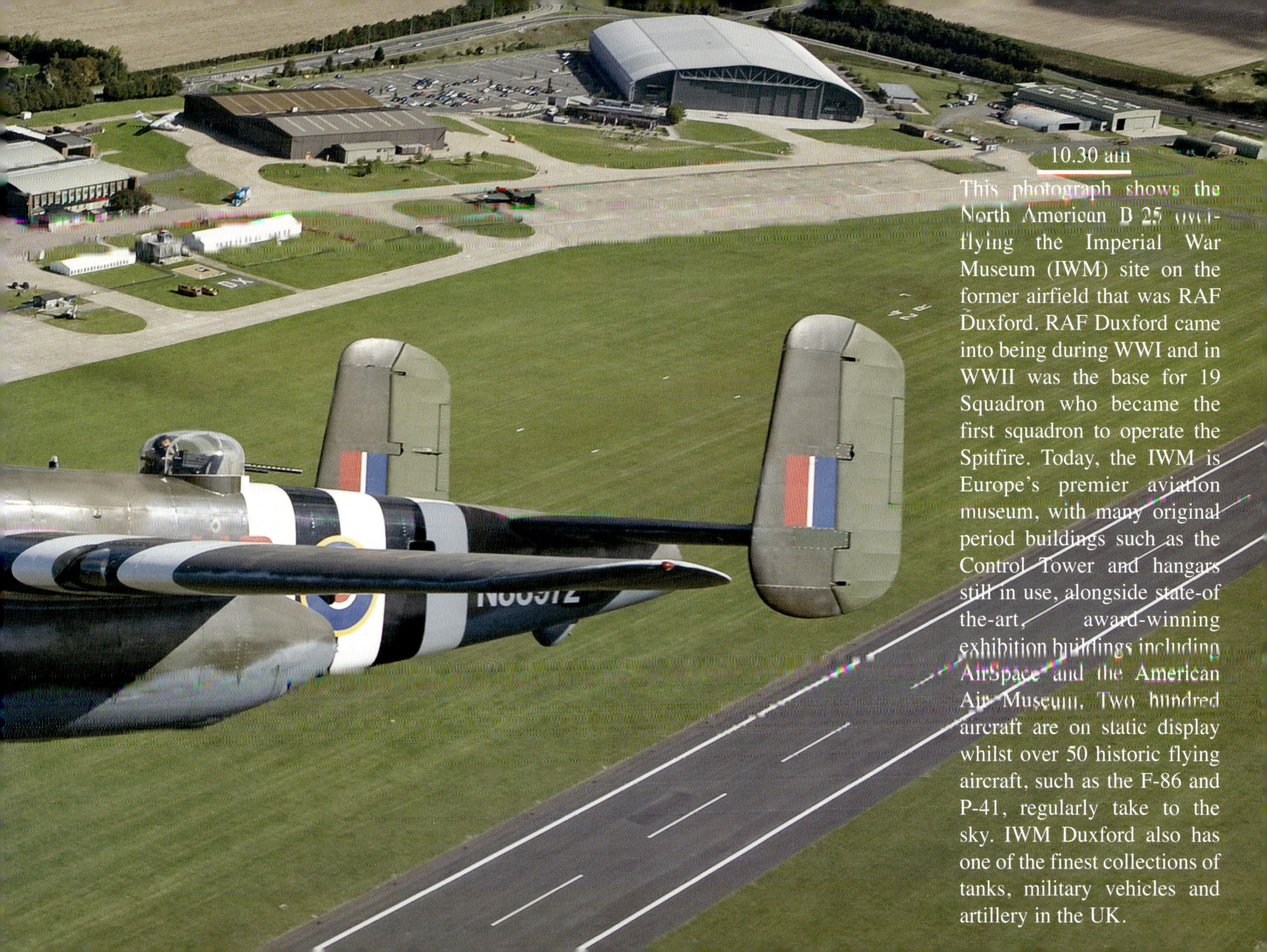

10.30 am

This photograph shows the North American B-25 over-flying the Imperial War Museum (IWM) site on the former airfield that was RAF Duxford. RAF Duxford came into being during WWI and in WWII was the base for 19 Squadron who became the first squadron to operate the Spitfire. Today, the IWM is Europe's premier aviation museum, with many original period buildings such as the Control Tower and hangars still in use, alongside state-of the-art, award-winning exhibition buildings including AirSpace and the American Air Museum. Two hundred aircraft are on static display whilst over 50 historic flying aircraft, such as the F-86 and P-41, regularly take to the sky. IWM Duxford also has one of the finest collections of tanks, military vehicles and artillery in the UK.

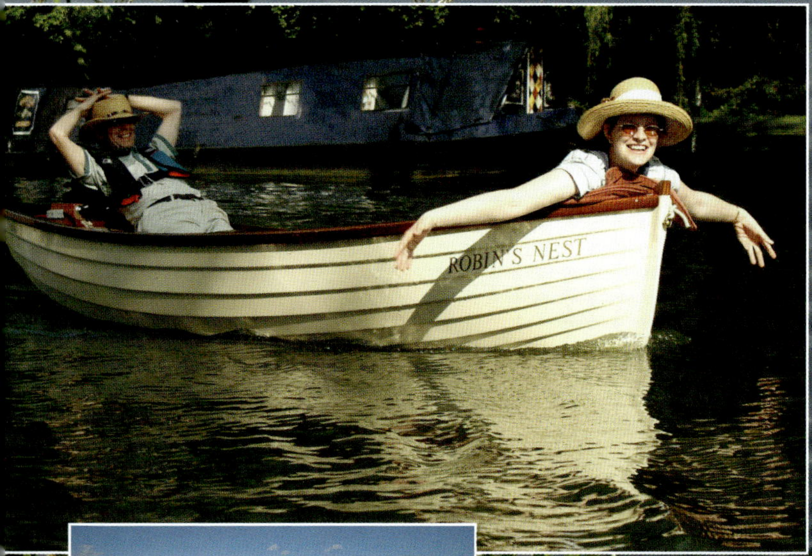

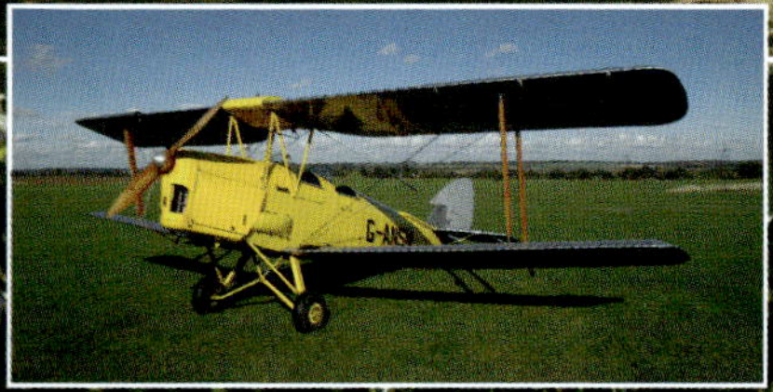

11 am

For those wishing to fly up and down the River Cam, hats have always been fashionable. The monochrome photograph was taken in May 1887 at an event that became known as the 'Bump' races. Side-by-side racing is not possible over a long distance on the narrow and winding River Cam, so the bumps format was introduced in the early 19th century as an exciting alternative. In bumping races, crews line up along the river

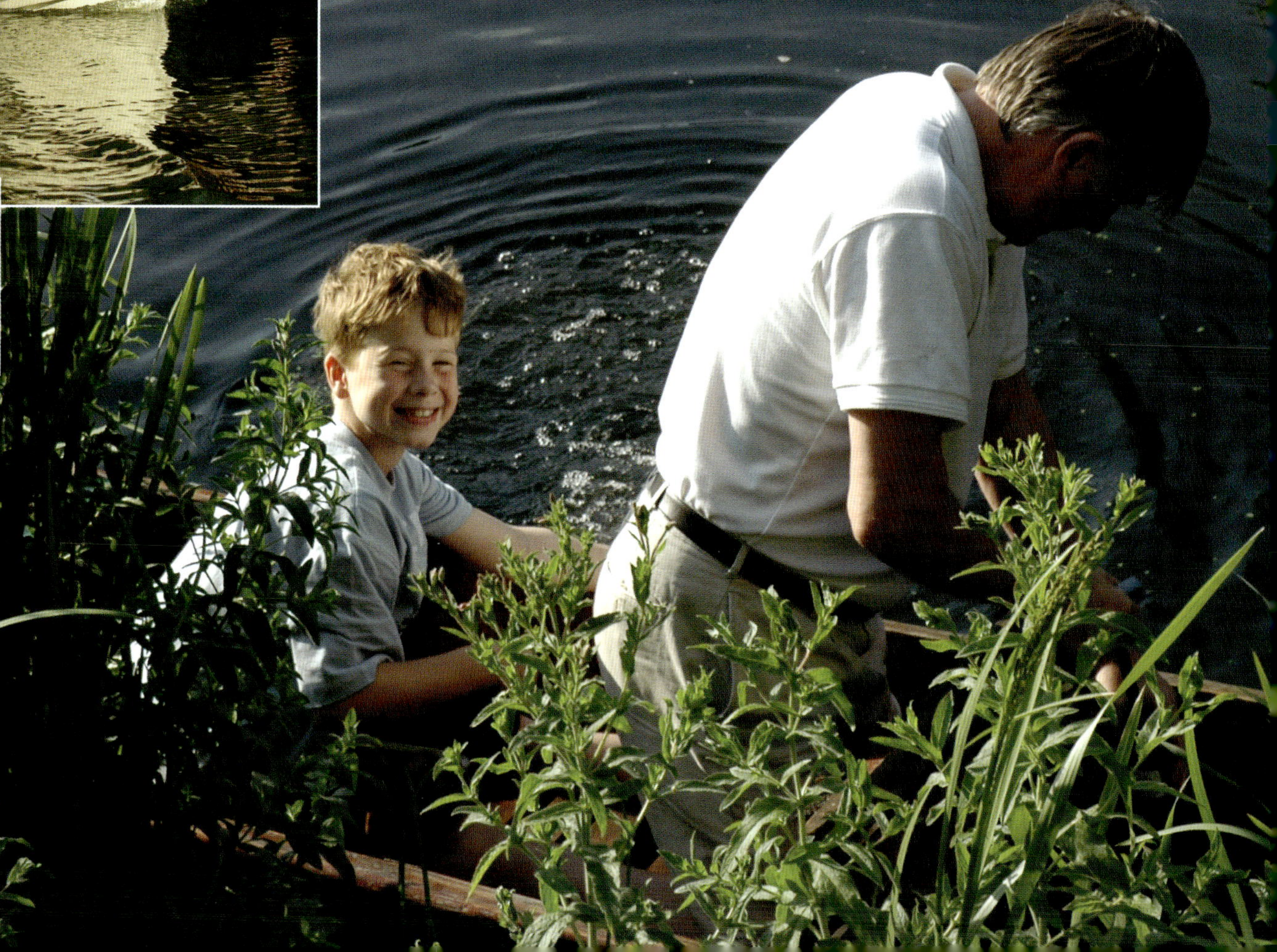

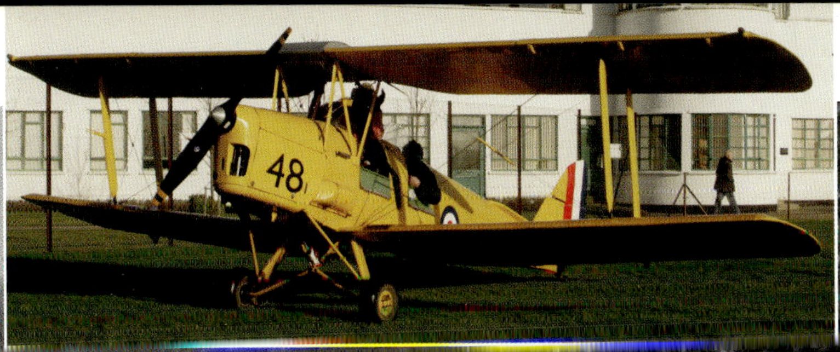

with one and a half boat lengths of clear water between them. On the start signal (the firing of a cannon) they chase each other up the river. When a bump occurs (when one crew is hit by its chasing crew), they pull over to allow the other crews to continue racing. The next day all crews involved in a bump swap places and the race is run again. After the four days of racing, the aim of the top crews is to be at the 'head of the river' i.e. they lead the first division.

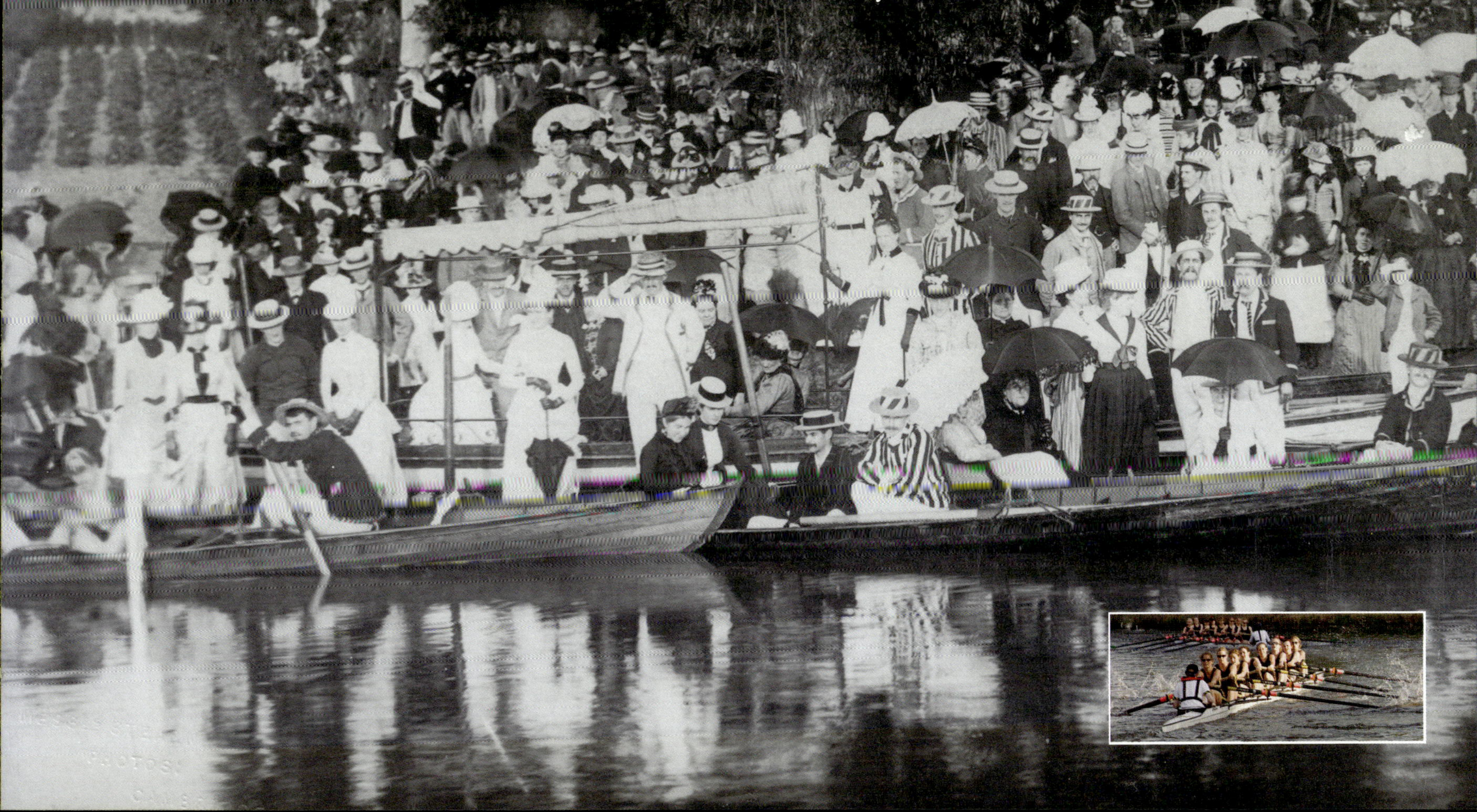

11.15 am

Cap, gowns and hats are worn by punting pilots while overhead, a pilot of an RAF Hercules, newly fitted with a refuelling probe by Marshalls, is climbing out from Cambridge Airport en route back to base.

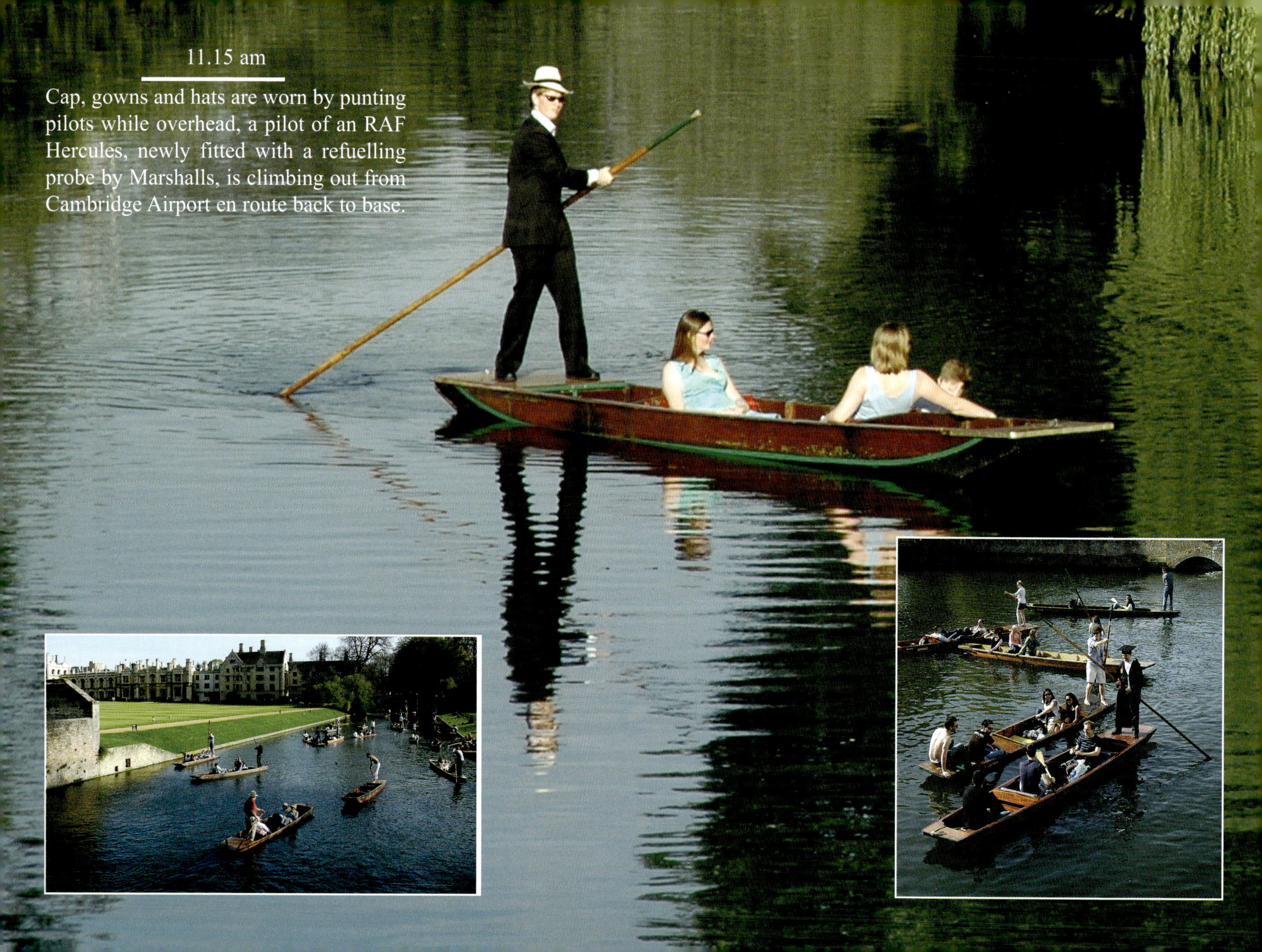

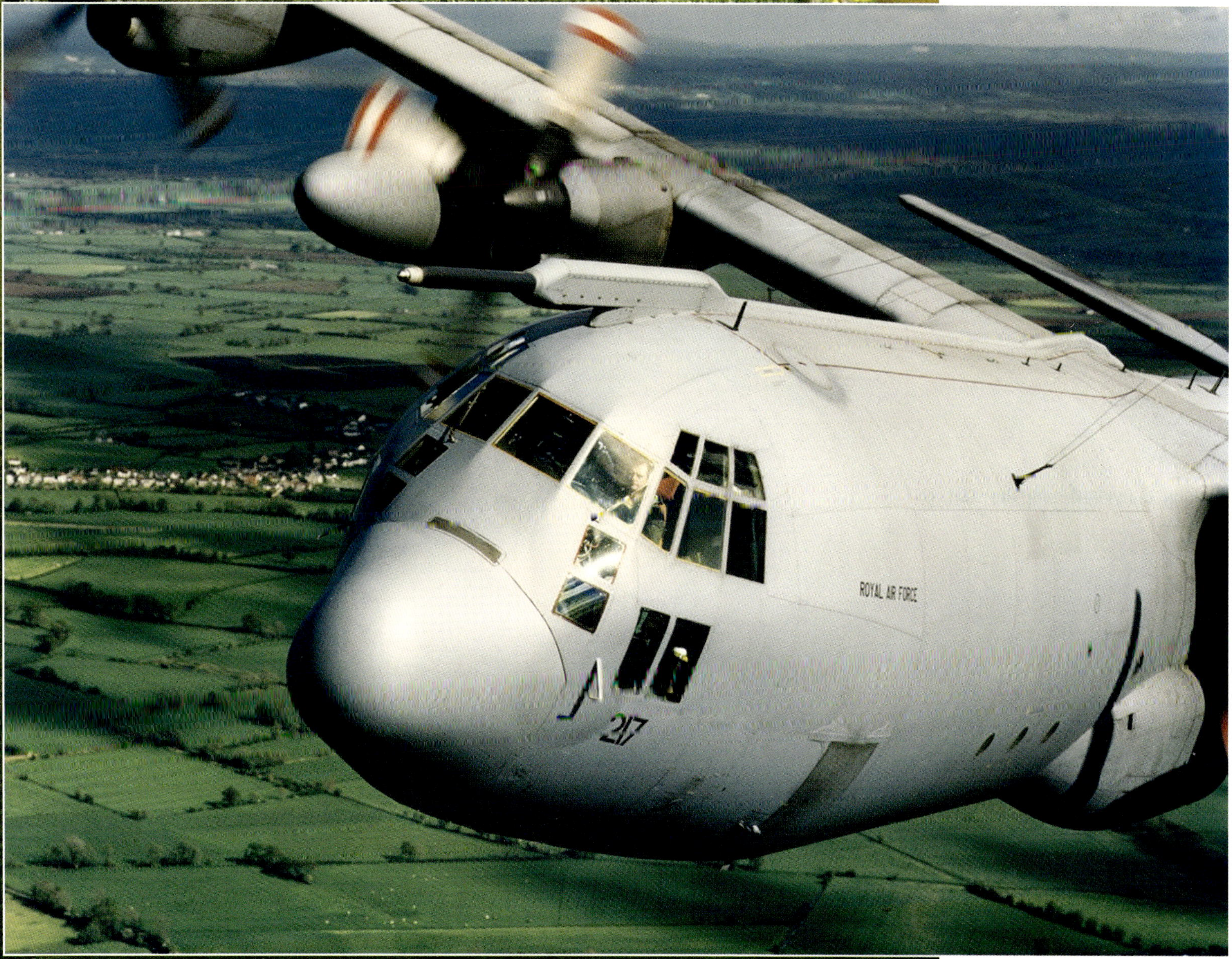
ROYAL AIR FORCE
217

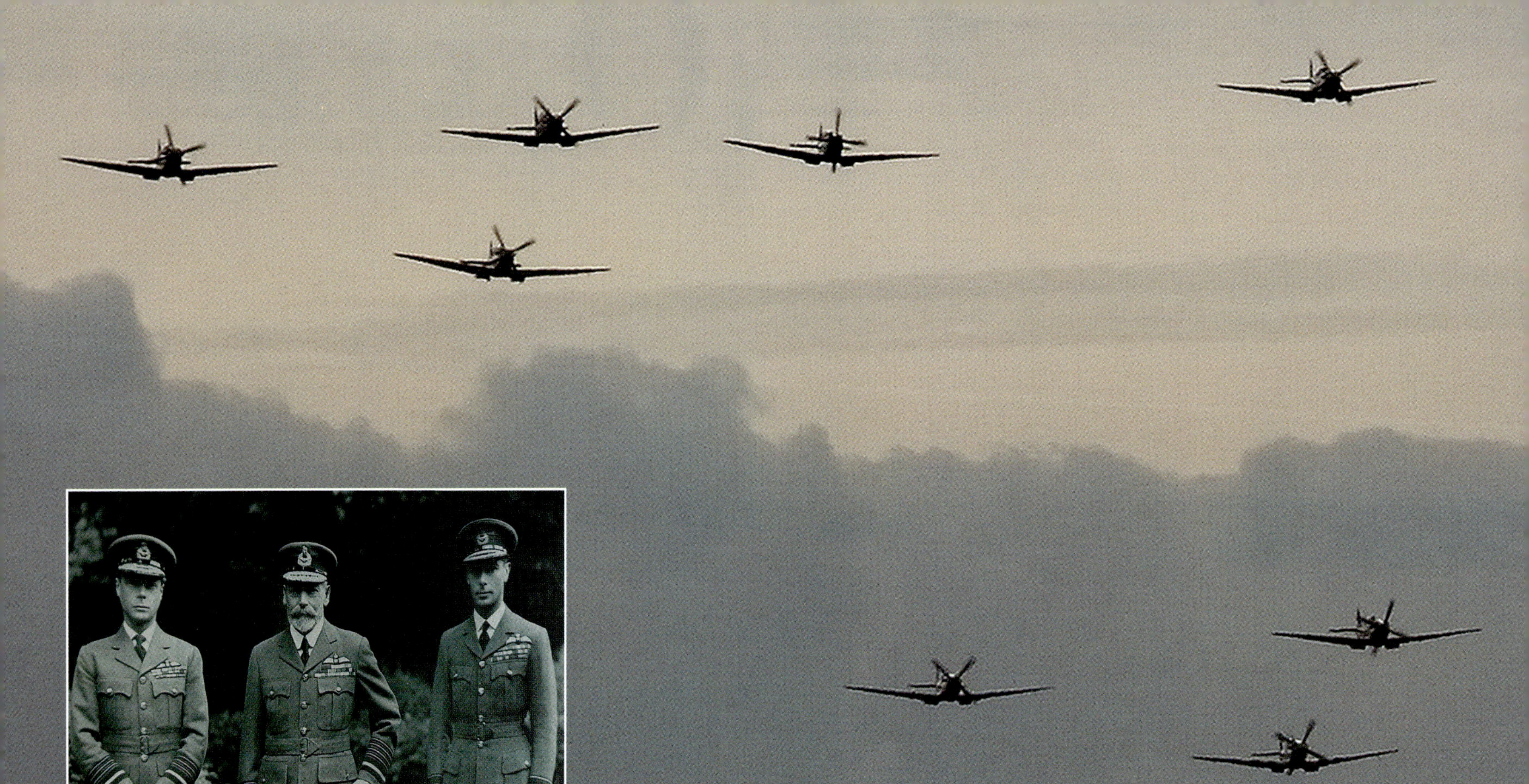

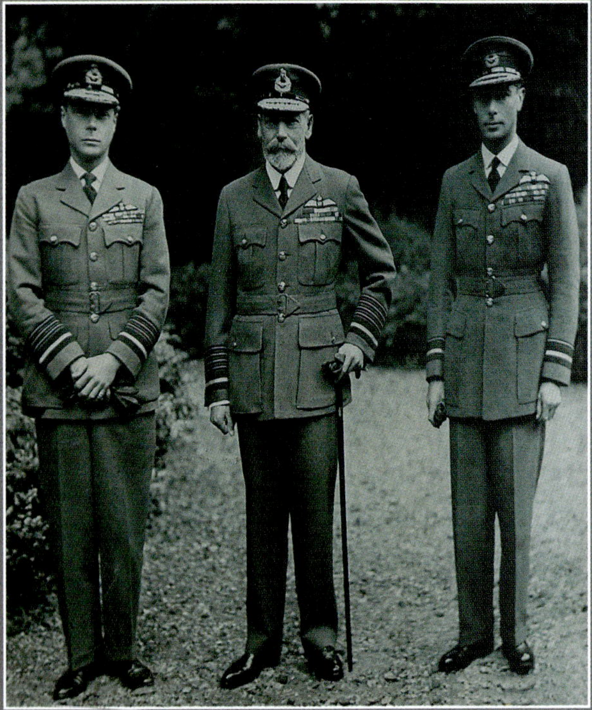

11.30 am

On the 4th September 2010, 40,000 people watched 16 Supermarine Spitfires overfly the former RAF airfield at Duxford during the annual September Air Show to commemorate the 70th anniversary of the RAF's finest hour - the Battle of Britain. RAF Duxford first opened in 1918 and in 1935 was the location of the Silver Jubilee celebrations of King George V, shown left with two of his sons, Prince Edward, later King Edward VIII and Prince Albert, later King George VI. Number 19 Squadron was resident at Duxford and gave a 'spirited' display and was the first to re-equip with Spitfires. A formation of 19 Squadron Spitfires is shown

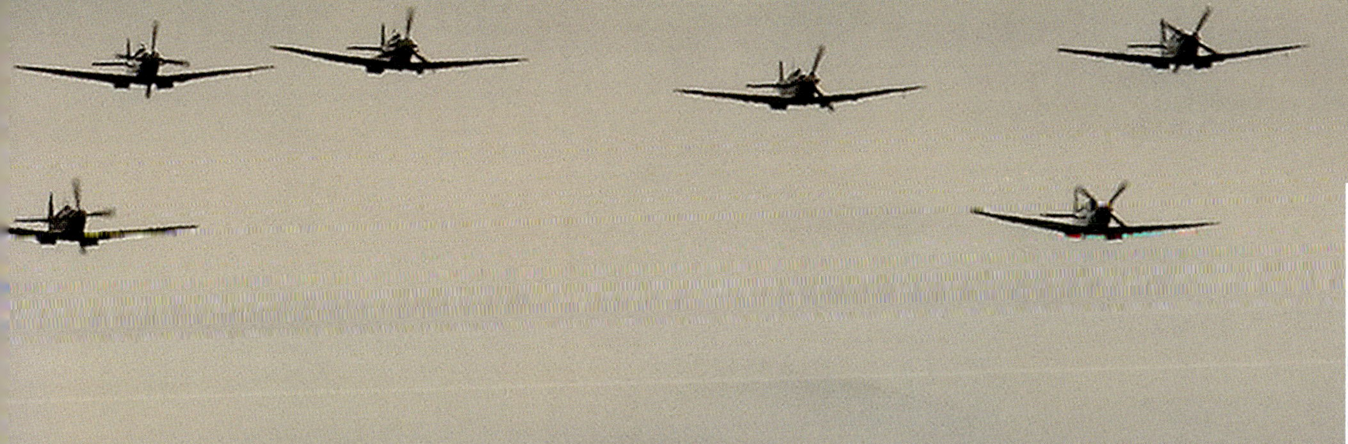

'Never in the field of human conflict was so much owed by so many to so few'. Winston Churchill, 20th August 1940, The House of Commons.

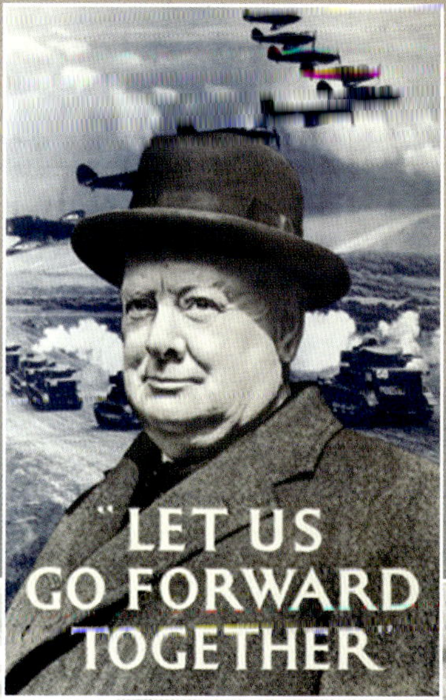

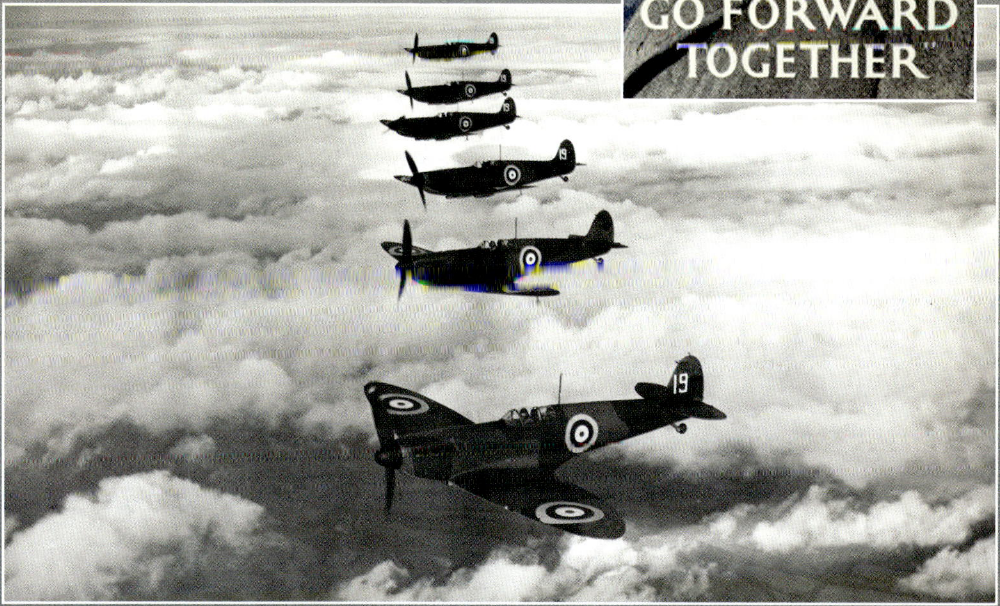

right. After WWII, Churchill College, a constituent college of Cambridge University was established in 1958 with a motto that reads simply 'Forward'. This motto was from Churchill's famous, call-to-arms, speech, 'Blood, toil, tears and sweat', given to the Commons on 13th May 1940 on his first day as new Prime Minister. In 1972, Churchill College was the first to admit ladies.

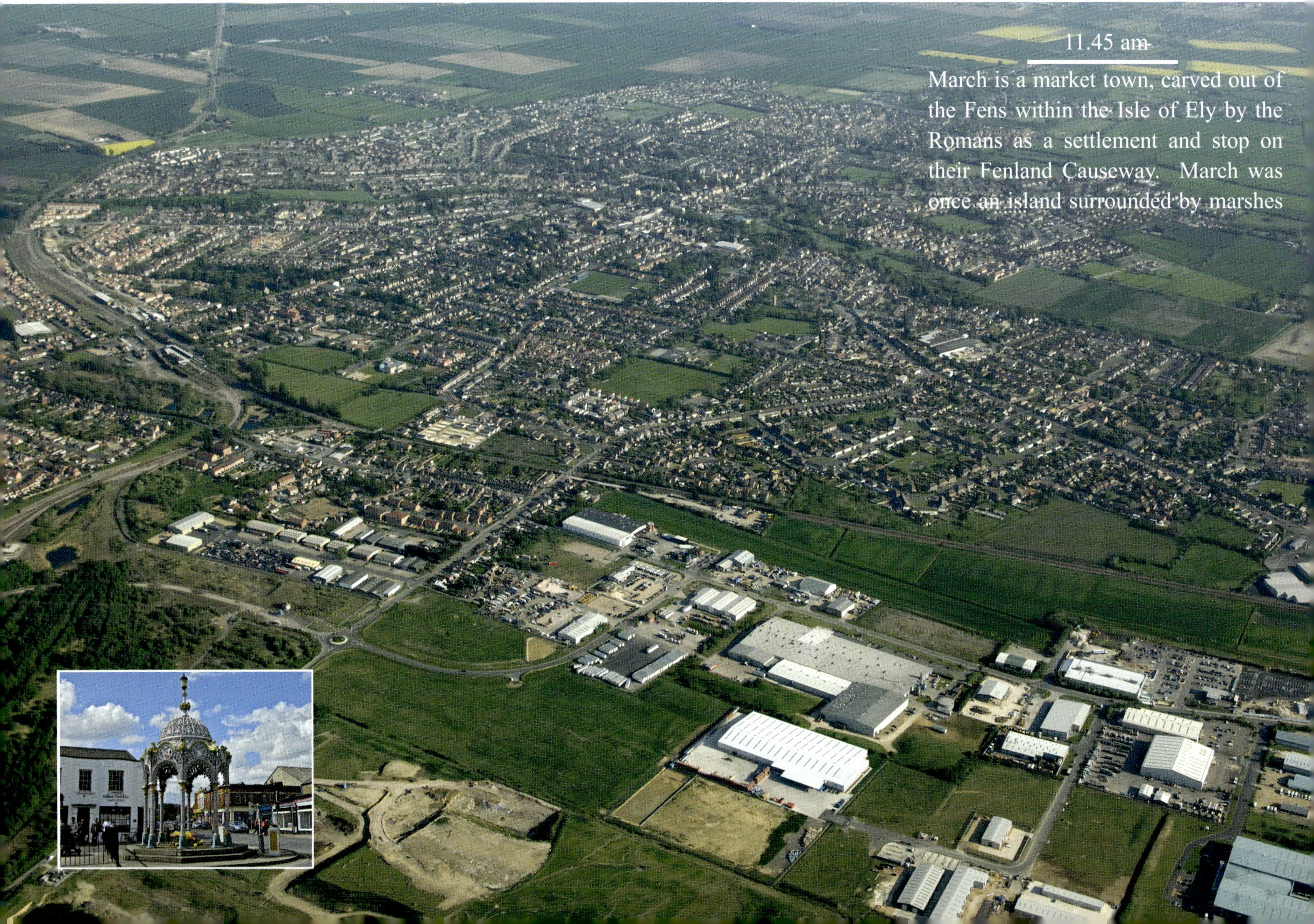

11.45 am

March is a market town, carved out of the Fens within the Isle of Ely by the Romans as a settlement and stop on their Fenland Causeway. March was once an island surrounded by marshes and occupied the second largest 'island' in the Great Level. As the land drained, the town grew and prospered as a trading, religious and a minor port. Today, it is a modern market town, administrative centre and a major railway junction. In the centre of March stands the Coronation Arch of King George V dedicated to his crowning in Westminster Abbey on the 22nd June 1911 and, almost 100 years later, on the 29th April 2011, Prince William and his bride, Catherine, became the Duke and Duchess of Cambridge. The extensive Great Fen Project, shown right, is the most exciting habitat restoration projects ever planned in Great Britain and will create a 3,700 hectare wetland almost midway between Huntingdon and Peterborough.

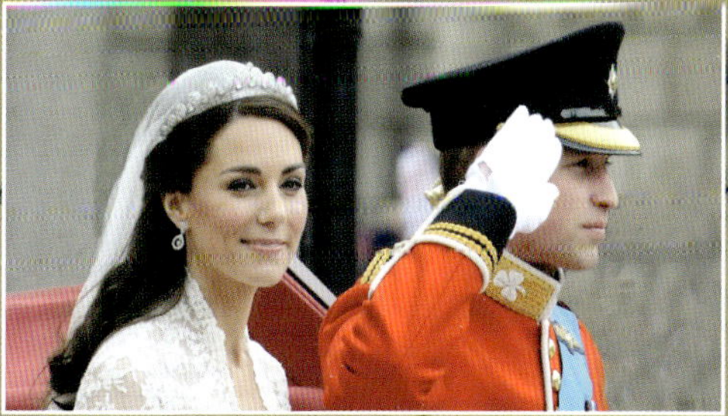

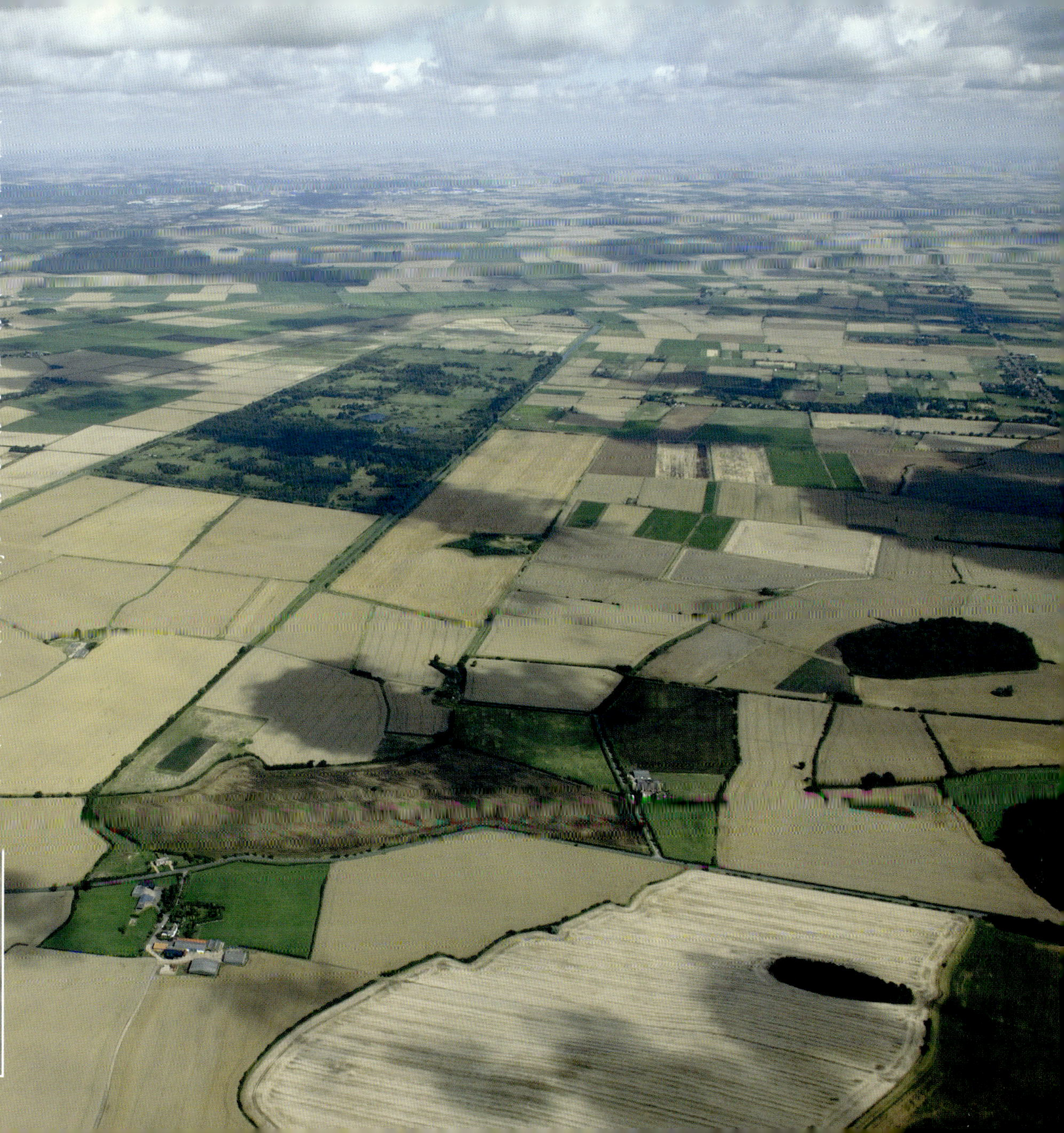

Chapter 3

Midday

12 pm

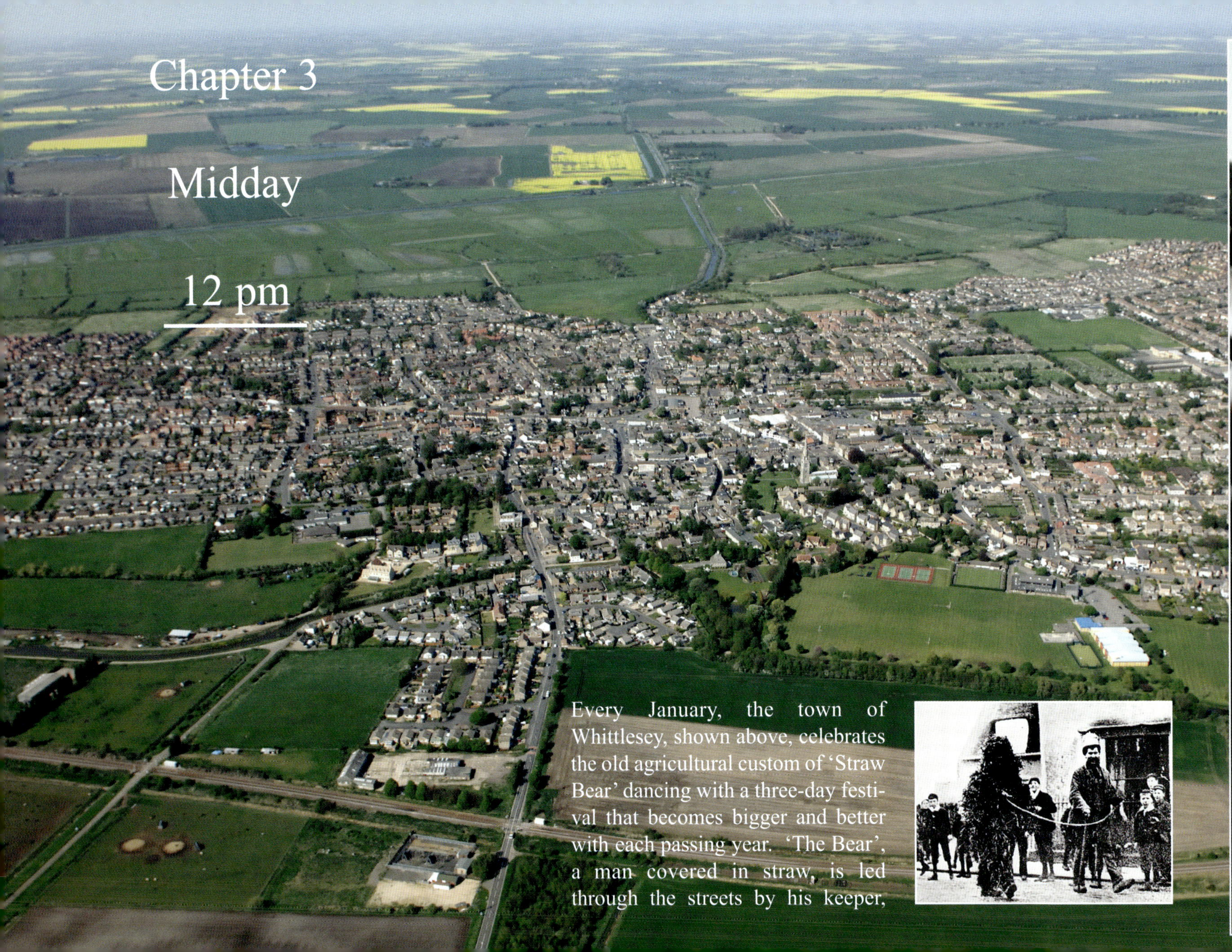

Every January, the town of Whittlesey, shown above, celebrates the old agricultural custom of 'Straw Bear' dancing with a three-day festival that becomes bigger and better with each passing year. 'The Bear', a man covered in straw, is led through the streets by his keeper,

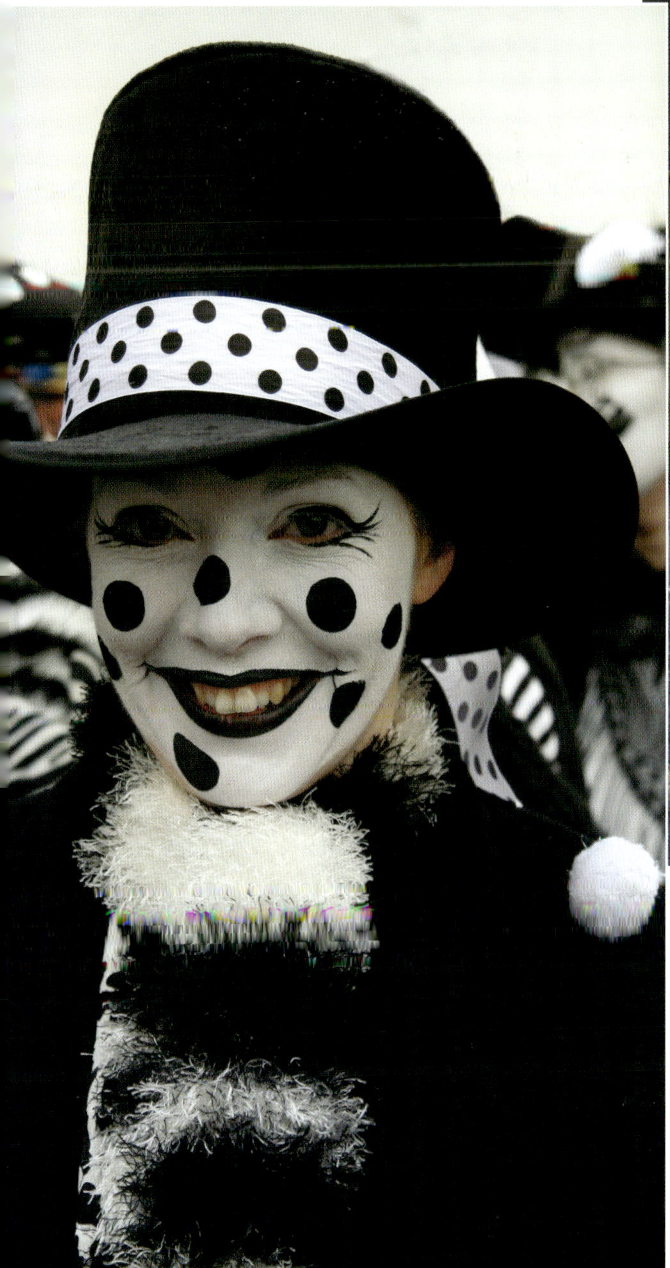

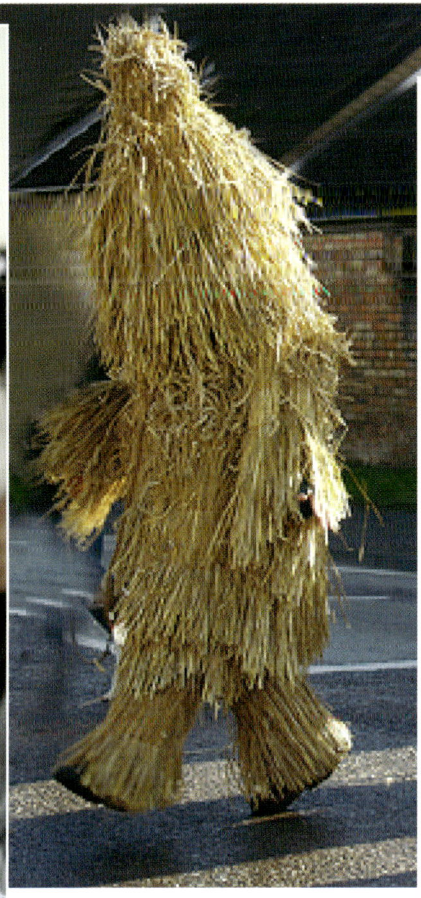

followed by a procession of over 250 musicians, dancers and performers touring the public houses around the route. The traditional procession takes place on a Saturday and events culminate on Sunday with the 'Straw Bear' being burnt.

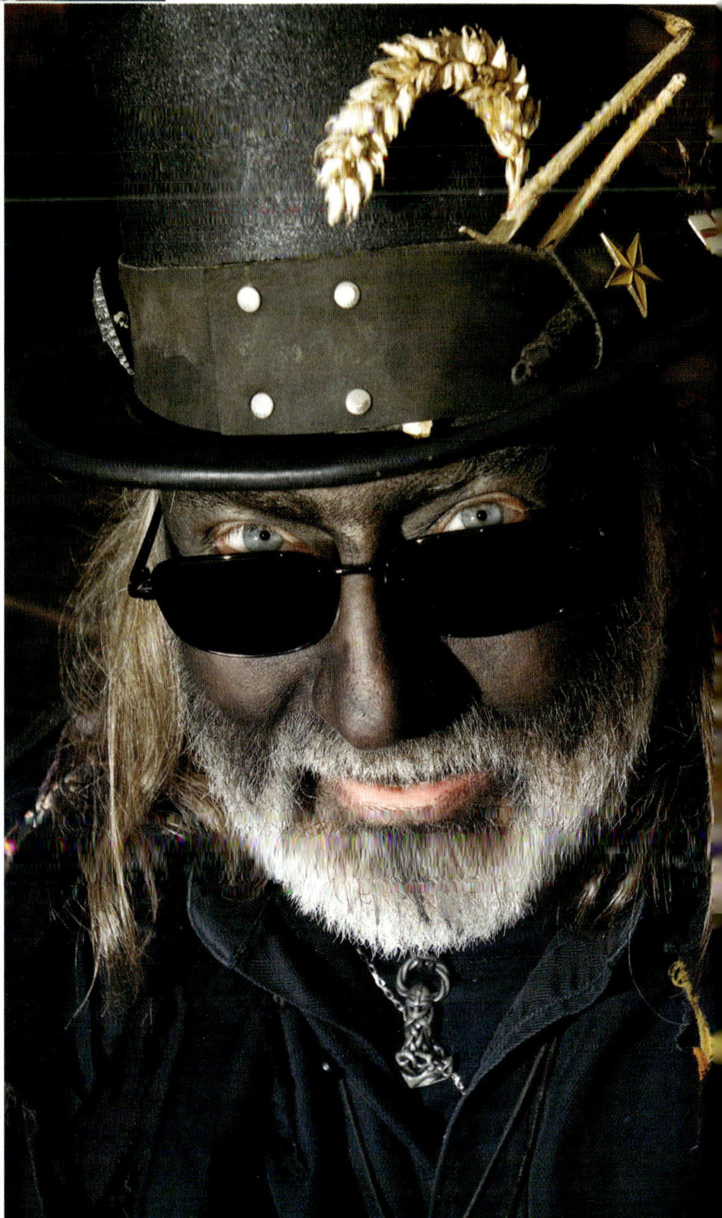

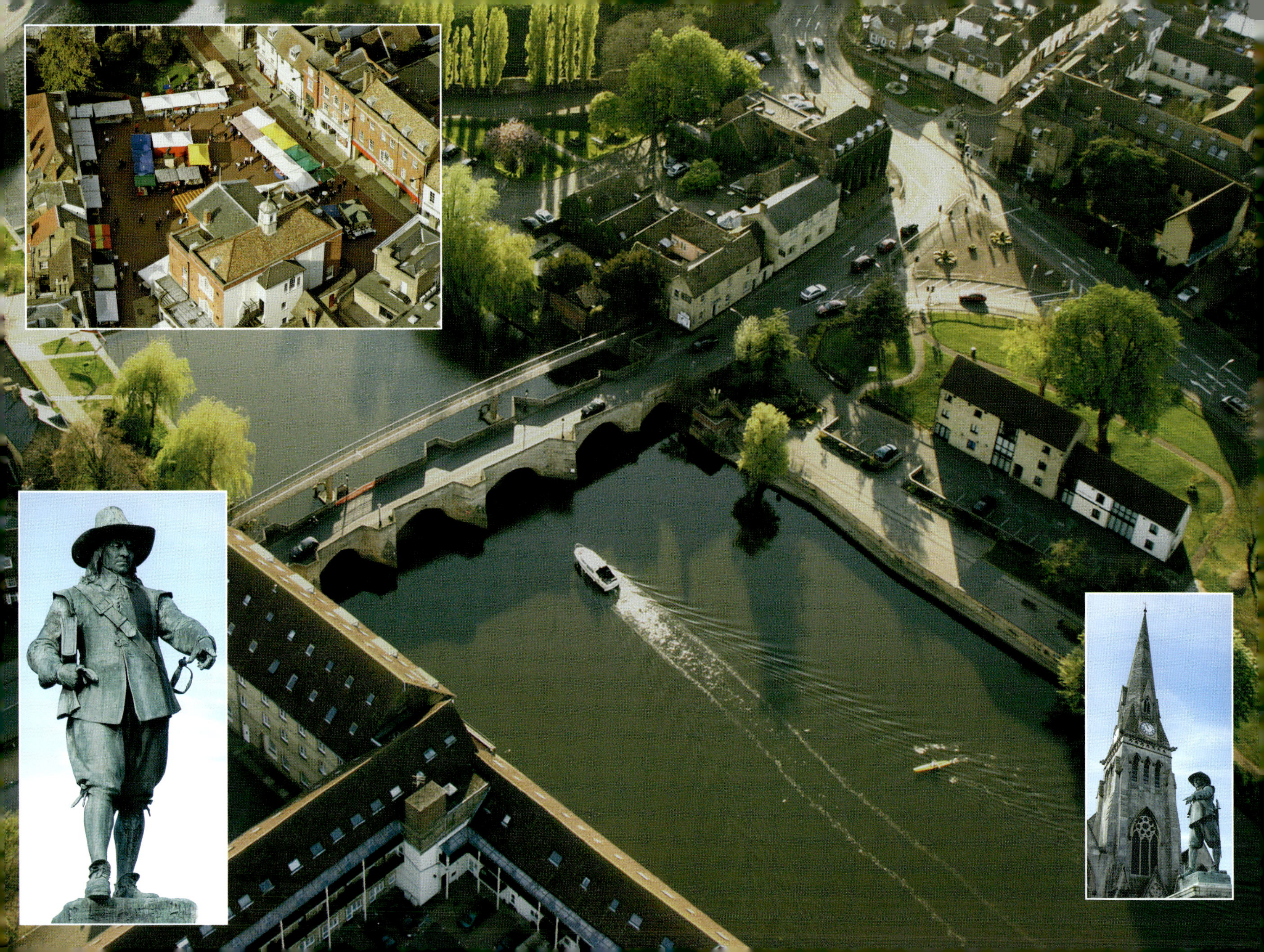

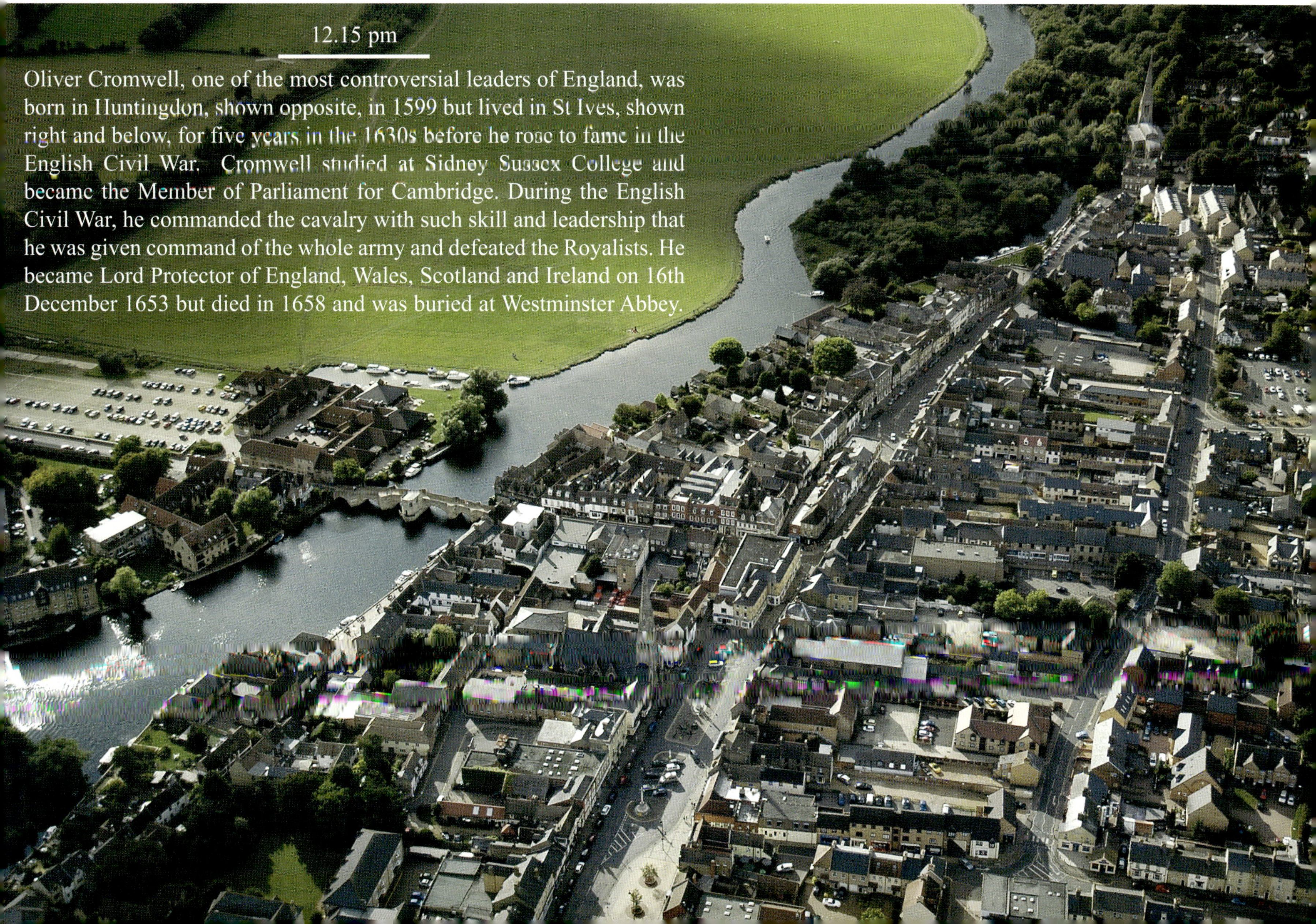

12.15 pm

Oliver Cromwell, one of the most controversial leaders of England, was born in Huntingdon, shown opposite, in 1599 but lived in St Ives, shown right and below, for five years in the 1630s before he rose to fame in the English Civil War. Cromwell studied at Sidney Sussex College and became the Member of Parliament for Cambridge. During the English Civil War, he commanded the cavalry with such skill and leadership that he was given command of the whole army and defeated the Royalists. He became Lord Protector of England, Wales, Scotland and Ireland on 16th December 1653 but died in 1658 and was buried at Westminster Abbey.

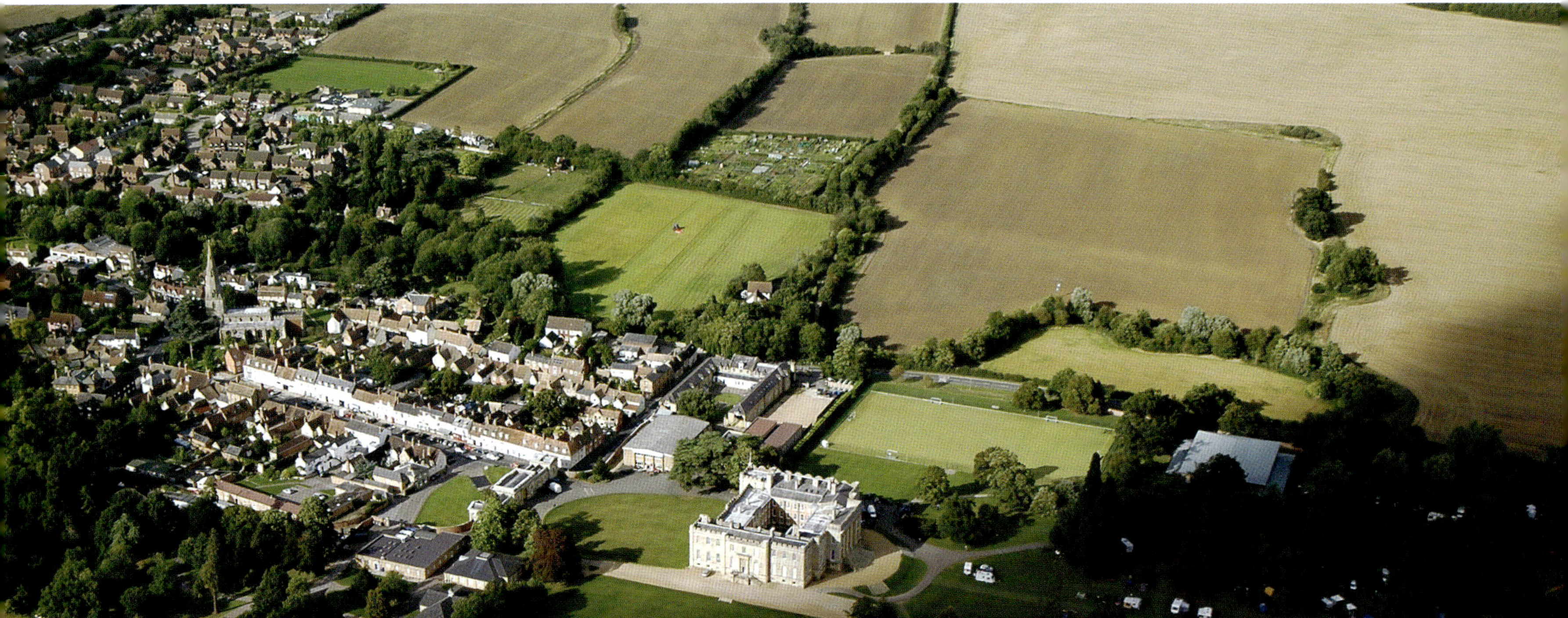

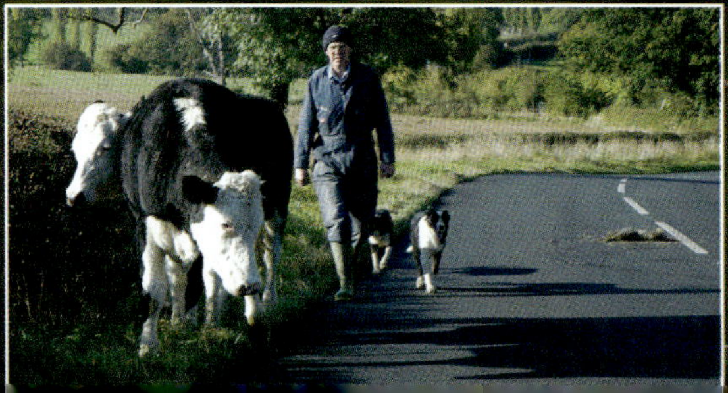

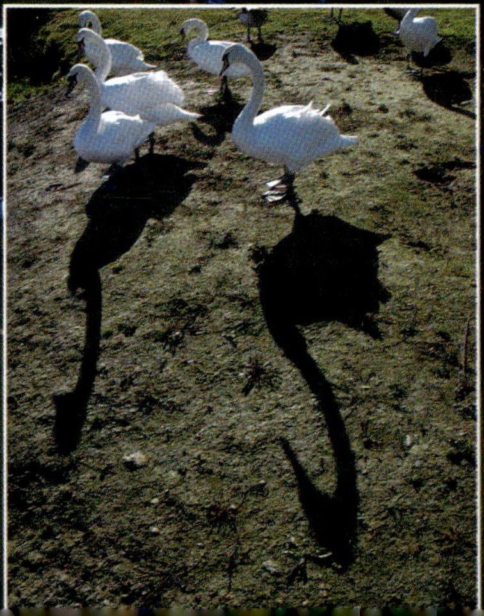

12.30 pm

Kimbolton Castle, above, is best known as the final home of Catherine of Aragon, the first wife of King Henry VIII. Queen Catherine was imprisoned and died at Kimbolton in 1536. Her body was buried in Peterborough Cathedral and it is said that her ghost walks upon the original floor levels which have been altered since her day. Hence, her ghost appears as the legs and lower body projecting from the ceiling on one floor with head and upper body gliding along the floor above! Kimbolton was originally a medieval castle but was converted into a stately home as the family seat of the Dukes of Manchester from 1615 until 1950 when it was sold to Kimbolton School by the 10th Duke of Manchester. It is open to the public during school holidays and weekends. During WWII, the castle was used by the Royal Army Medical Corps long before helicopters were used to rescue patients - now a daily occurrence throughout the County.

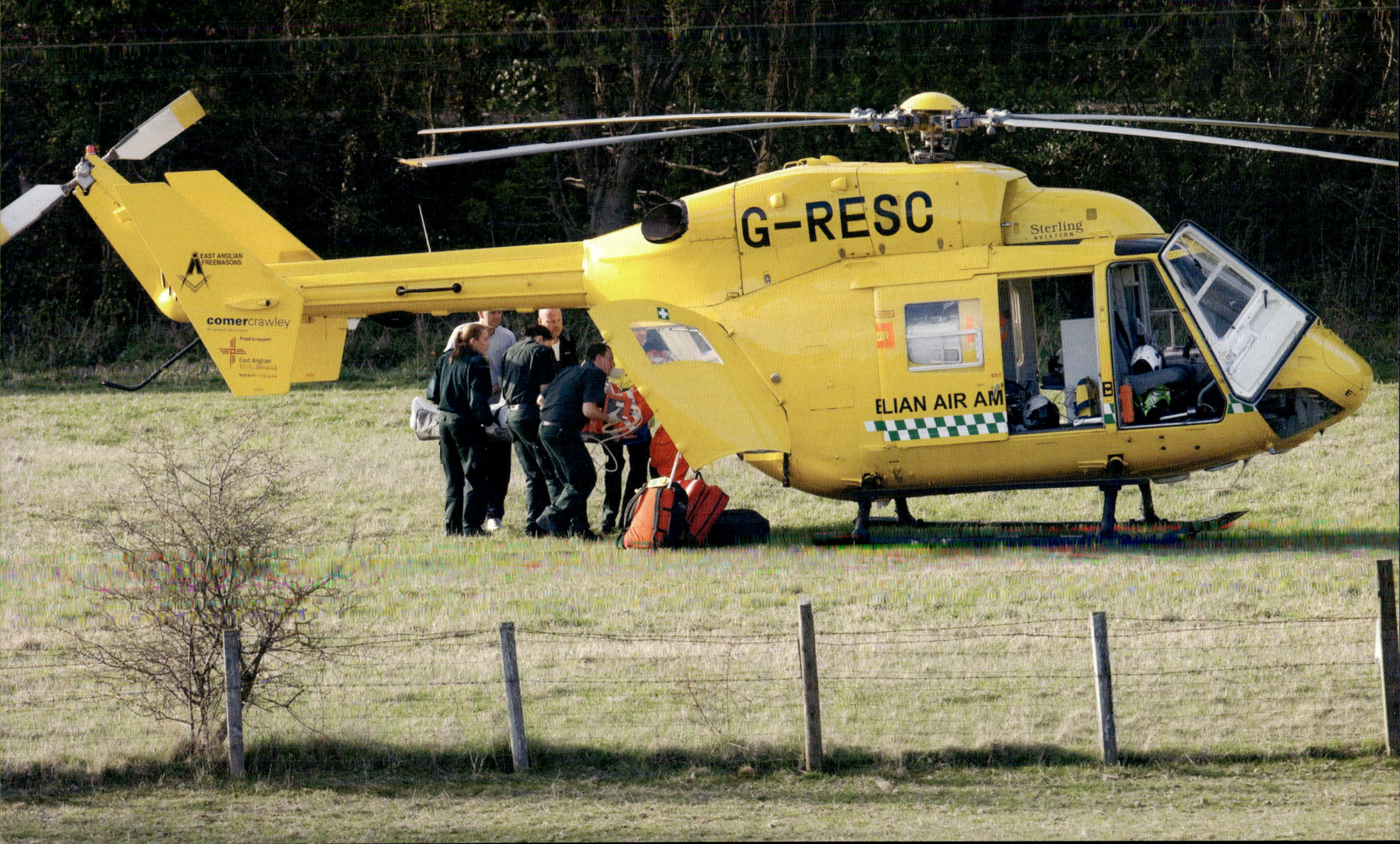

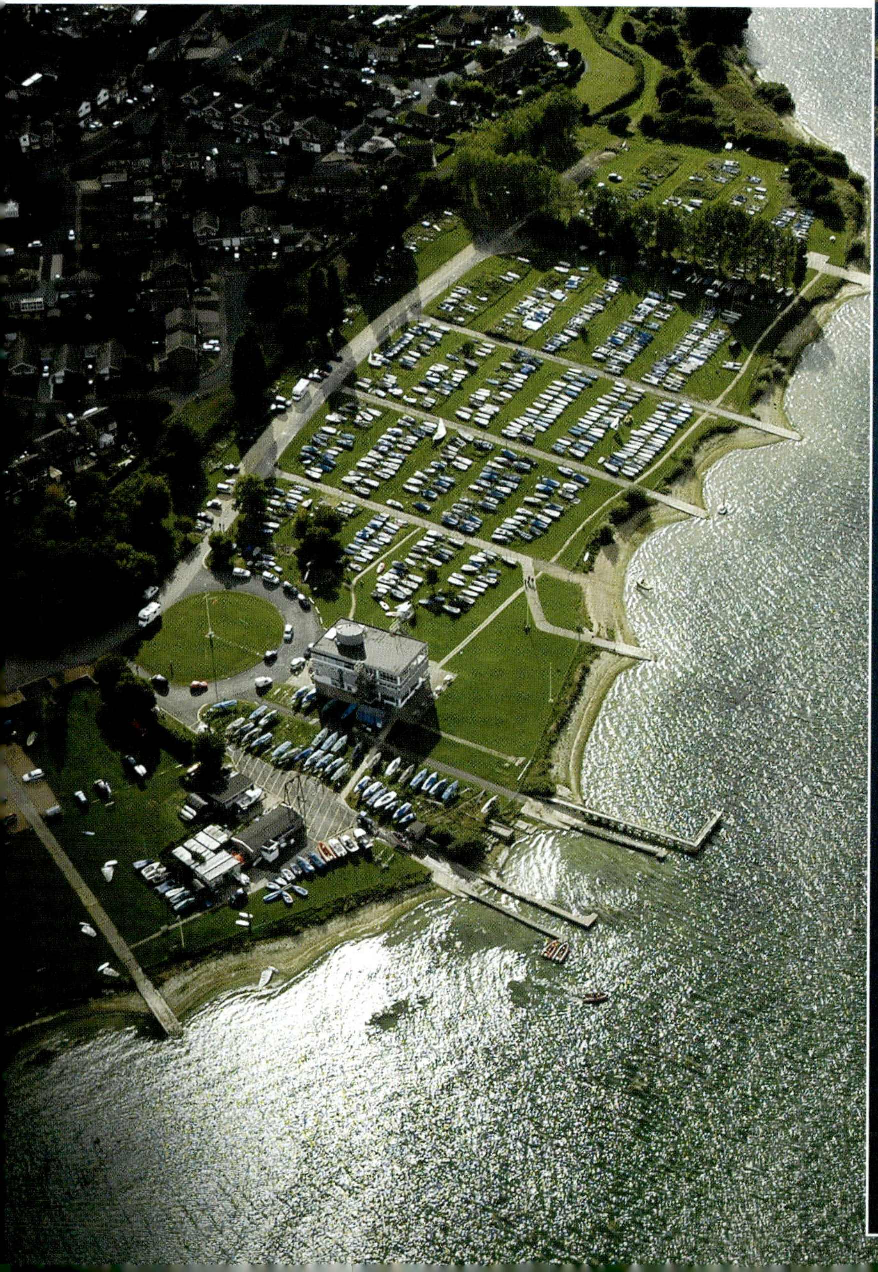

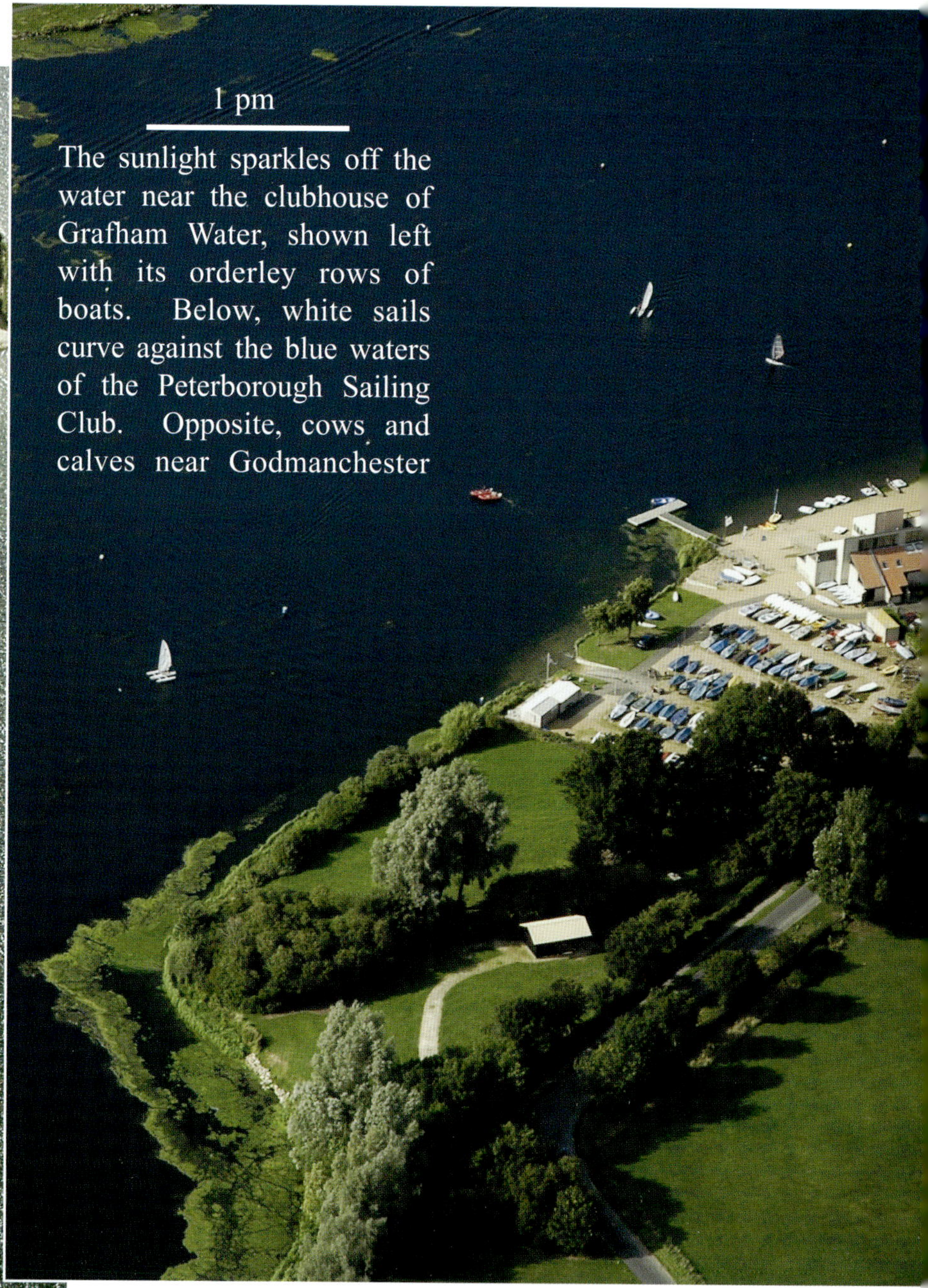

1 pm

The sunlight sparkles off the water near the clubhouse of Grafham Water, shown left with its orderley rows of boats. Below, white sails curve against the blue waters of the Peterborough Sailing Club. Opposite, cows and calves near Godmanchester

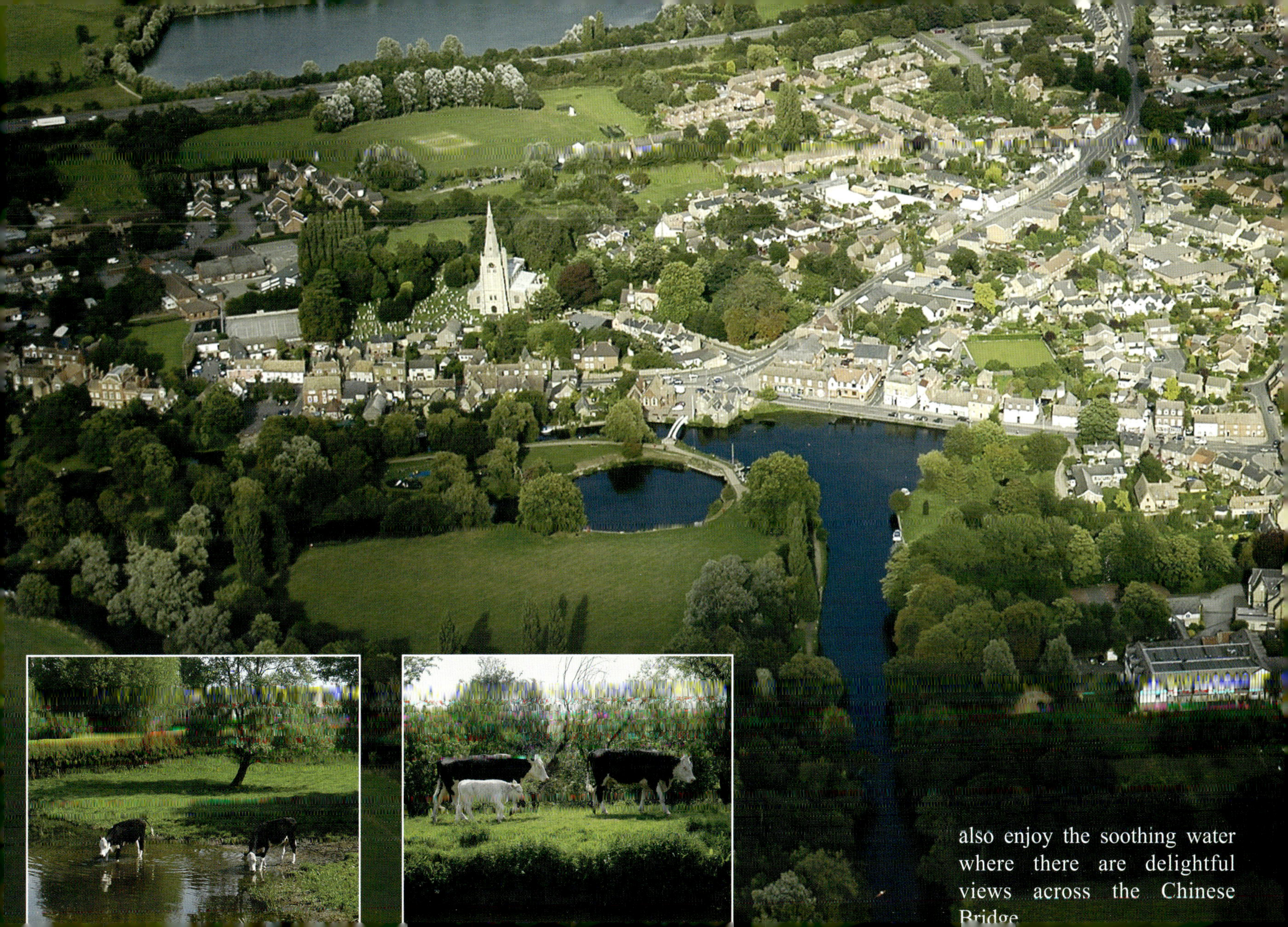

also enjoy the soothing water where there are delightful views across the Chinese Bridge

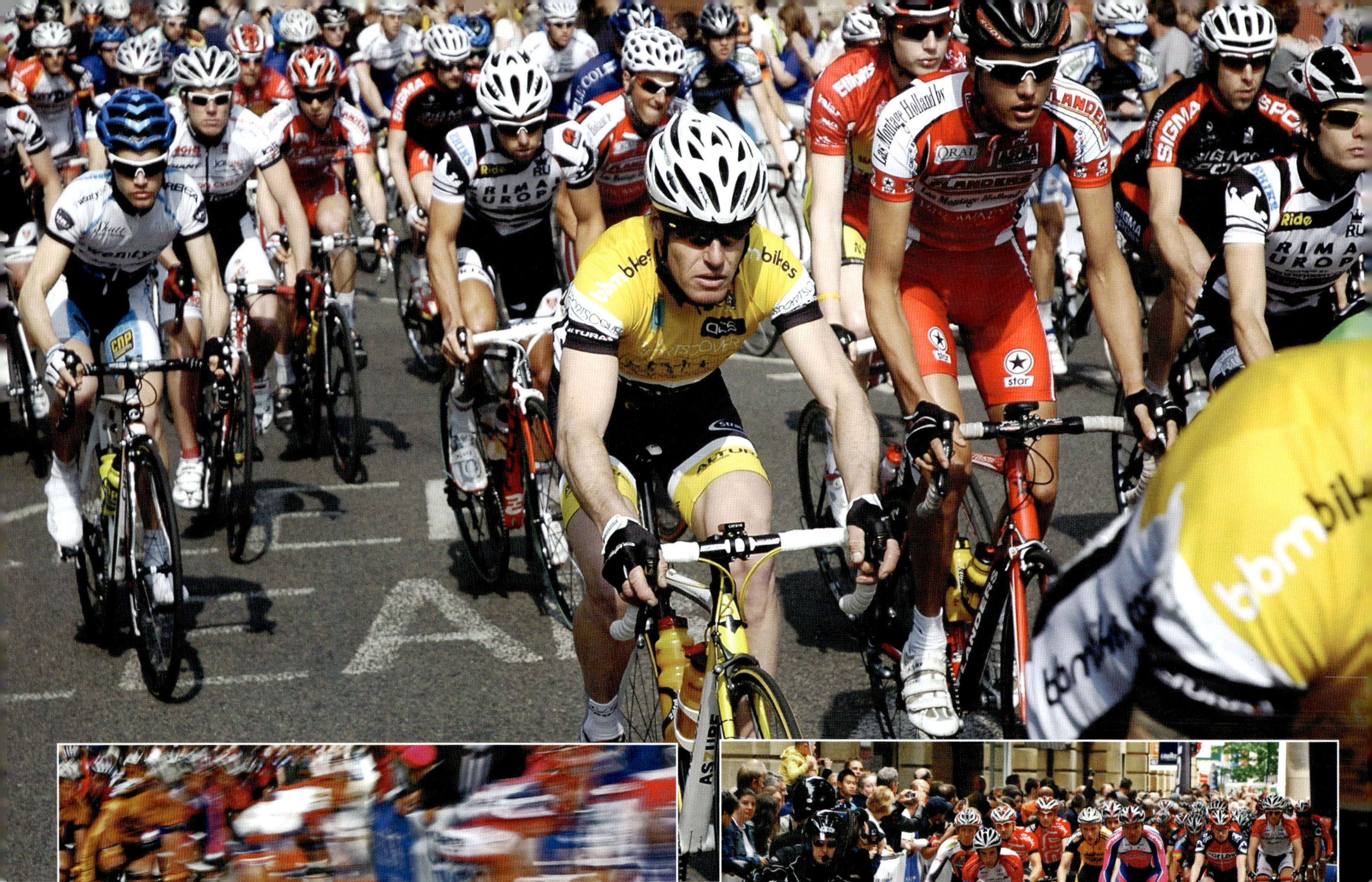
SIGMA
FLANDERS
star
bbmbikes
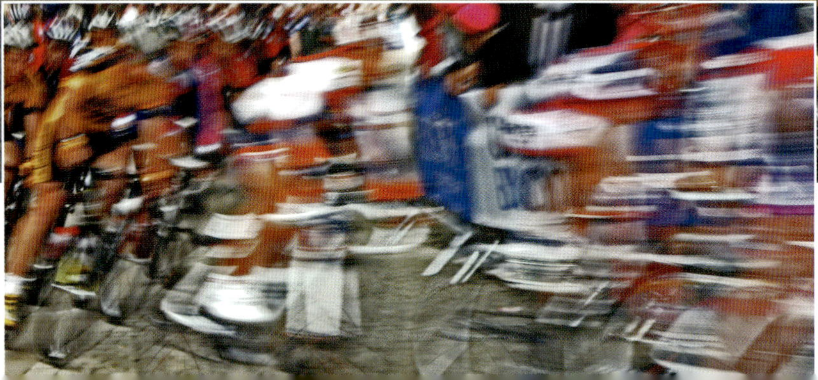
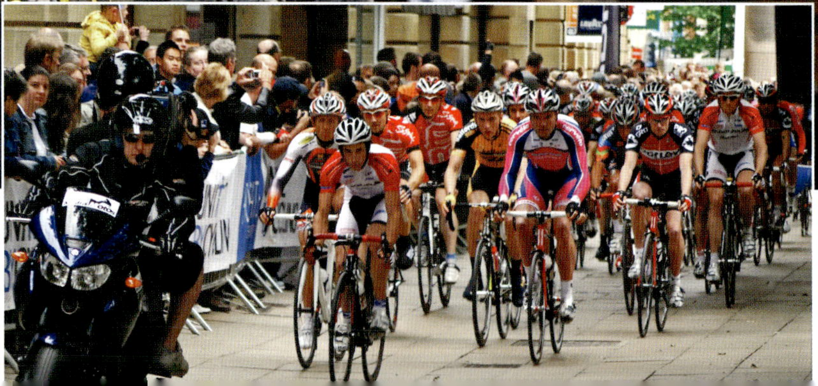

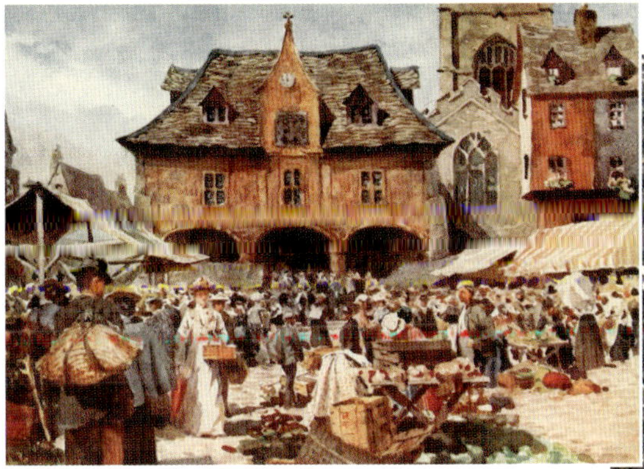

1.15 pm

This aerial view of Peterborough, right, shows how the Cathedral dominates the skyline. It is the oldest building in Peterborough near the magnificent 17th century Guildhall, shown above, which itself was built shortly after the restoration of King Charles II. The iconic Guildhall is supported by columns to provide an open ground floor for the butter and poultry markets. Later, the old Market Place was renamed Cathedral Square. Today, Peterborough is one of [illegible] city-centre cycle challenges which make up the Halfords Tour Series. Teams race through Cathedral Square, Cowgate, Bourges Boulevard and Bridge Street at speeds of around 30mph, viewed by thousands of spectators.

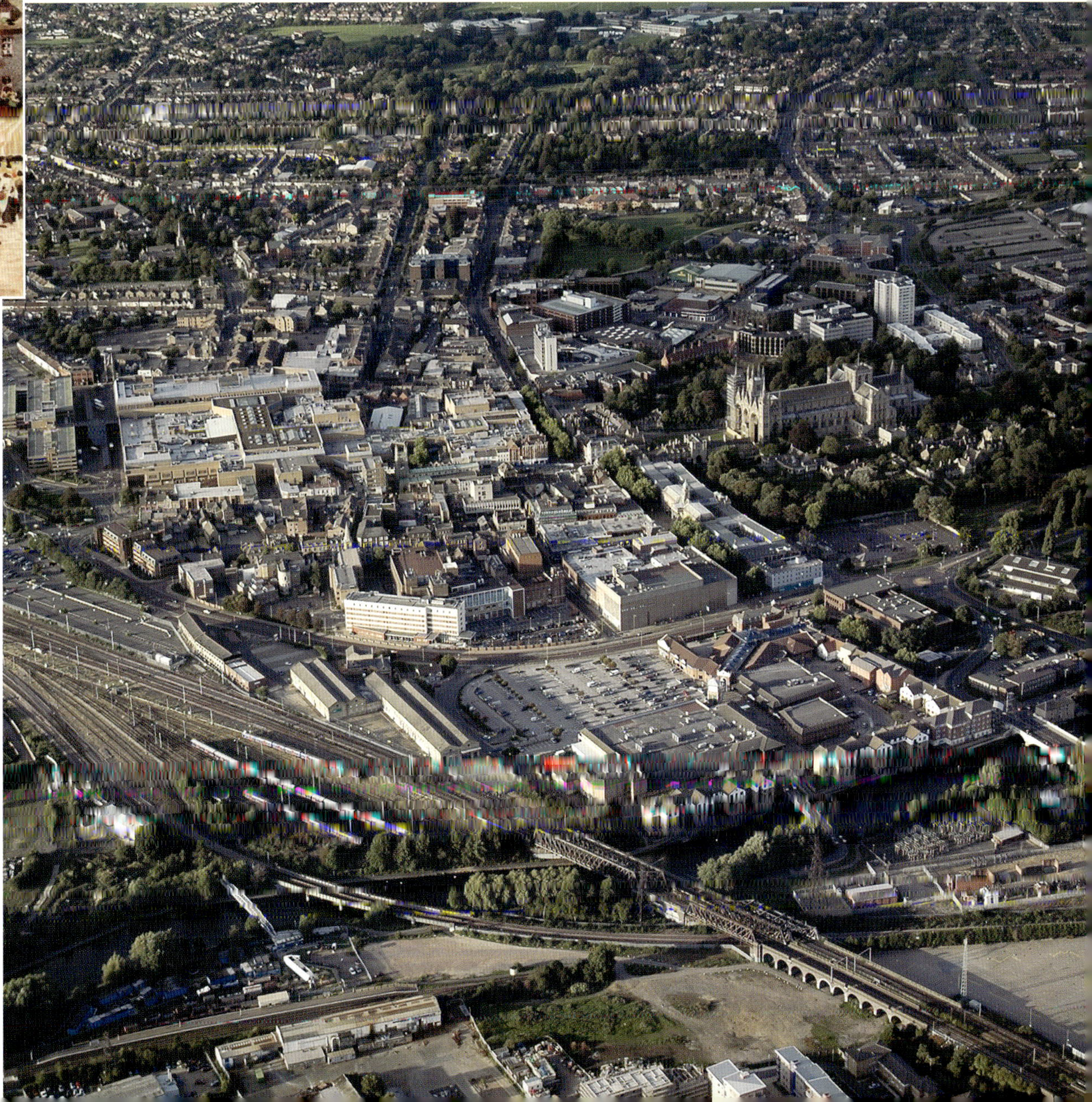

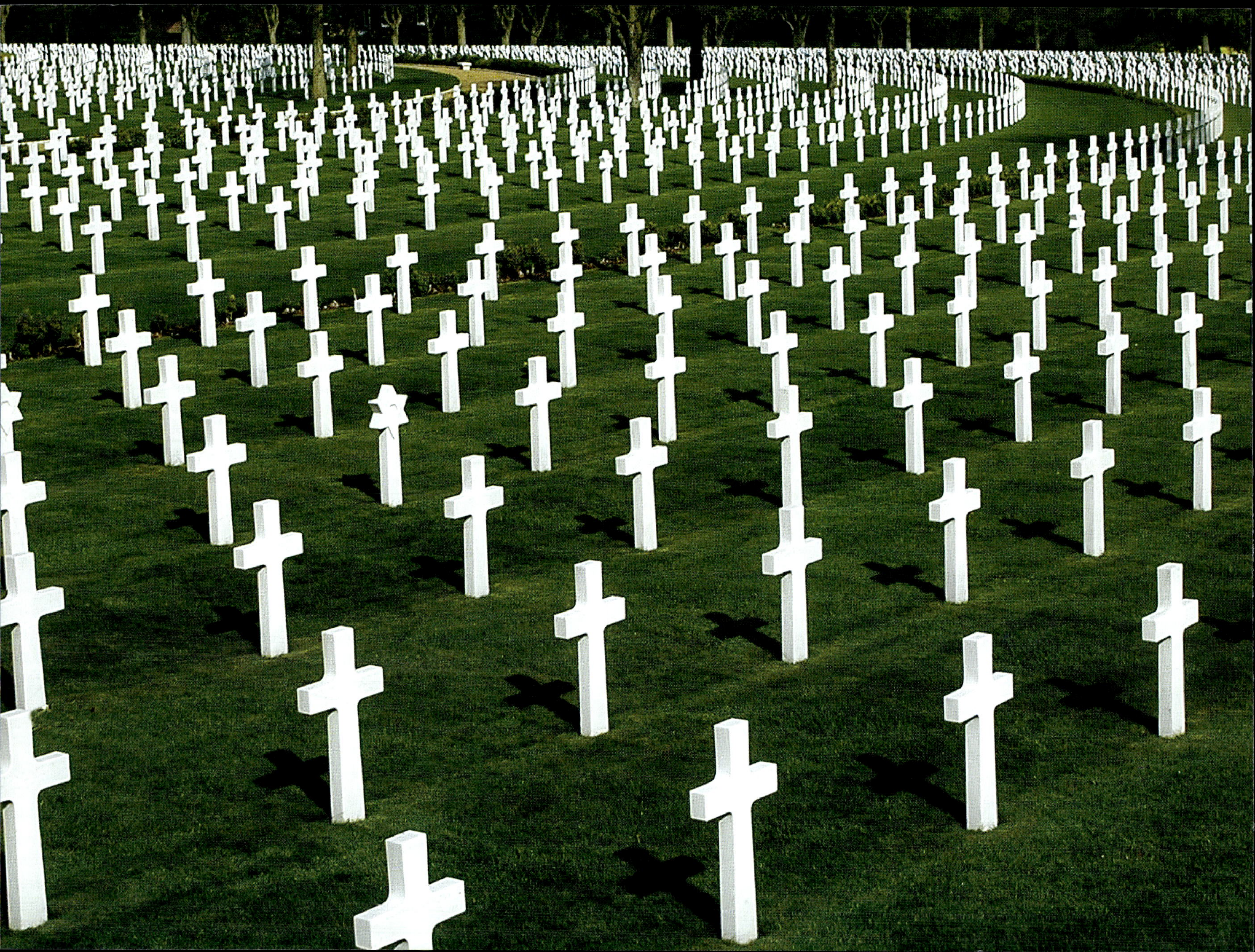

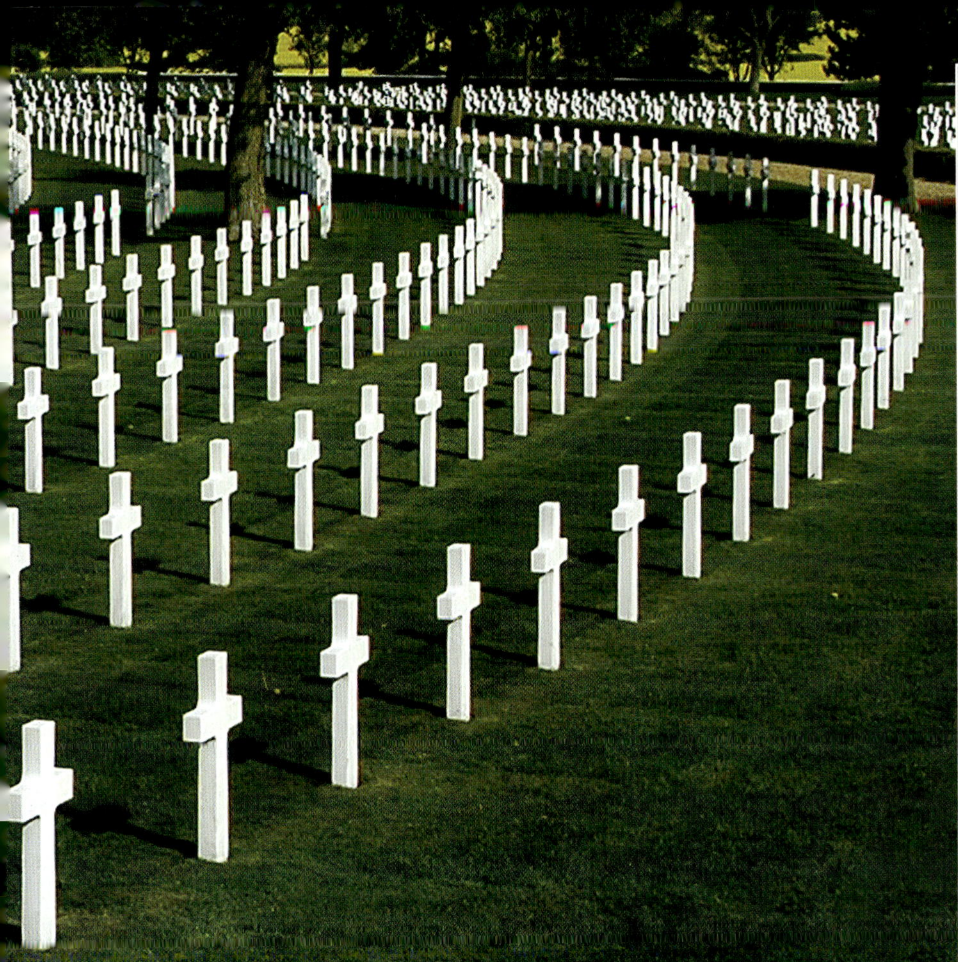

1.30 pm

During WWII, B-17 and B-24 bombers of the 8th Air Force, made 500,000 bombing missions. Initially, the bombers flew without fighter escort and suffered heavy losses. Here they commence the long turn back to their bases in England. 290,000 US servicemen were lost in WWII and they are commemorated here at Madingley, just outside Cambridge where 'Old Glory', the US Flag, itself based on the English origins of George Washington, flies forever in their memory.

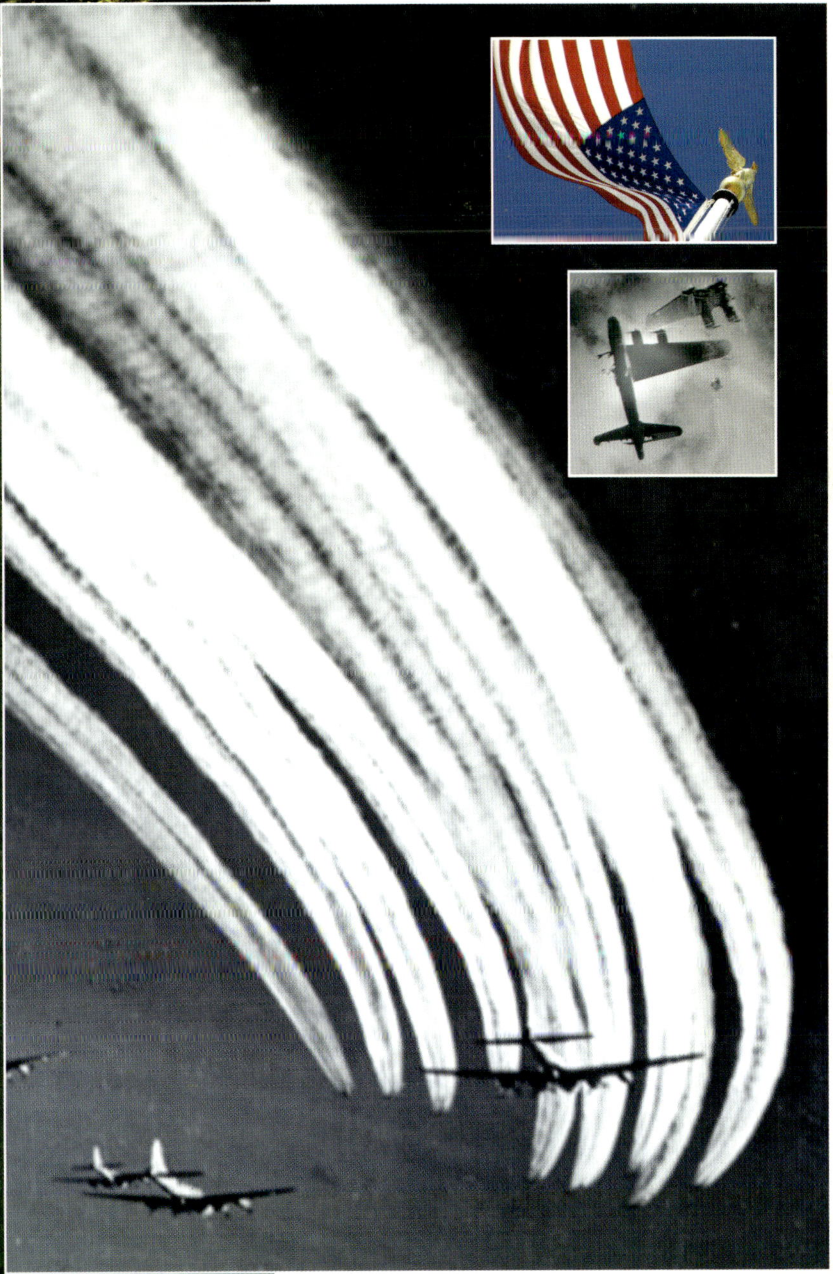

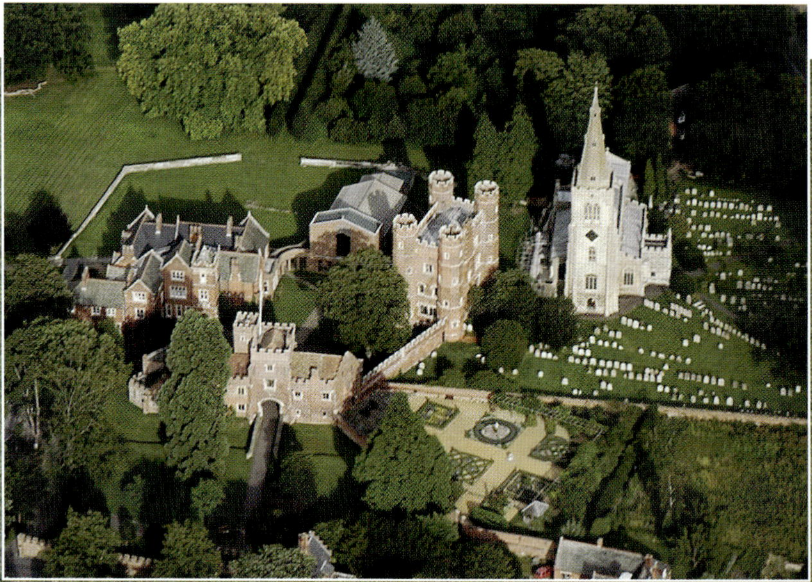

2.0 pm

Buckden Towers or Buckden Palace as it was once known was listed in the Doomsday list in 1086 as the property of the Bishop of Lincoln. Around 1225 another house was built by Hugh De Welles on the site. This work was completed by Robert Grosseteste, Bishop of Lincoln along with the addition of the Great Hall. However, the building work by both men was mostly destroyed in 1291 by a fire leaving only foundations behind. In 1480, the Tower was built by Bishop Rotherham and more building was completed by Bishop John Russell. By 1595 Bishop Chaderton had left Buckden as he couldnít afford to run it and after falling into disrepair, John Williams, Bishop of Lincoln, returned and restored Buckden. In 1640, after the restoration of the Monarchy, Buckden was returned to the See of Lincoln and Bishop Sanderson restored the property. In 1838, the buildings were destroyed and any valuables were sold by the ecclesiastical commissioners to raise funds. In 1872, the present Buckden Towers were built by Arthur Wellington Marshall and designed by Robert Edis, who also designed Sandringham House. In World War I Buckden was used as a hospital and after the war it was sold to Dr Robert Holmes Edleston who rebuilt the northern part of the inner Gatehouse. In World War II Buckden housed evacuees. In 1956 Buckden was given to the Claretian Missionaries who undertook restoration and new building work. In 1970, the St Claret Centre opened for conferences and spiritual retreats. Restoration of the towers and gardens has been ongoing ever since. The old Great North Road ran through Buckden and was the location of the famous 'Buckden speed trap'

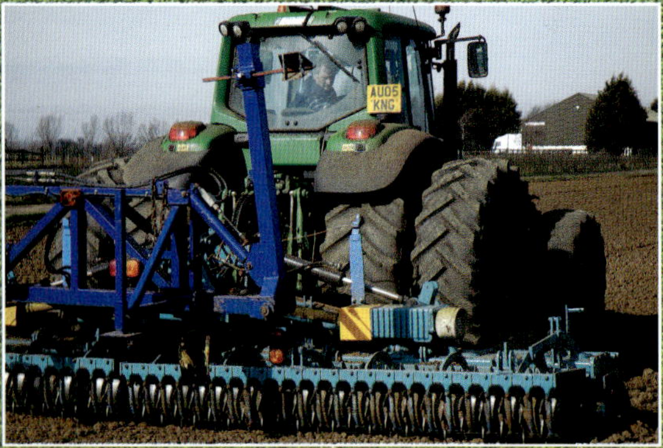

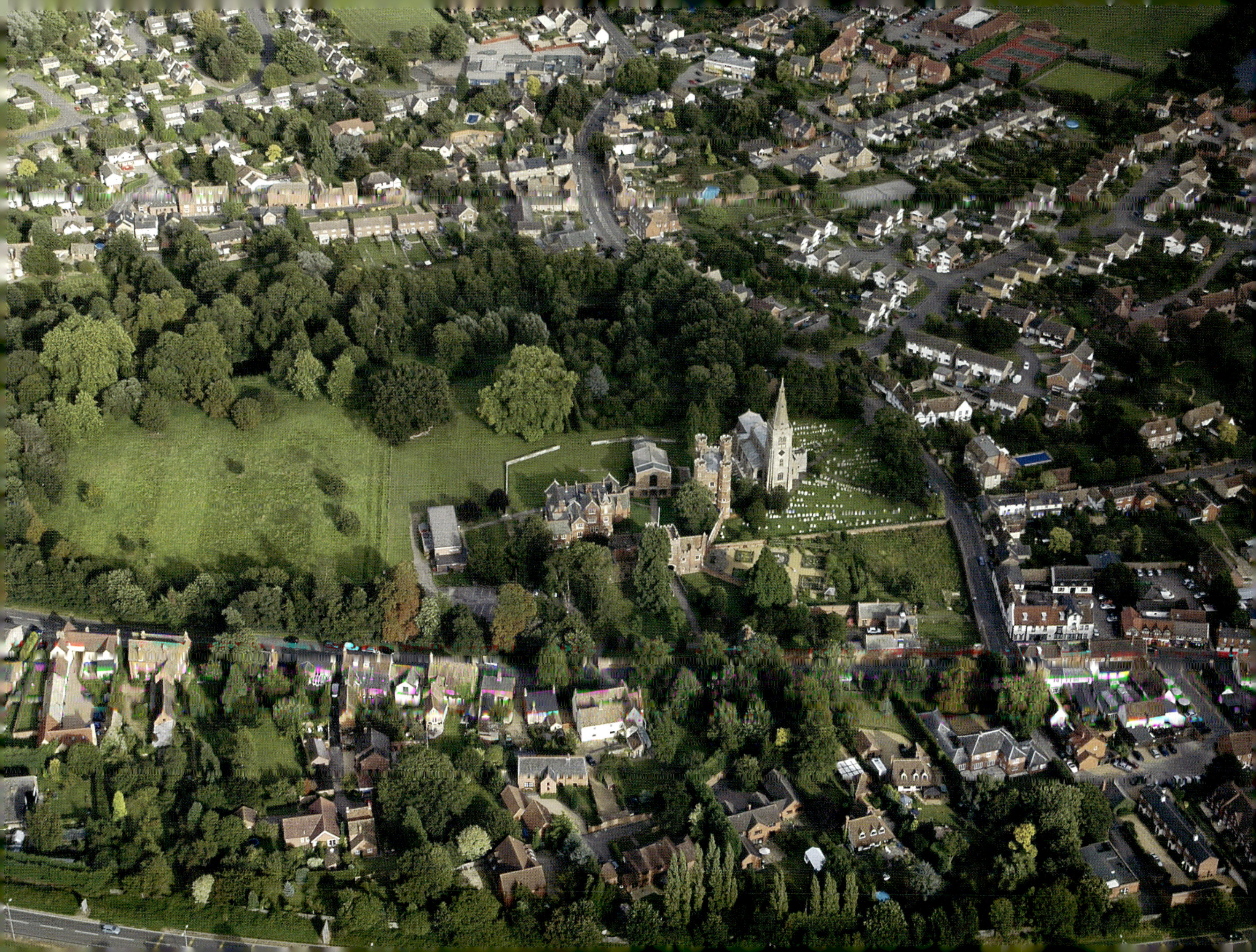

2.30 pm

From 1932 to 1963, this vintage fire engine was in service in Wisbech, which is renowned for elegant Georgian architecture and for the distinctive monument to Thomas Clarkson, shown just beyond the bridge. It was designed by Gilbert Scott, who also built the Albert Memorial. In 1881, the monument was erected in honour of Clarkson who was the driving force behind the abolition of slavery. Clarkson had entered Cambridge in 1775 and wrote a Latin essay competition on the question 'Is it lawful to make slaves of others against their will?' Clarkson's translated essay was published in London and William Wilberforce took up the challenge in parliament - the Slavery Abolition Act came into force in 1883.

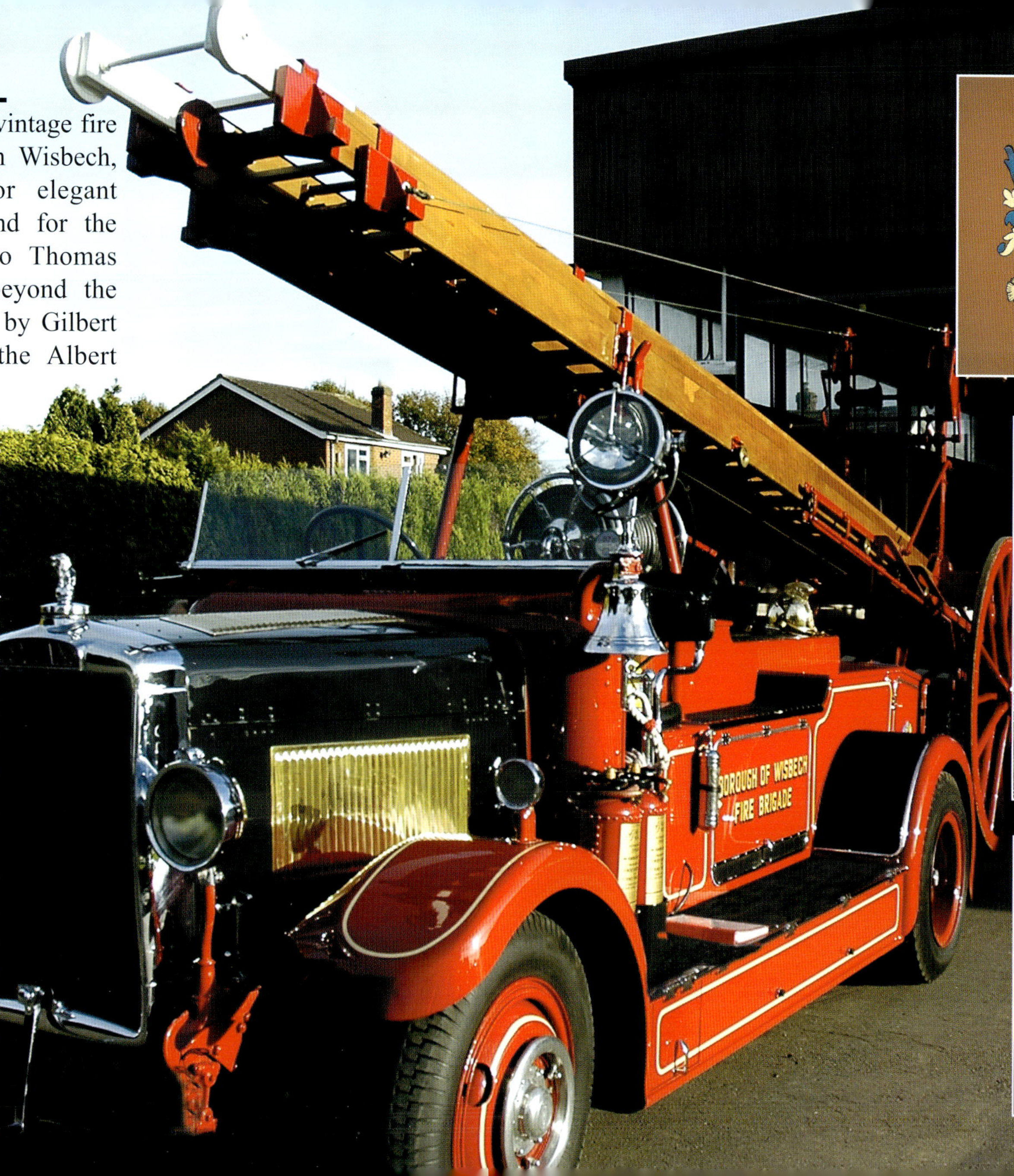

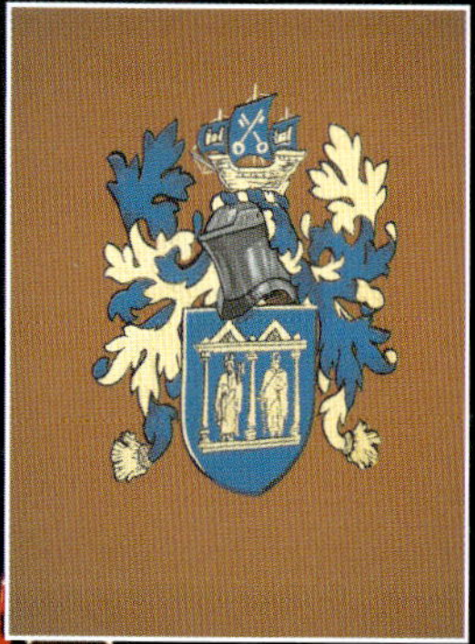

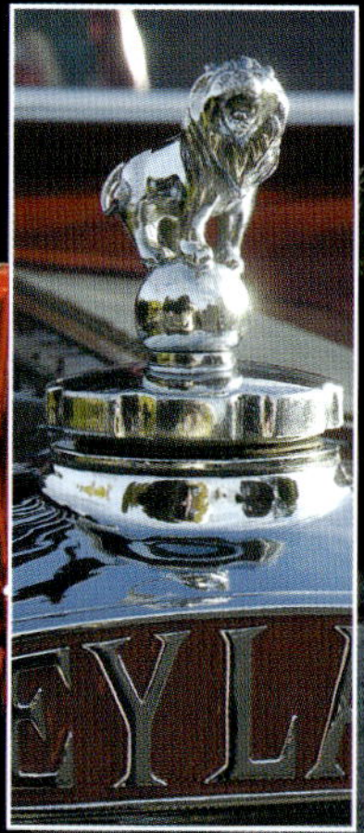

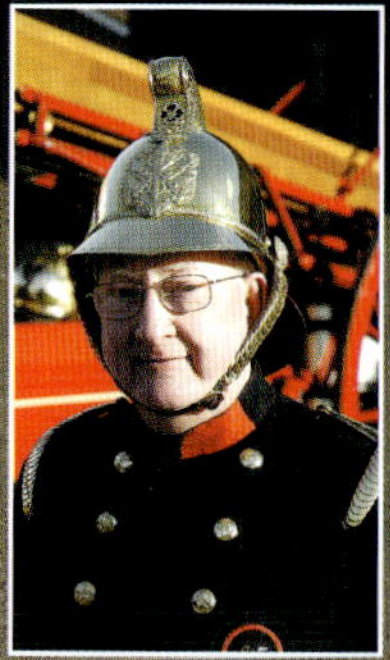

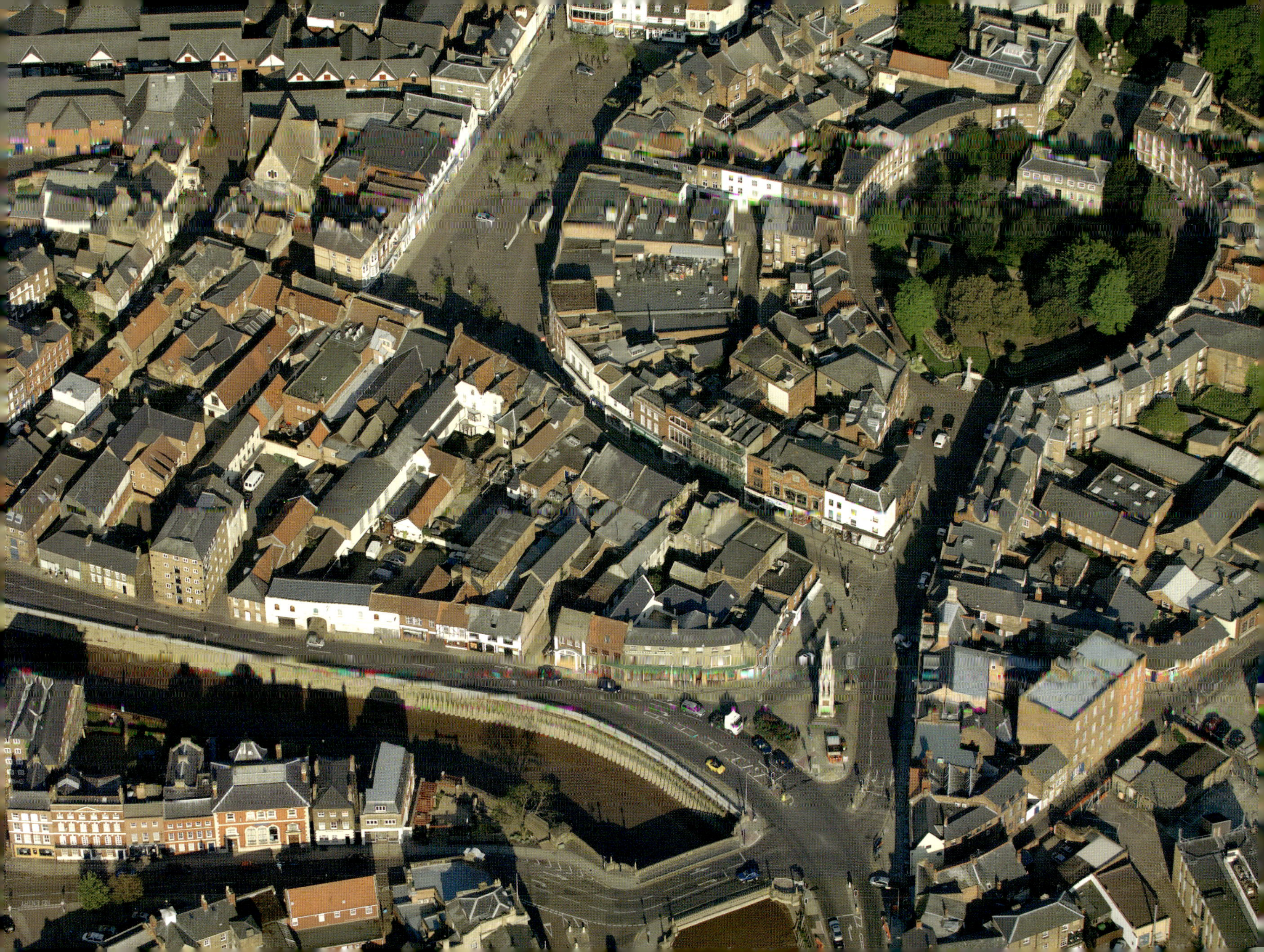

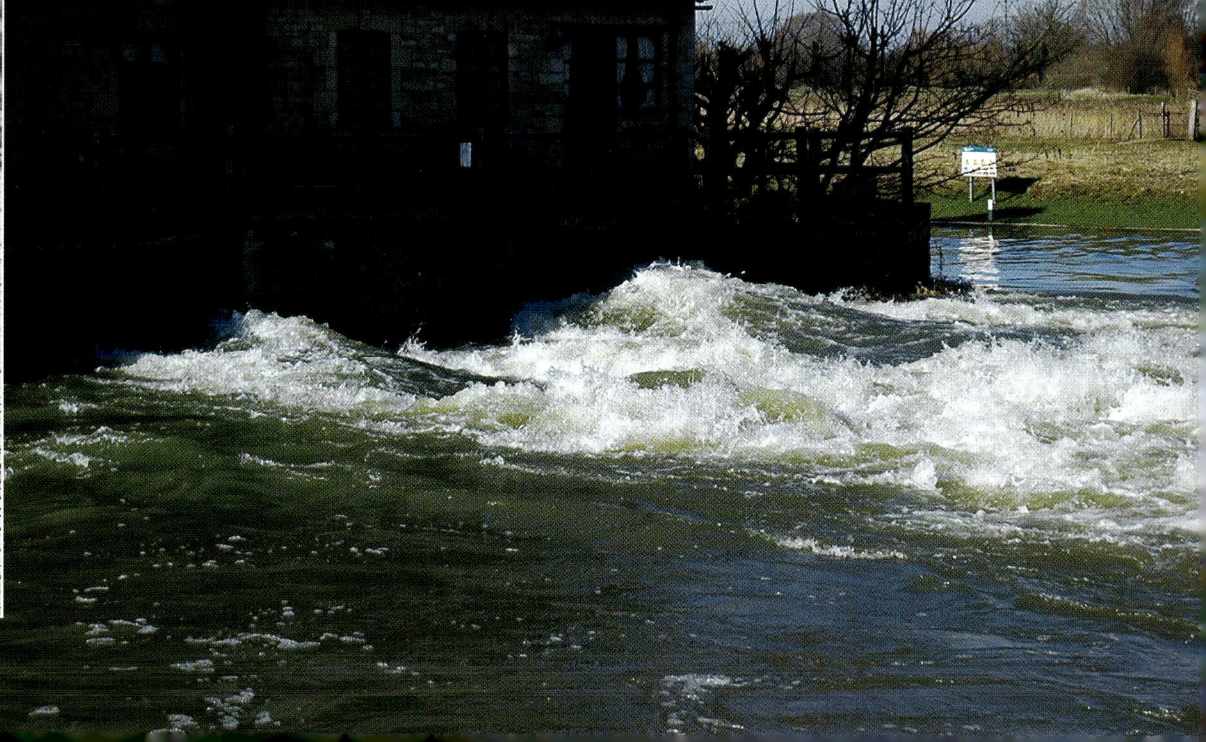

Chapter 4

Afternoon

3 pm

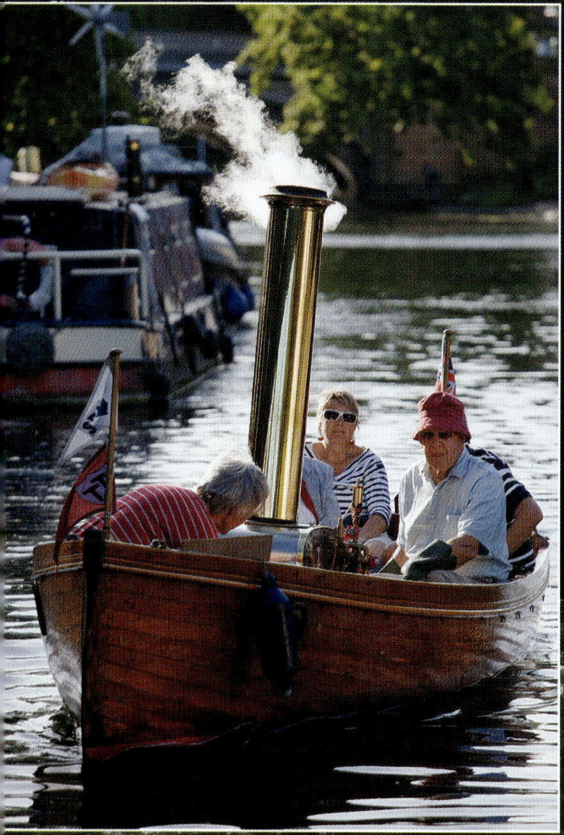

In the hamlet of Water Newton stands a huge disused water mill, originally built in 1791 by J Compton and Sons, to sustain the growing population of the area. Water power was the main source of energy to mill flour until steam power was introduced in the industrial age. The mill was constructed with coursed limestone rubble and freestone dressings, topped by Collyweston stone slated roofs and a red pantiled roof. The mill was converted into a shop and dwellings in 1986 and although not used, some of the machinery is still intact including two water wheels - one of which was huge for its time of construction with a diameter of 14 feet. Inset, the crew of a restored steam boat enjoy a day out on the River Cam.

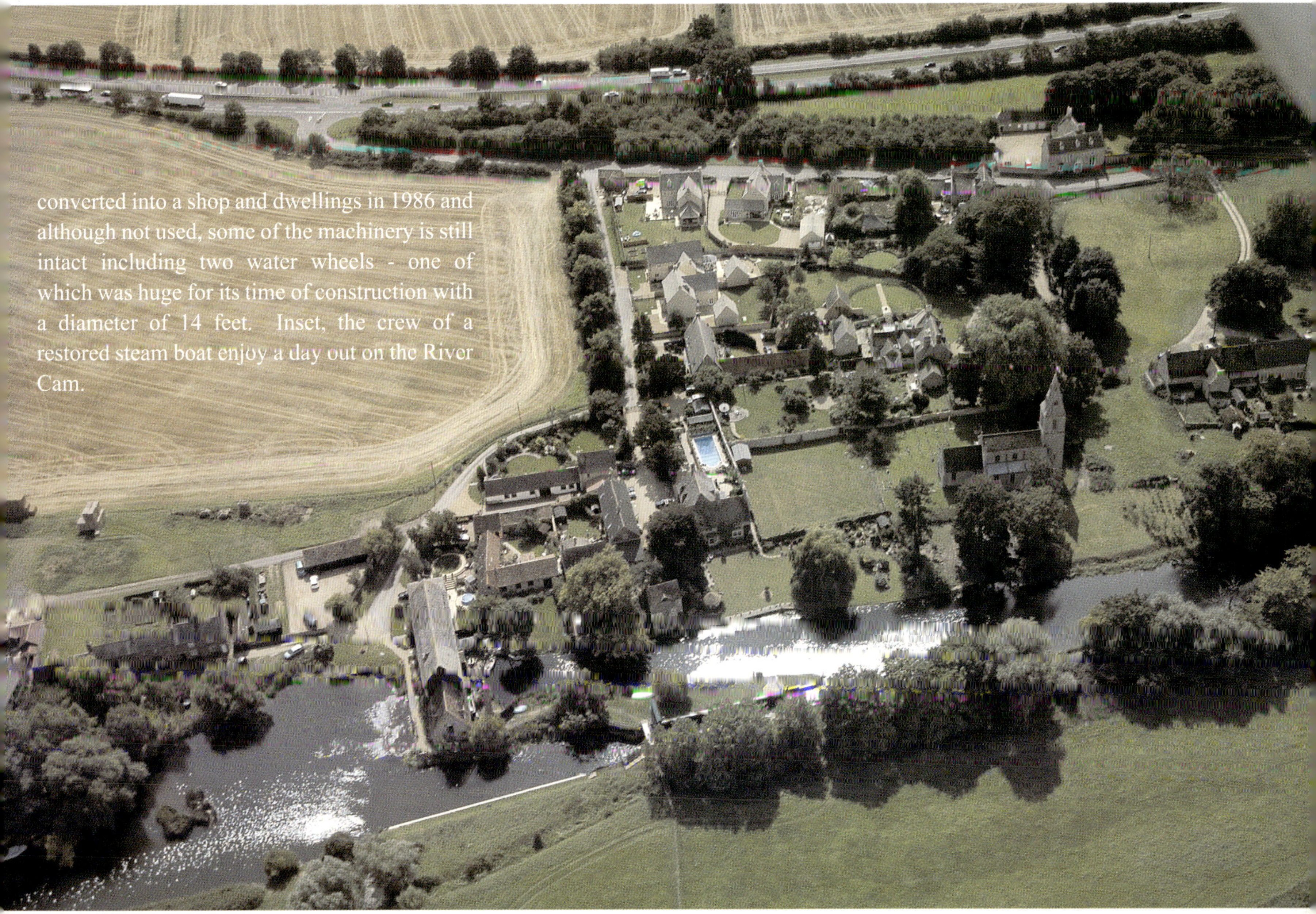

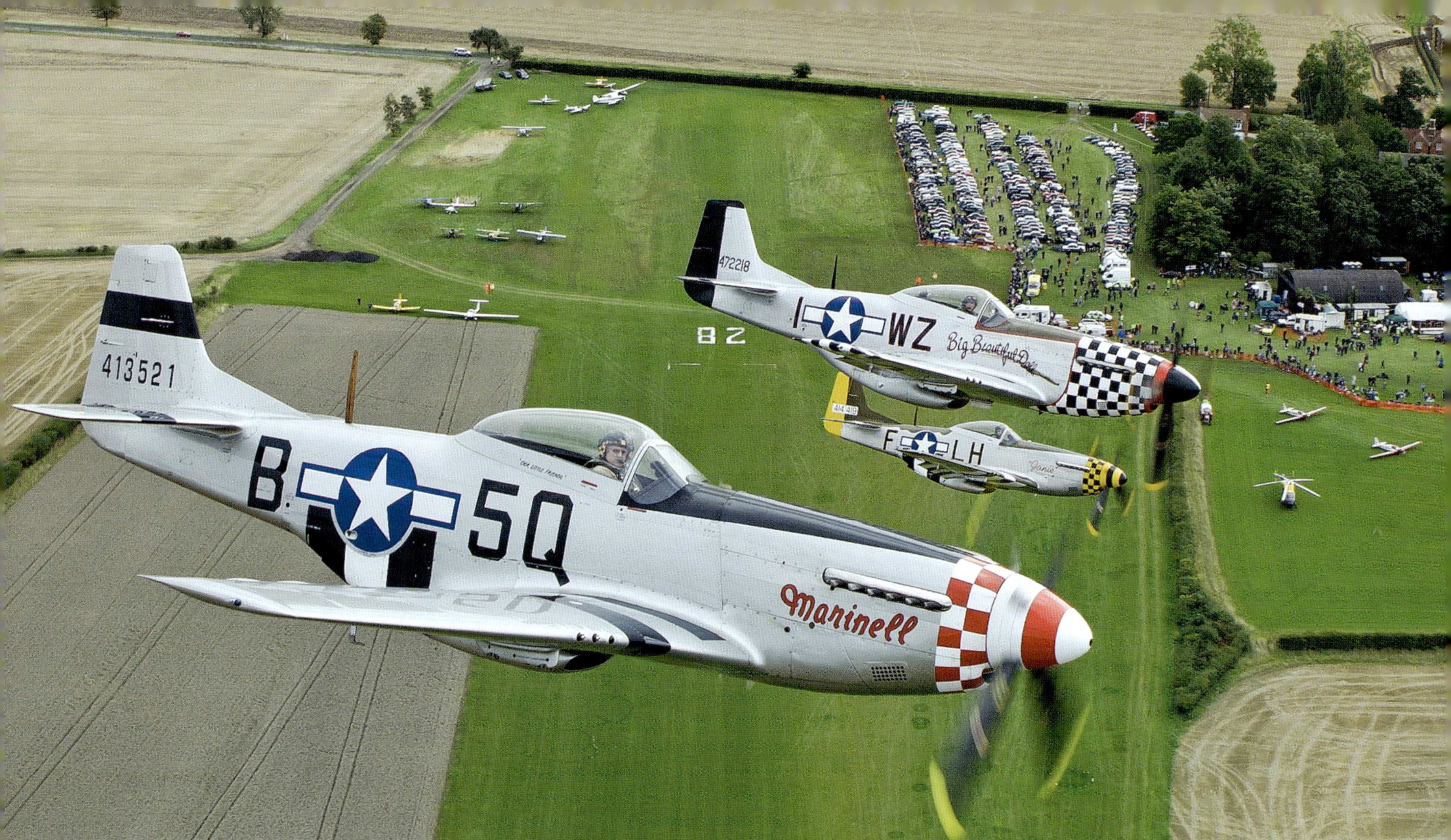

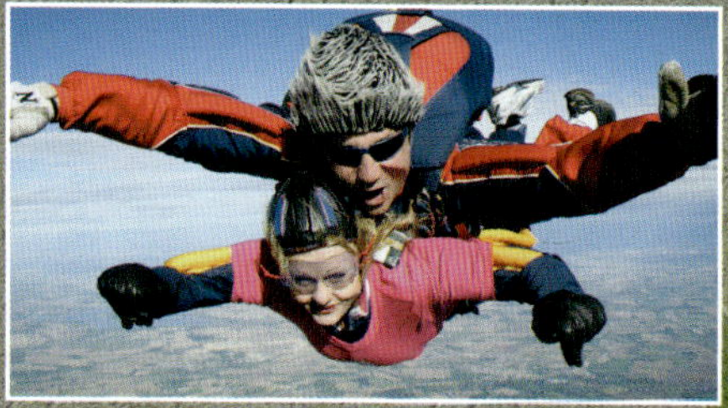

3.30 pm

The annual 'Children In Need' autumn airshow at Little Gransden airfield continues to raise record breaking sums - despite the variations of the British Summer weather. At the most northerly part of the County, three young ladies have leapt from a Cessna Caravan parachute plane 12,000 feet above Sibson airfield to raise funds for Breast Cancer

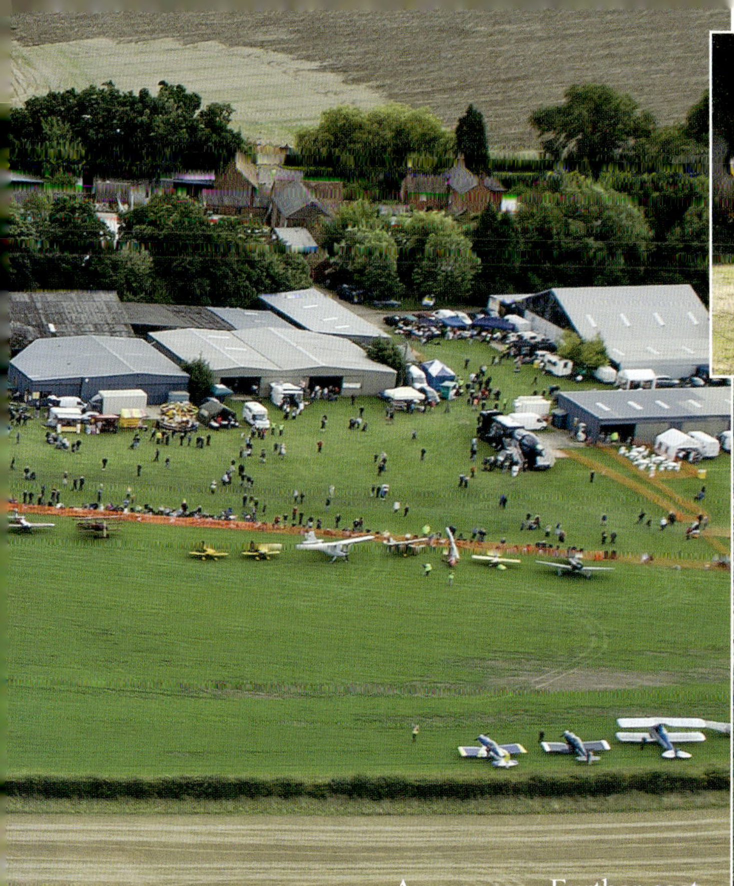

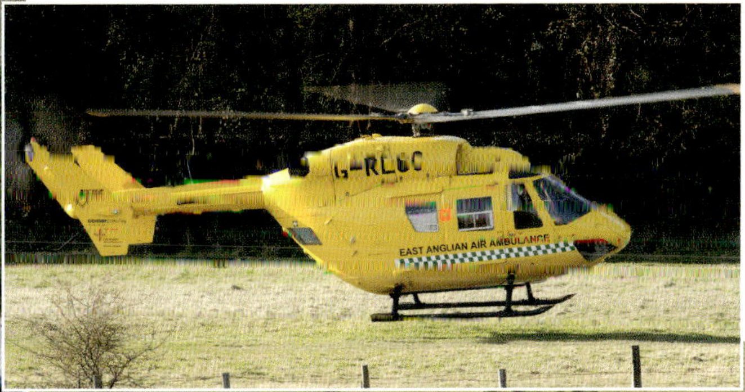

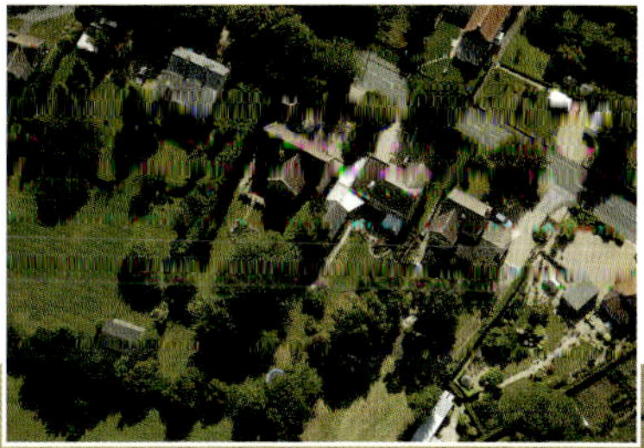

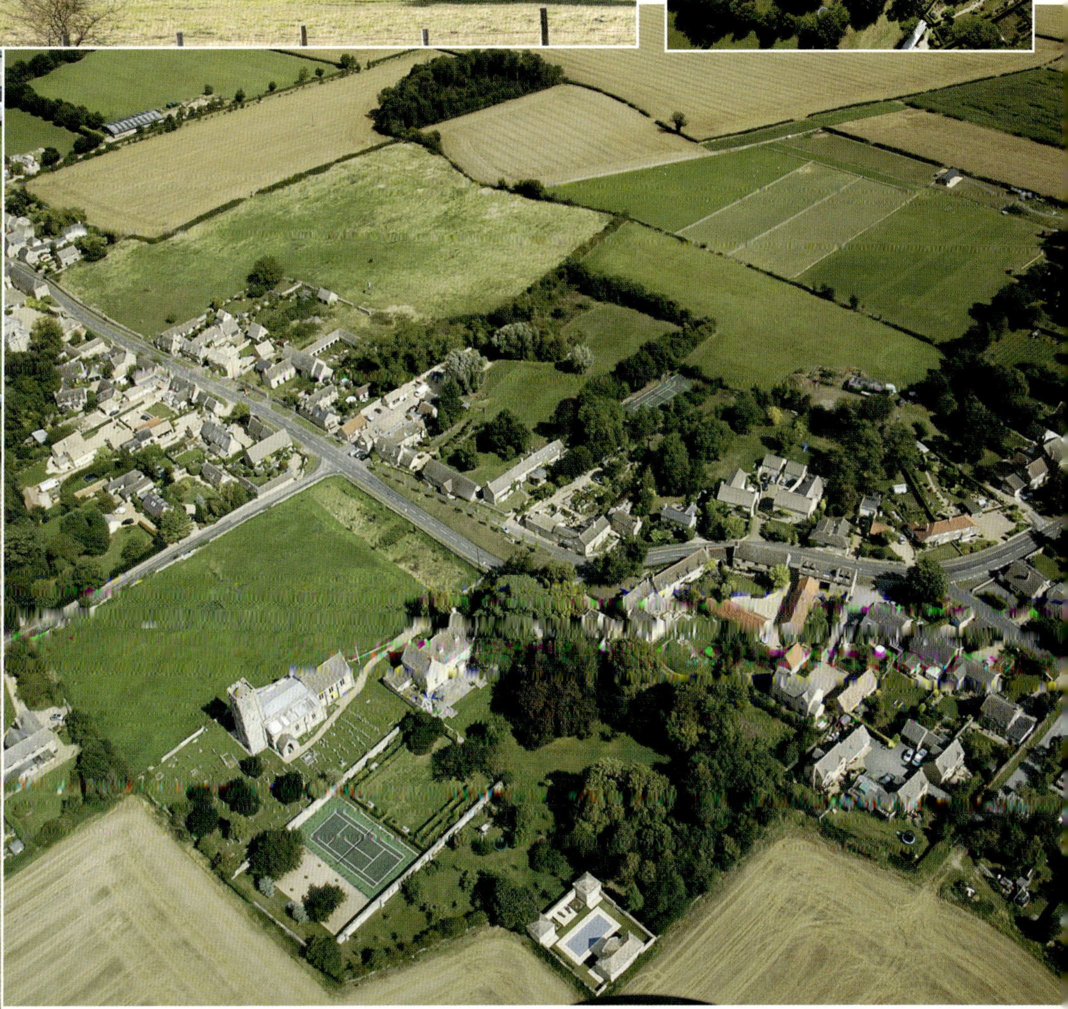

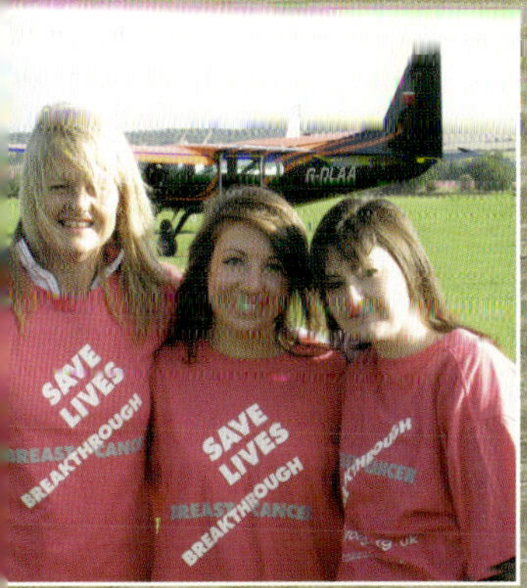

Awareness. Further east, the Air Ambulance lifts from the fields near the village of Ufford, where a ground-based ambulance cannot reach. It carries a fallen rider at speeds of 150 mph, to be at the hospital within ten minutes flying time, within the 'Golden' hour.

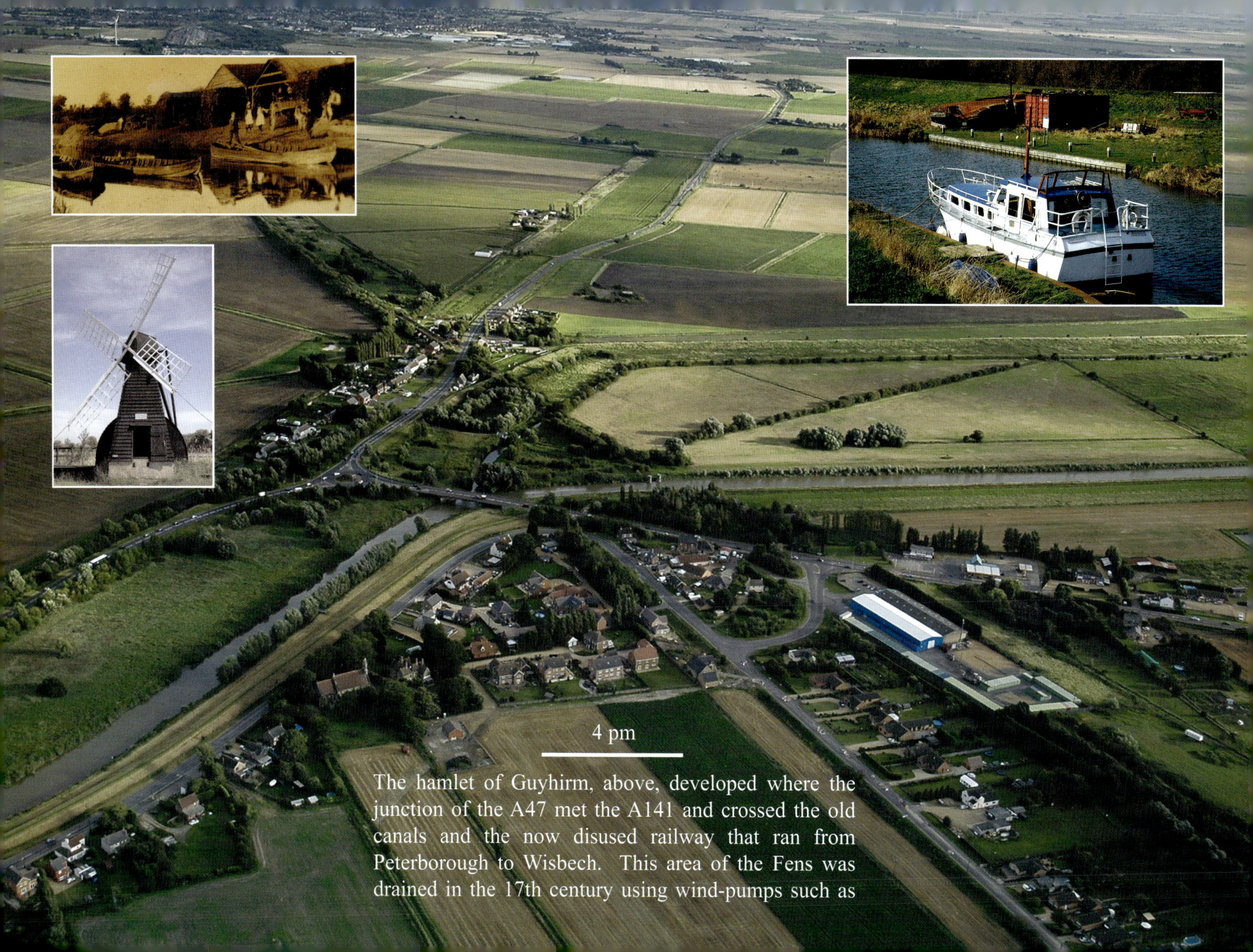

4 pm

The hamlet of Guyhirm, above, developed where the junction of the A47 met the A141 and crossed the old canals and the now disused railway that ran from Peterborough to Wisbech. This area of the Fens was drained in the 17th century using wind-pumps such as

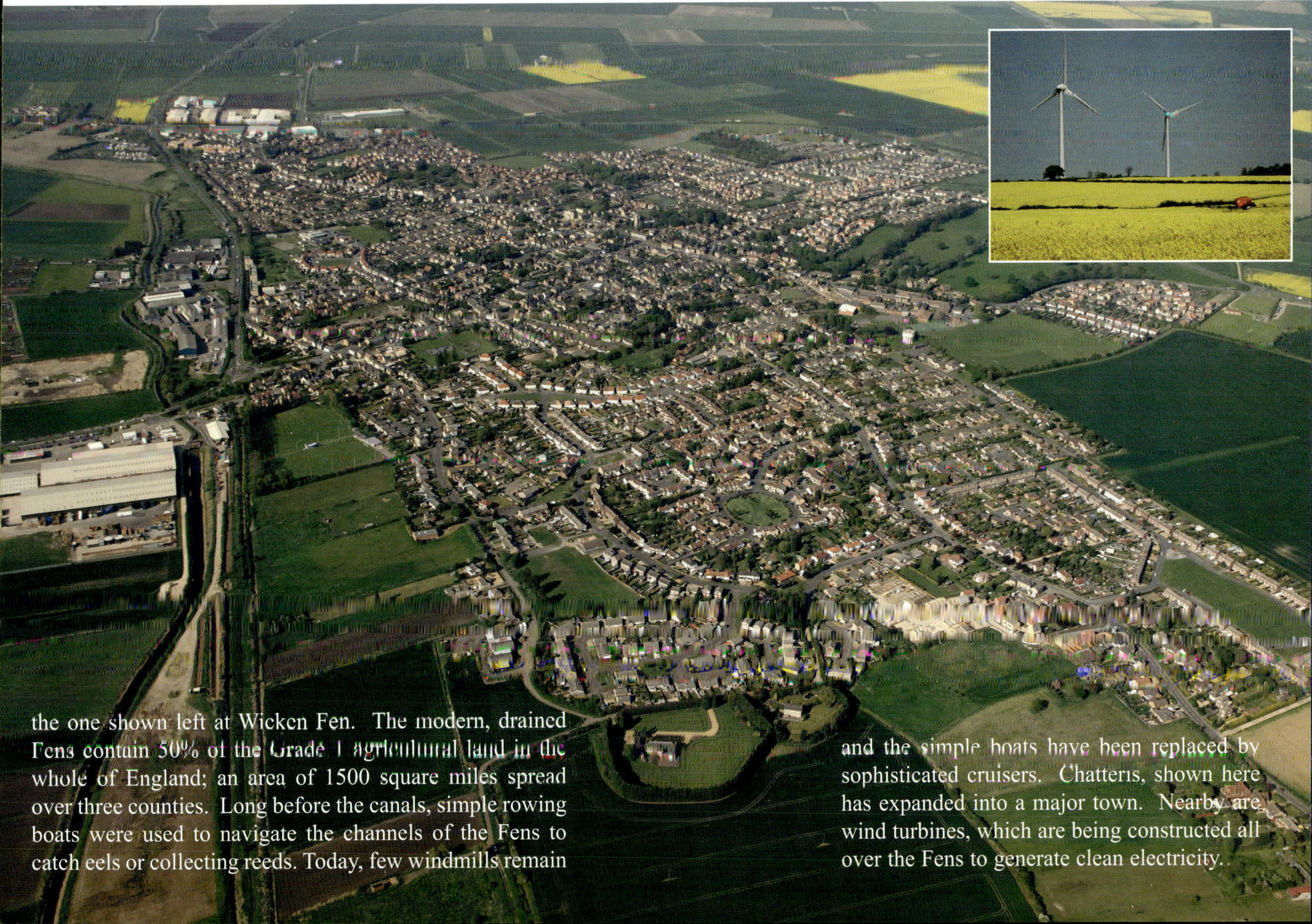

the one shown left at Wicken Fen. The modern, drained Fens contain 50% of the Grade 1 agricultural land in the whole of England; an area of 1500 square miles spread over three counties. Long before the canals, simple rowing boats were used to navigate the channels of the Fens to catch eels or collecting reeds. Today, few windmills remain and the simple boats have been replaced by sophisticated cruisers. Chatteris, shown here has expanded into a major town. Nearby are wind turbines, which are being constructed all over the Fens to generate clean electricity.

4.30 pm

On the 17 May 1943, a B-17F Flying Fortress, serial number 41-24485, named 'Memphis Belle' became the first bomber of the US 8 Air Force to complete 25 missions over Europe. The aircraft was part of the 324 Bomb Squadron of the 91 Heavy Bomb Group based at RAF Bassingbourne. Lt Robert Morgan, the bomber Captain and his crew of nine airmen, had named their ship 'Memphis Belle' after Morgan's girlfriend, Margaret Polk, who lived in Memphis, Tennessee. The 'nose-art' had been inspired by a drawing by George Petty in a 1941 edition of Esquire magazine. In May 1943, long-range fighter escorts, such as Mustangs, Thunderbolts & Lightnings, were not capable of flying all the way to distant targets. Hence, the daylight bombers endured heavy flak and determined enemy fighters deep in Germany. At this time, the odds were very much against any crew completing 25 missions.

However, the crew of the 'Memphis Belle' were the first of many to beat the odds. The crew flew the ' Memphis Belle' back to the USA and embarked on a war-bond fundraising tour.

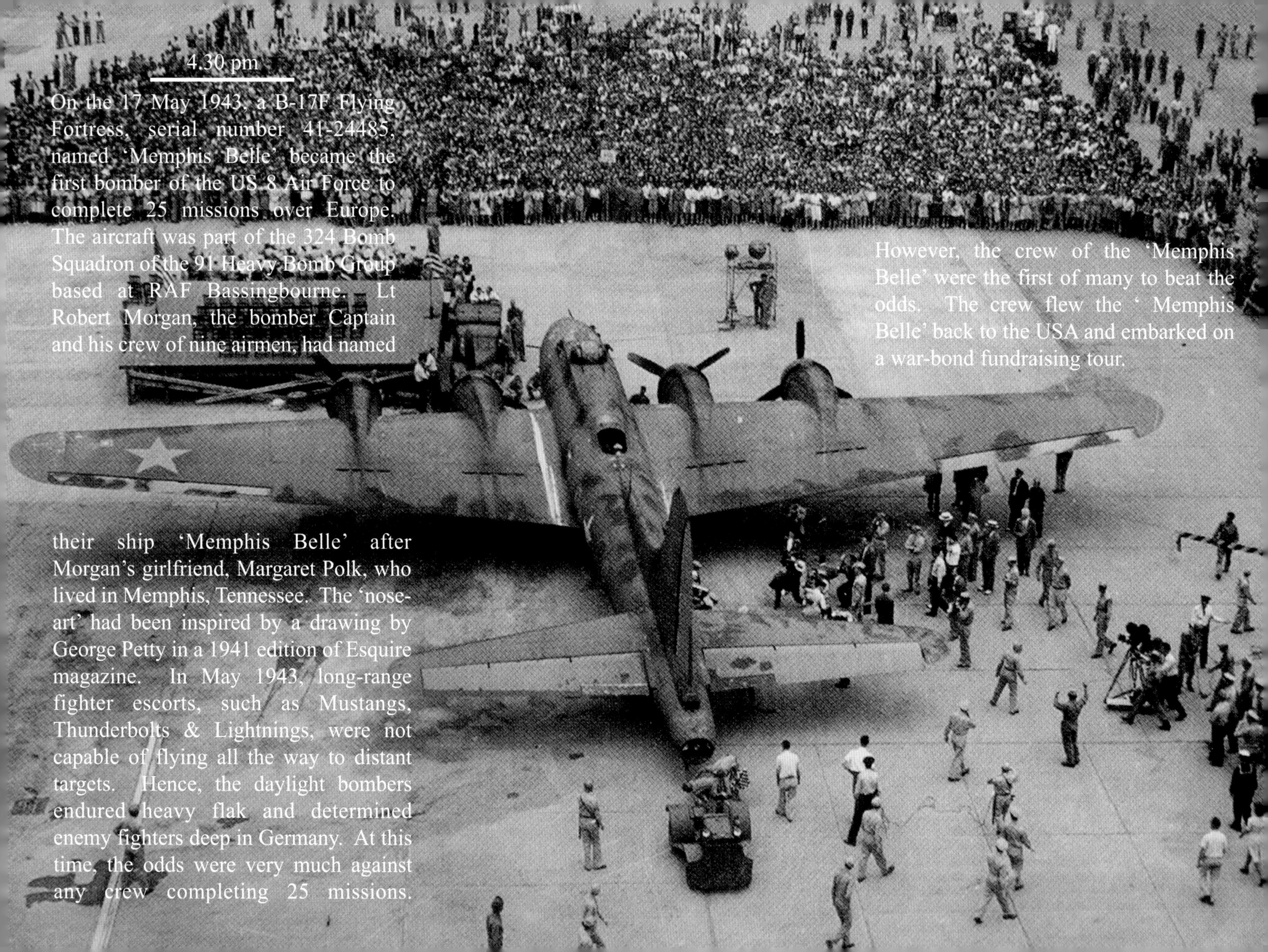

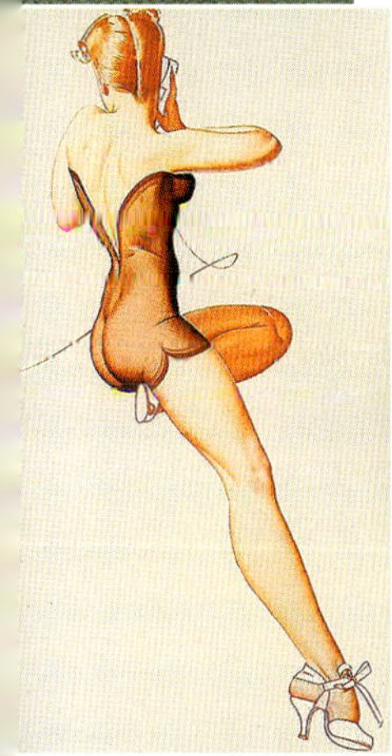

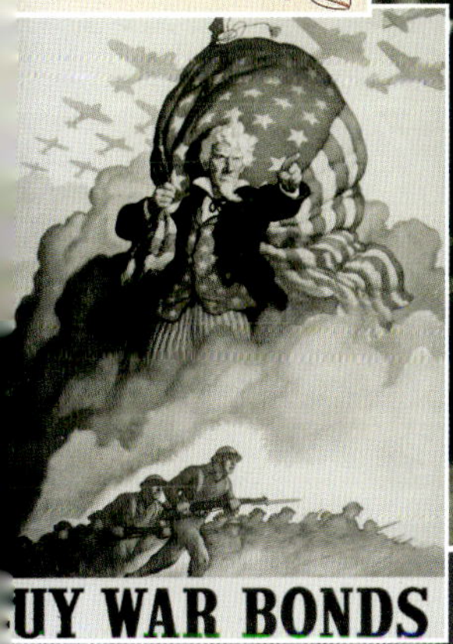
UY WAR BONDS

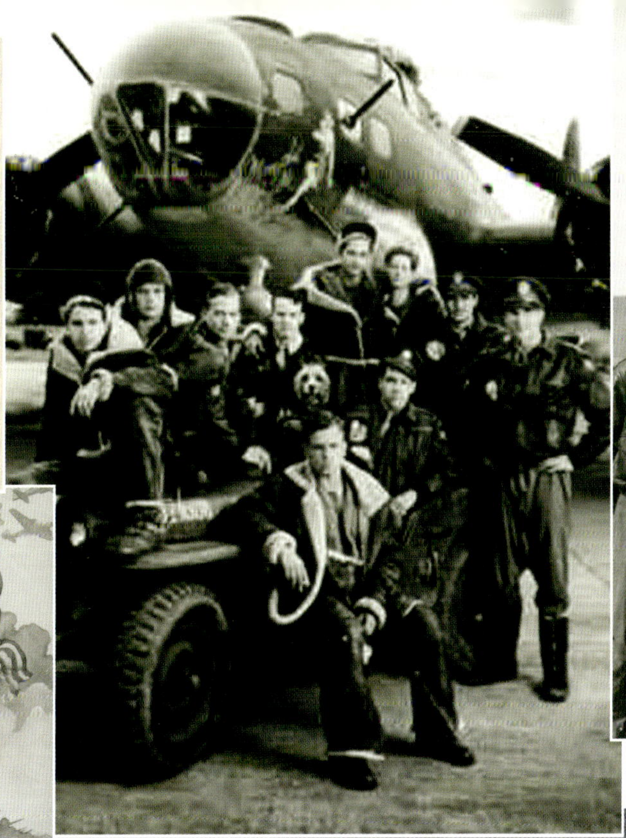

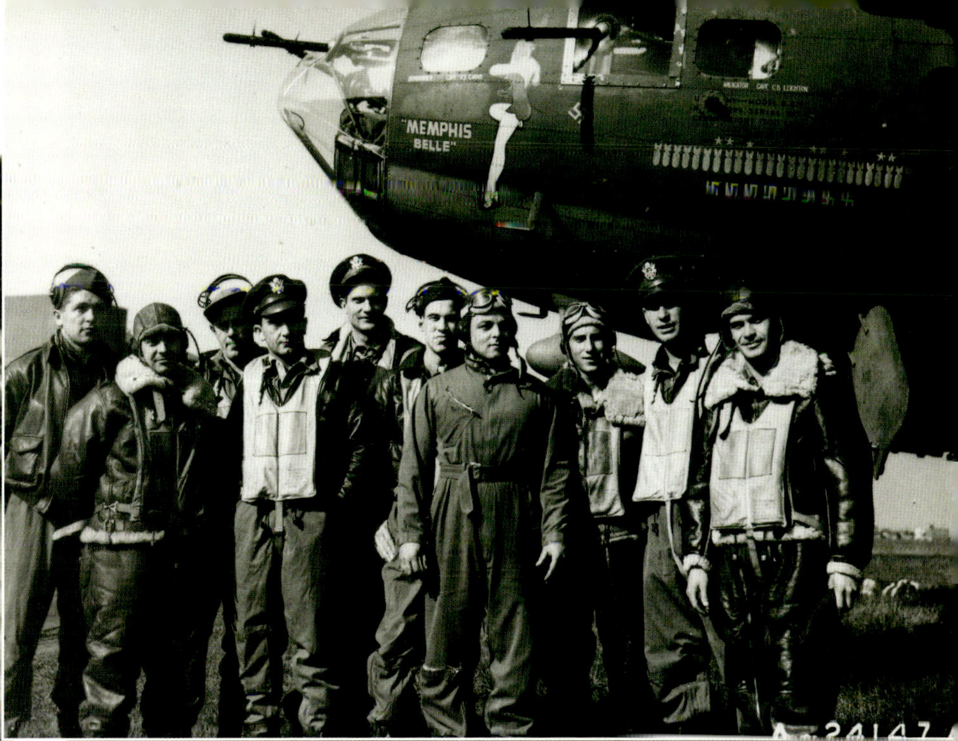
"MEMPHIS
BELLE"

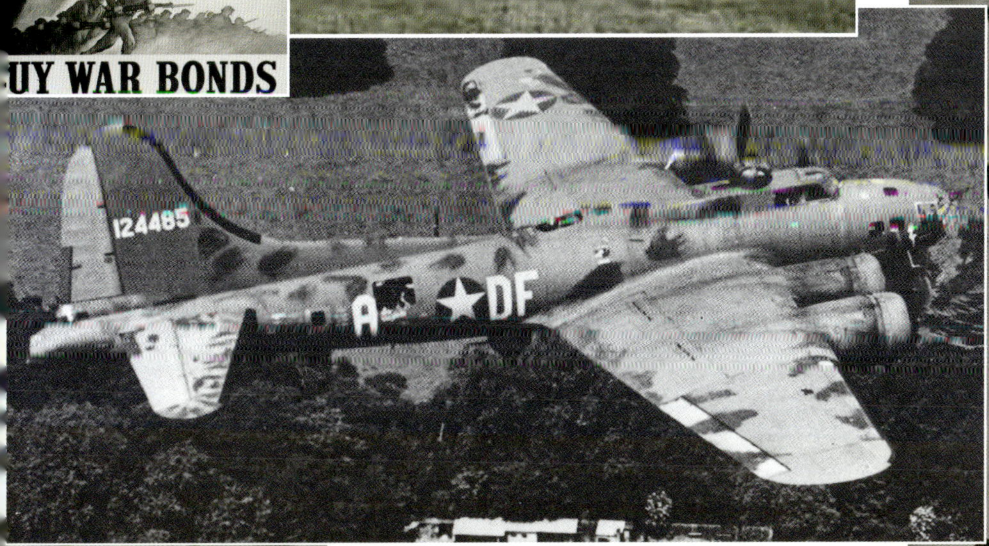
124485
A DF

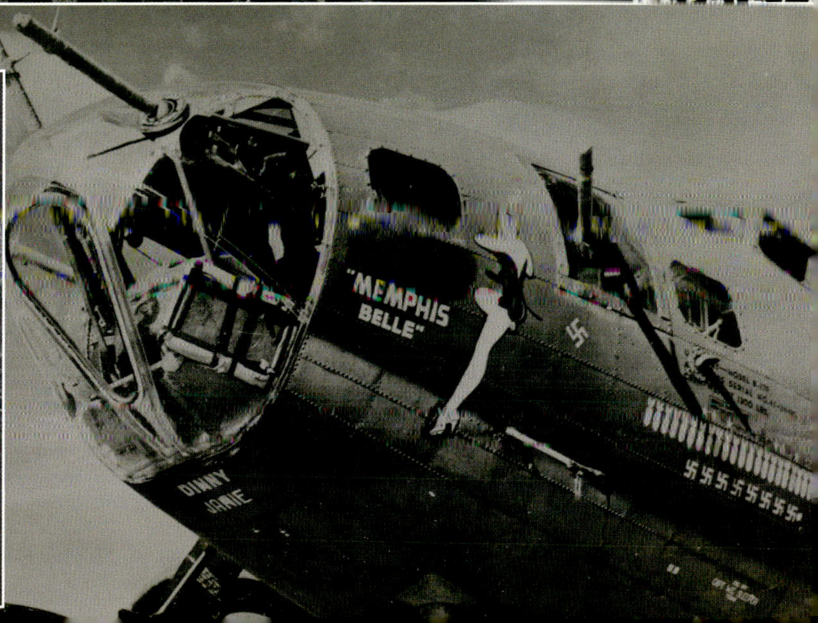
"MEMPHIS
BELLE"
DINNY
JANIE

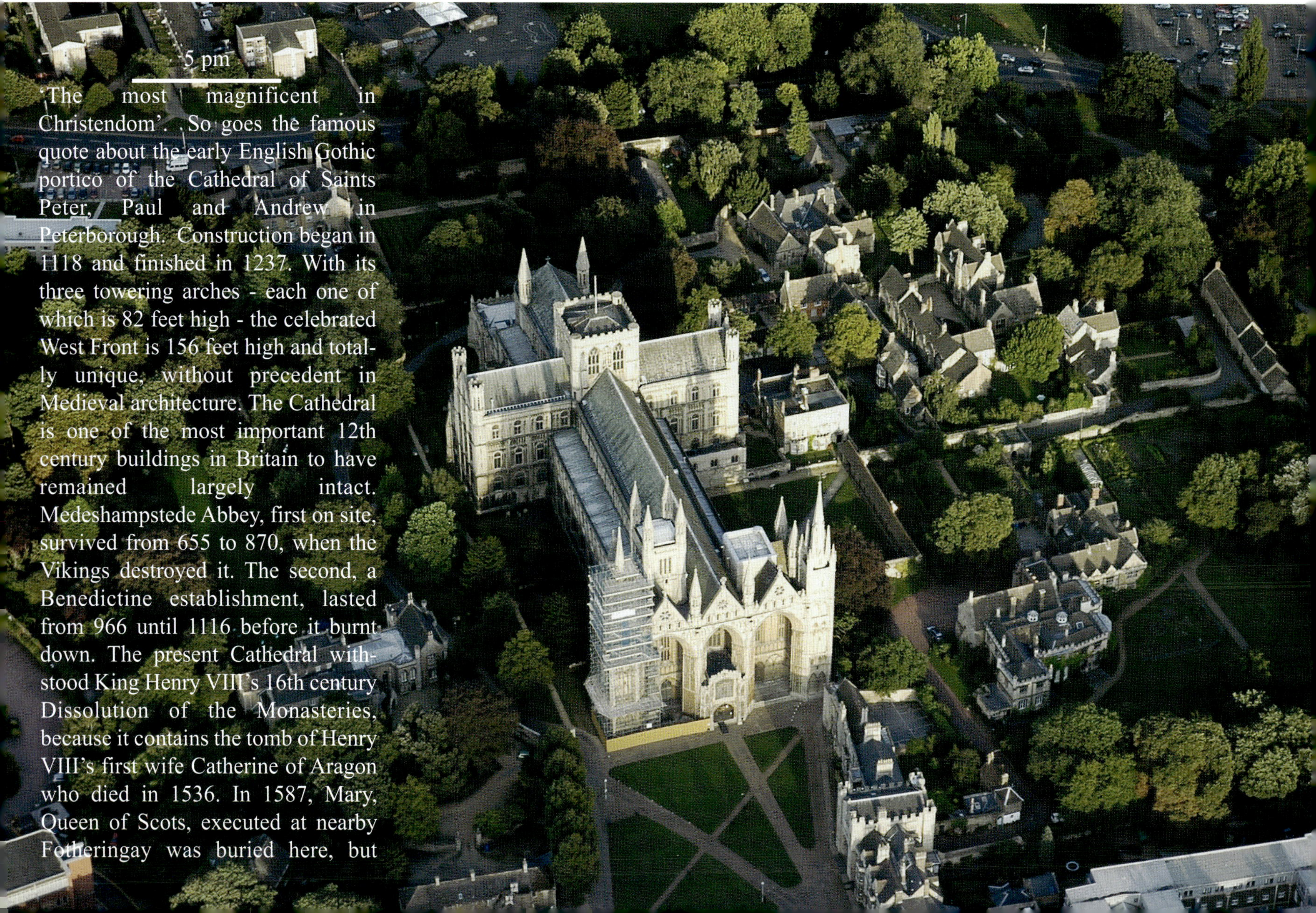

5 pm

'The most magnificent in Christendom'. So goes the famous quote about the early English Gothic portico of the Cathedral of Saints Peter, Paul and Andrew in Peterborough. Construction began in 1118 and finished in 1237. With its three towering arches - each one of which is 82 feet high - the celebrated West Front is 156 feet high and totally unique, without precedent in Medieval architecture. The Cathedral is one of the most important 12th century buildings in Britain to have remained largely intact. Medeshampstede Abbey, first on site, survived from 655 to 870, when the Vikings destroyed it. The second, a Benedictine establishment, lasted from 966 until 1116 before it burnt down. The present Cathedral withstood King Henry VIII's 16th century Dissolution of the Monasteries, because it contains the tomb of Henry VIII's first wife Catherine of Aragon who died in 1536. In 1587, Mary, Queen of Scots, executed at nearby Fotheringay was buried here, but later moved to Westminster Abbey on the orders of her son, King James I. Seven miles to the north west of Peterborough is the village of Barnack, shown, right, where the stone to build the both Peterborough and Ely Cathedral was quarried. Today, the exhausted ground is known as 'Barnack Holes', an overgrown area used by walkers with their dogs, even in the winter snow.

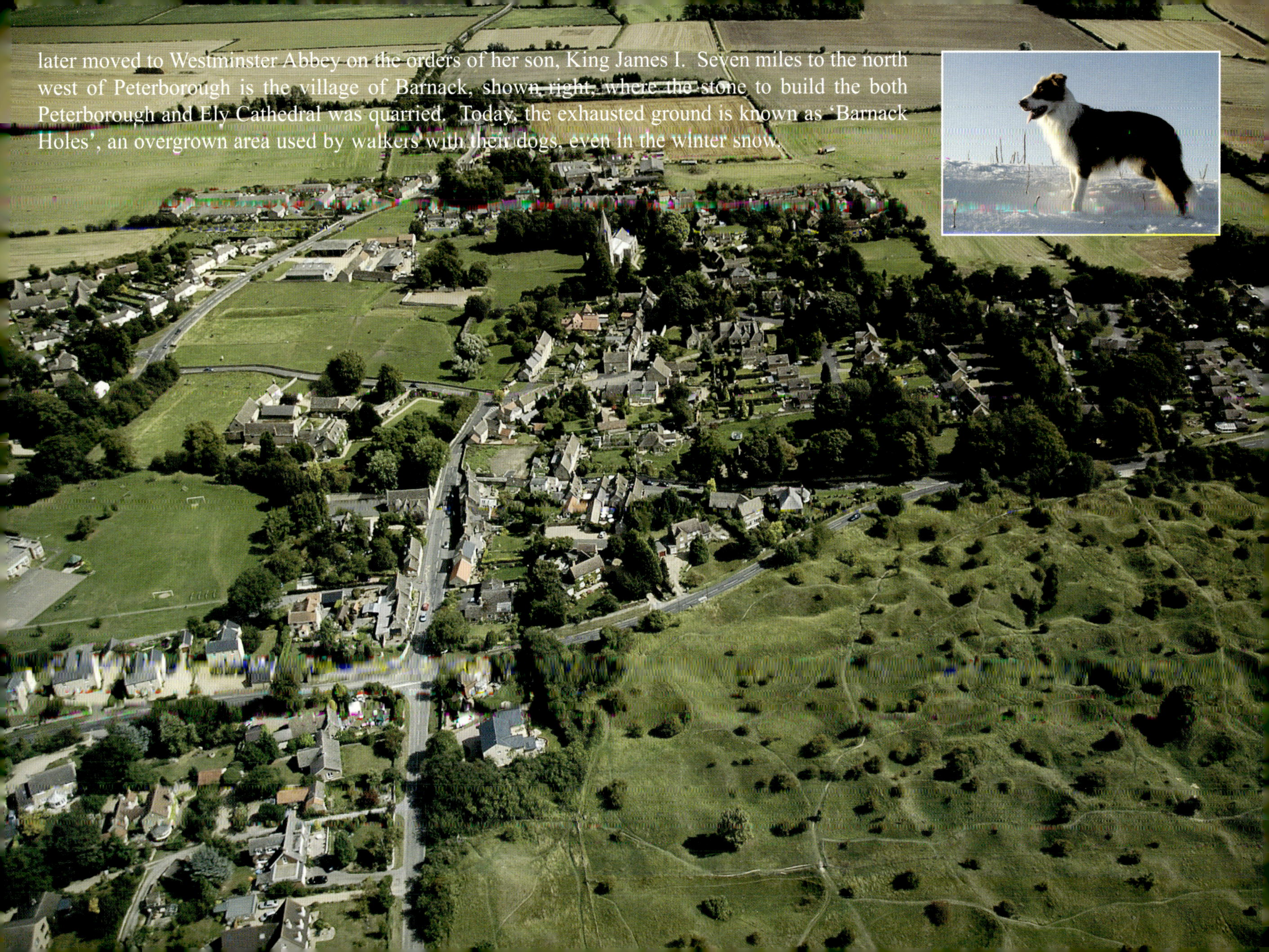

5.15 pm

Below, changing punting and rowing styles on the River Cam against an impressive backdrop. Opposite, Hinchinbrooke House, situated on the outskirts of Huntingdon is an impressive Tudor building built on the site of a 12th century Norman church which was converted to a Benedictine nunnery in 1200. The remains of the nunnery can still be seen within the house with the stone coffins

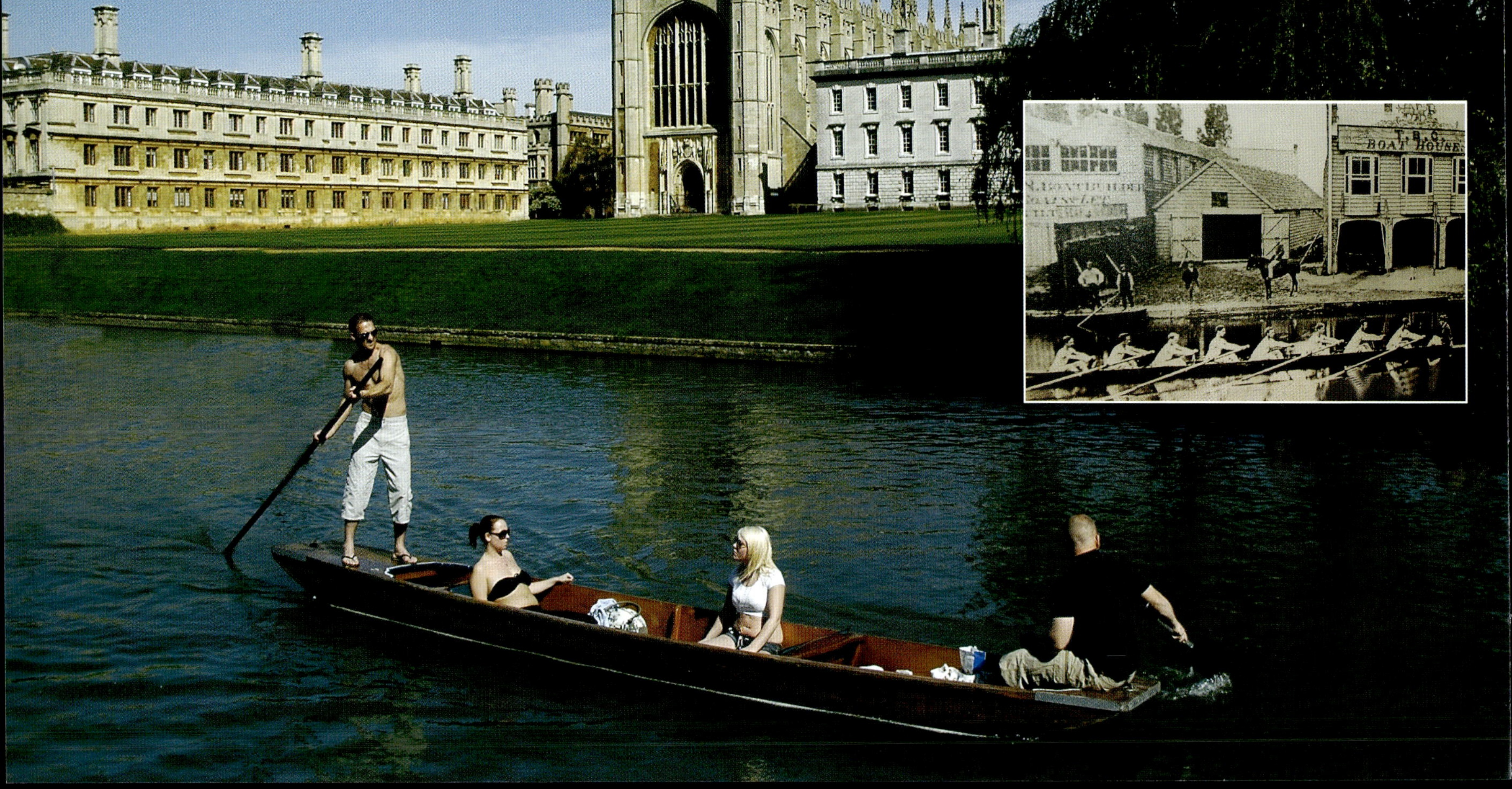

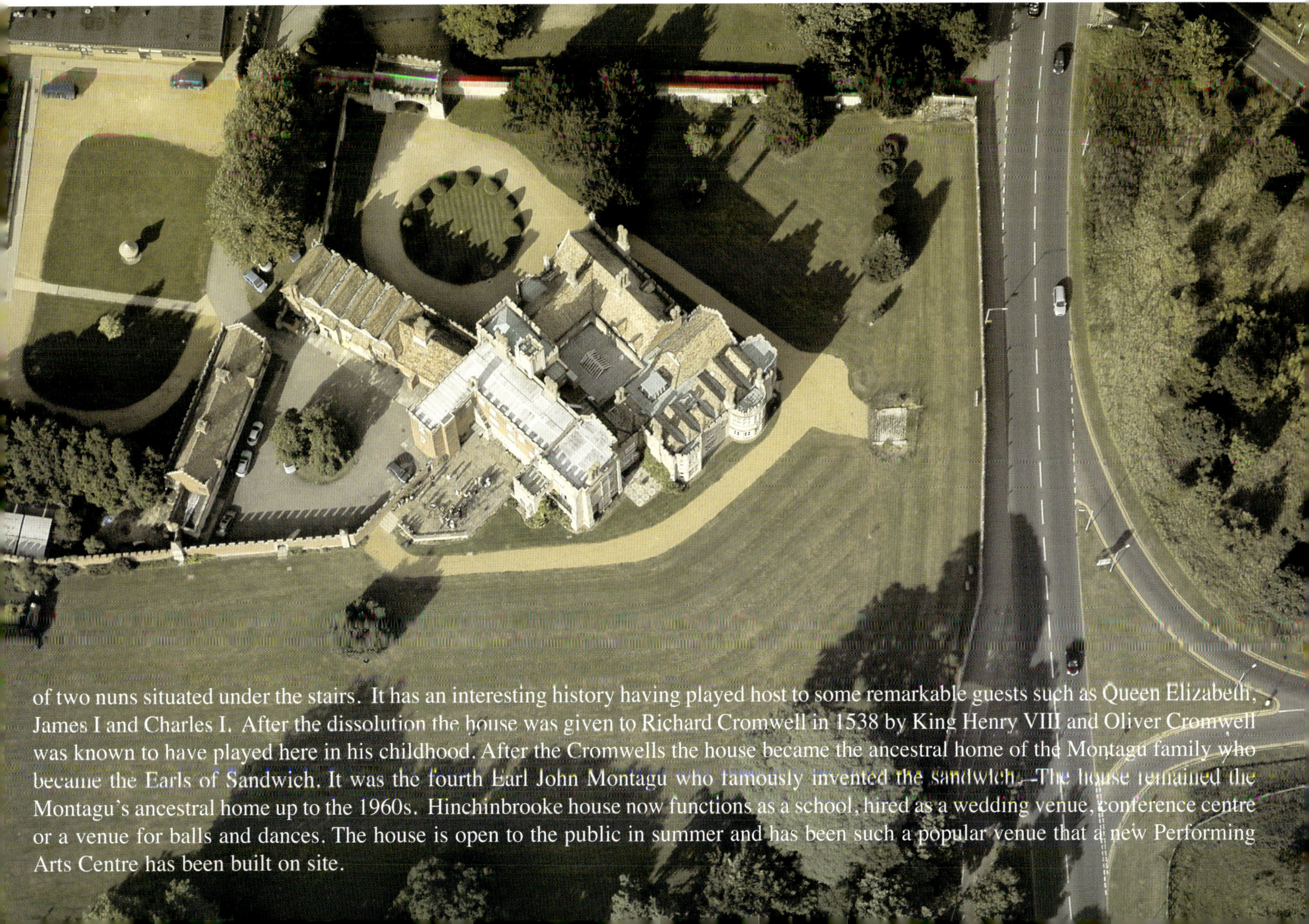

of two nuns situated under the stairs. It has an interesting history having played host to some remarkable guests such as Queen Elizabeth, James I and Charles I. After the dissolution the house was given to Richard Cromwell in 1538 by King Henry VIII and Oliver Cromwell was known to have played here in his childhood. After the Cromwells the house became the ancestral home of the Montagu family who became the Earls of Sandwich. It was the fourth Earl John Montagu who famously invented the sandwich. The house remained the Montagu's ancestral home up to the 1960s. Hinchinbrooke house now functions as a school, hired as a wedding venue, conference centre or a venue for balls and dances. The house is open to the public in summer and has been such a popular venue that a new Performing Arts Centre has been built on site.

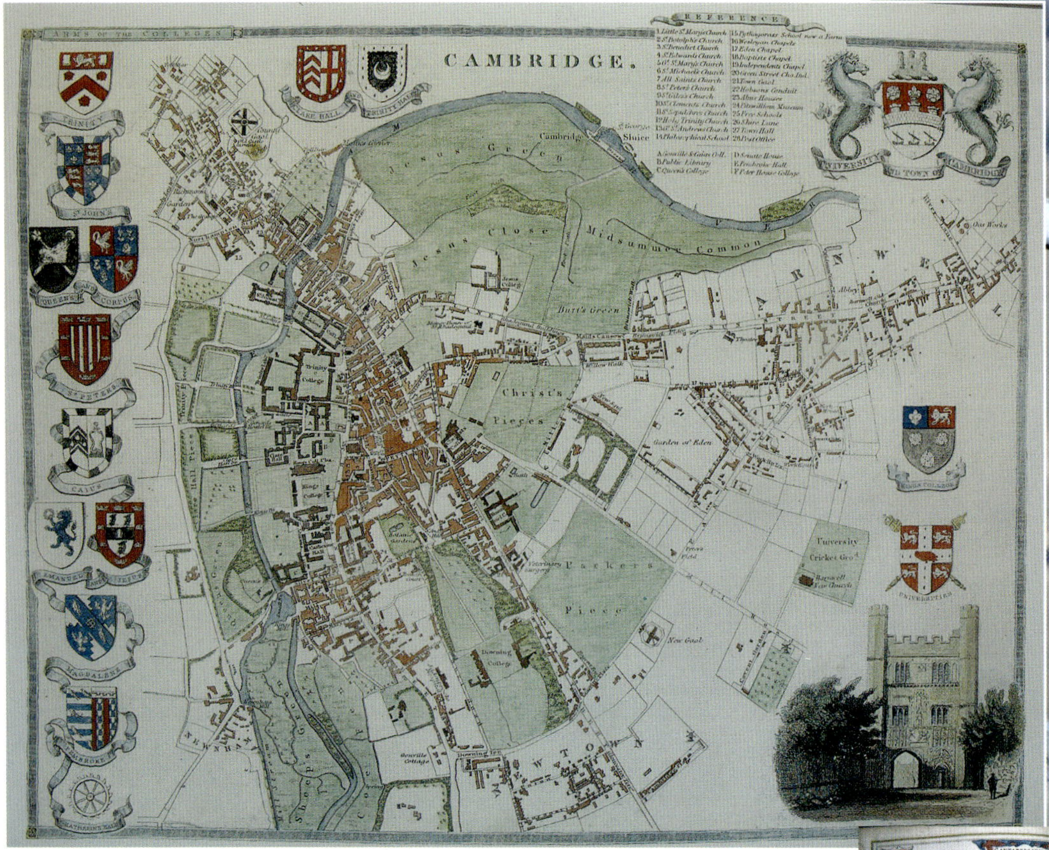

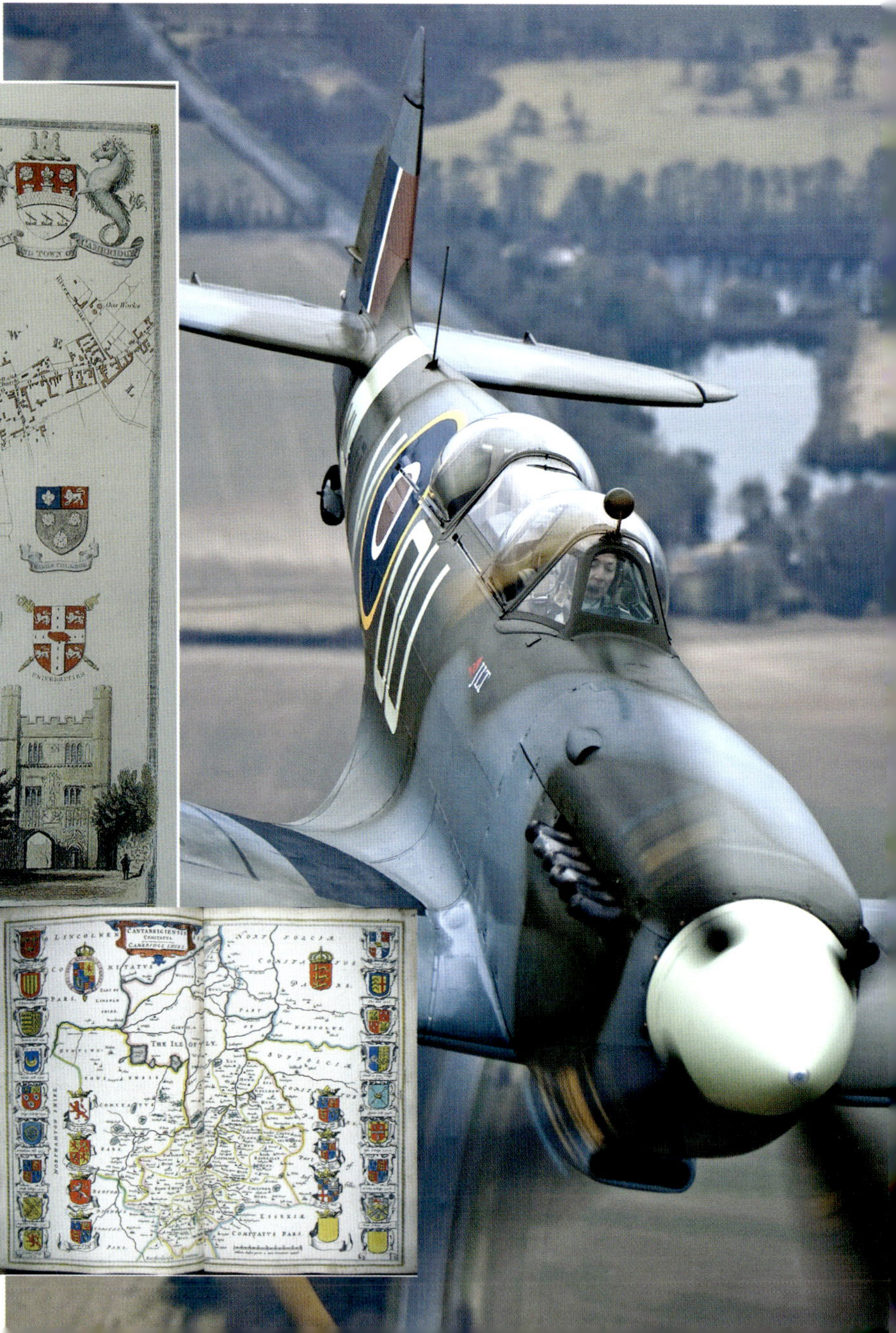

5.30 pm

Cambridge University was founded in 1209 when students left Oxford and settled in Cambridge where Peterhouse was founded in 1284 and is the oldest surviving college. Kings College Chapel, one of the most memorable vistas in the world, was started in 1446 in the 'Perpendicular' style by King Henry VII and completed by King Henry VIII in 1515. He also built the grandest college in Cambridge – Trinity, long before Spitfires flew over Cambridge.

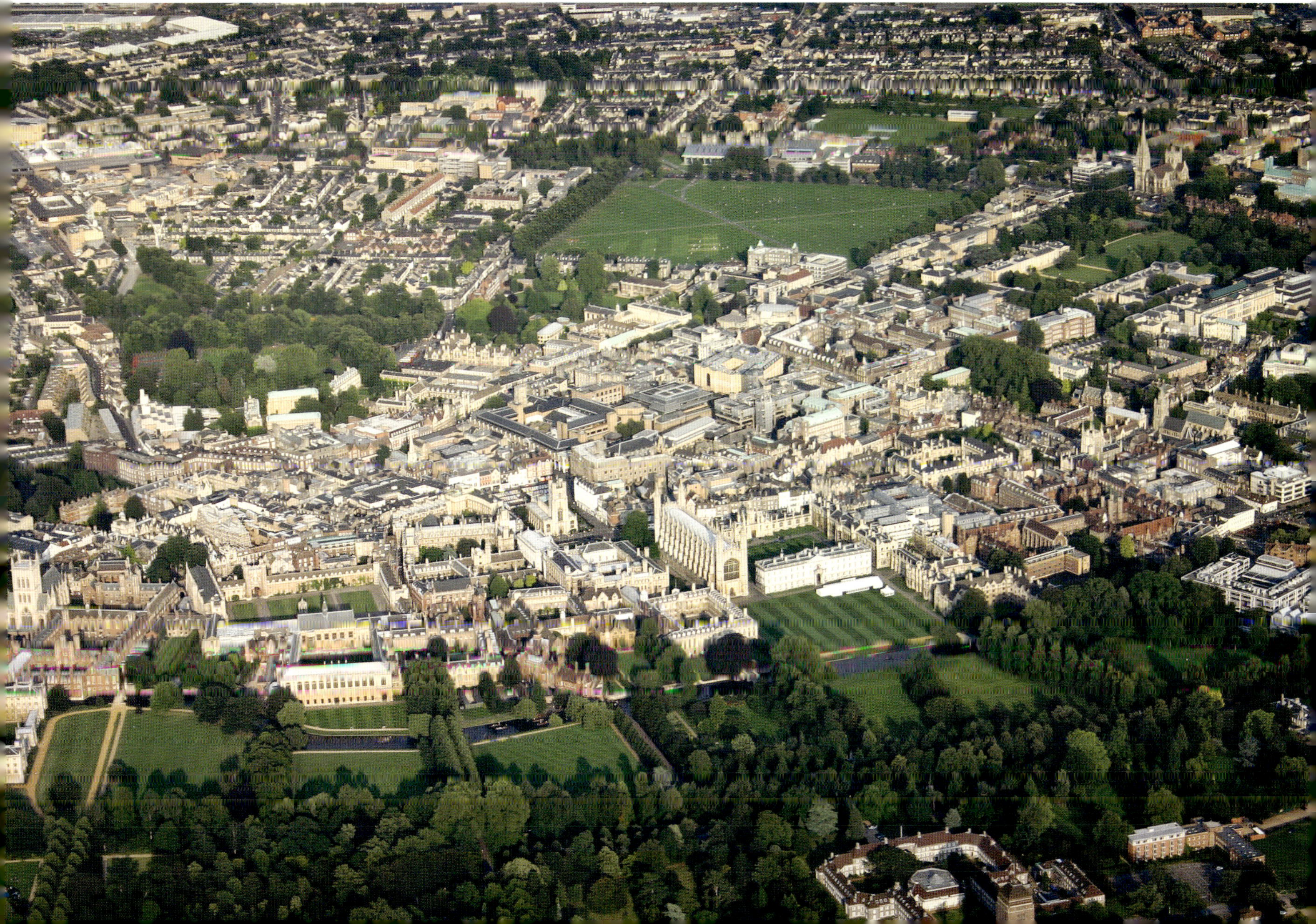

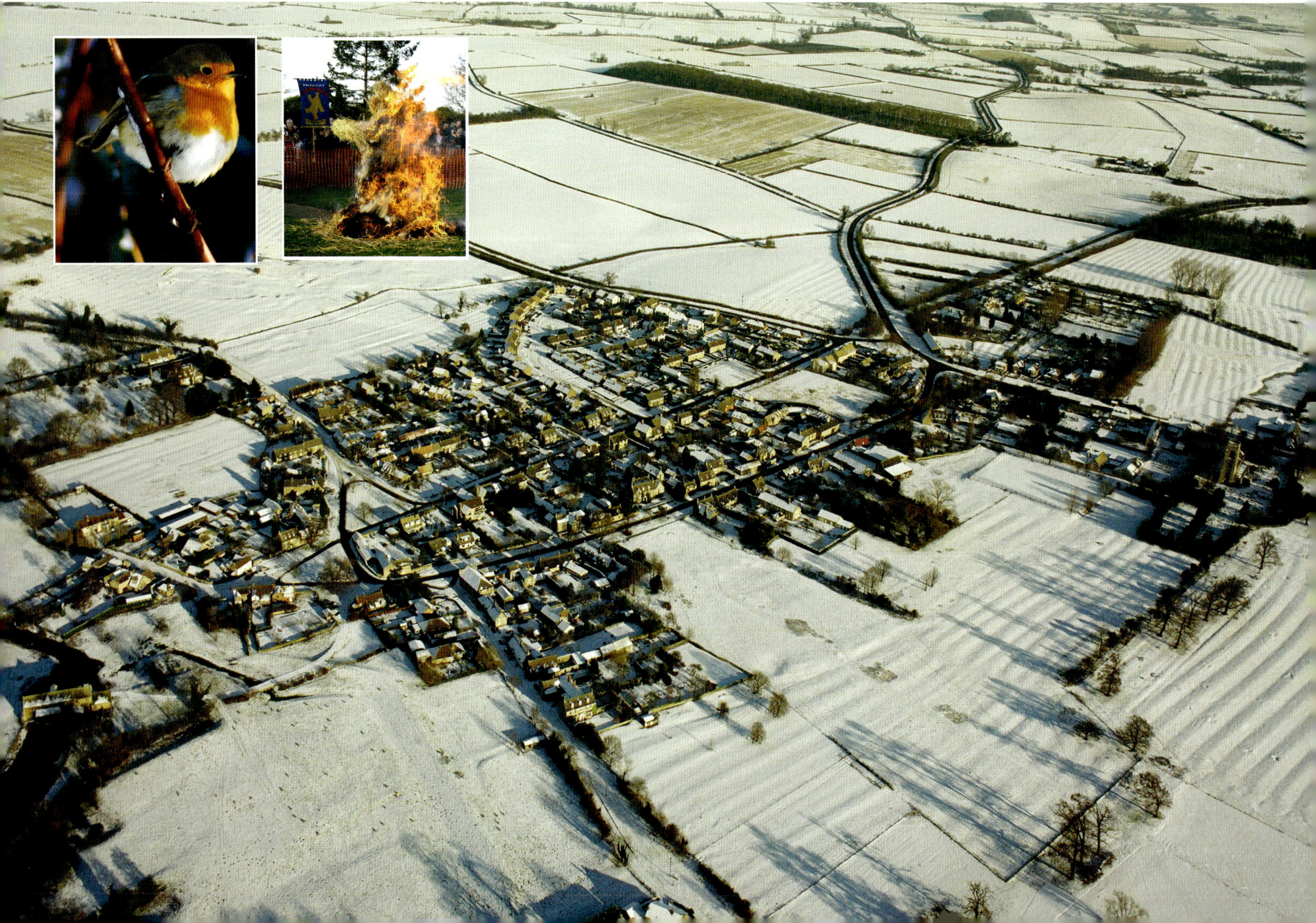

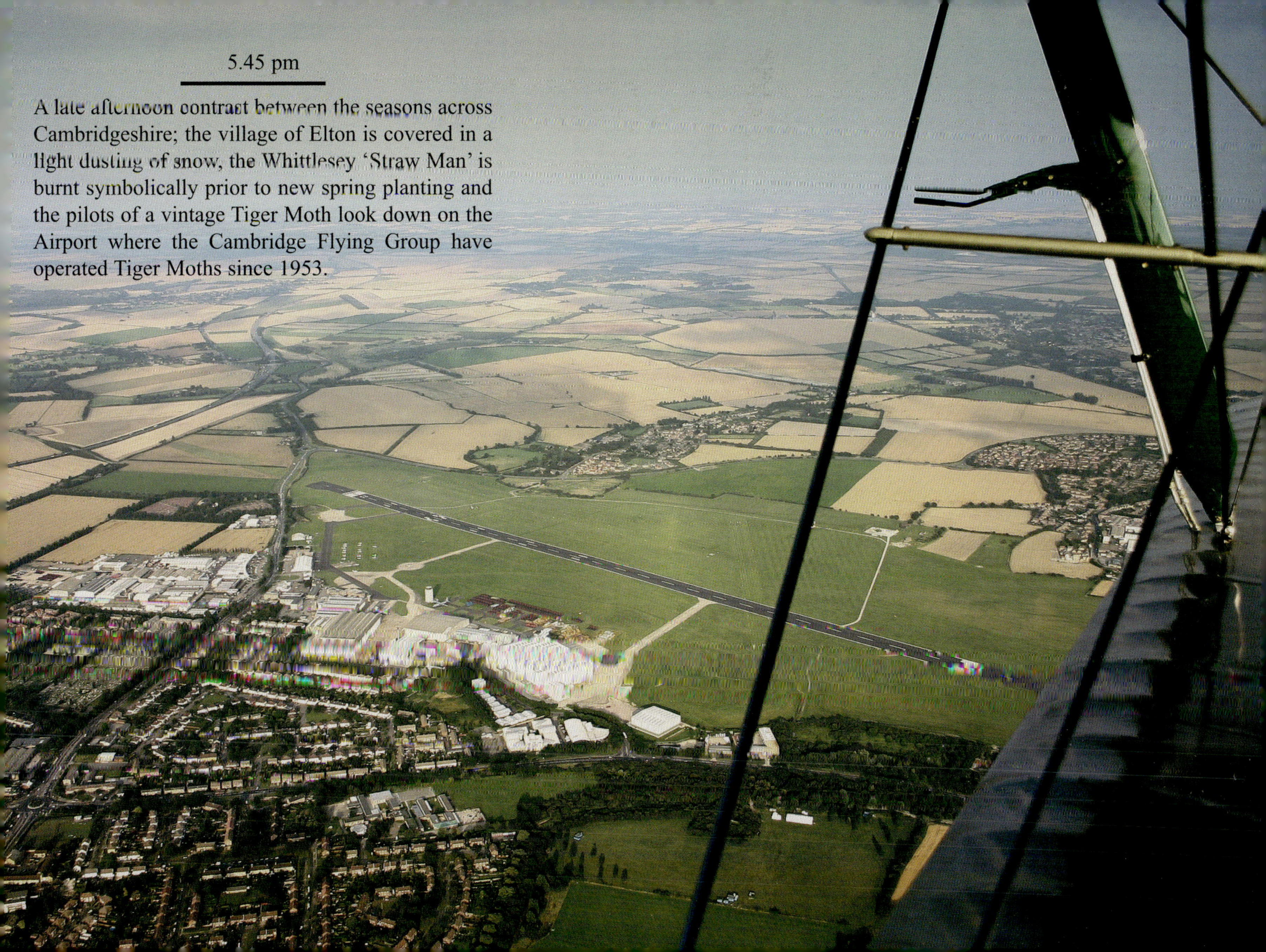

5.45 pm

A late afternoon contrast between the seasons across Cambridgeshire; the village of Elton is covered in a light dusting of snow, the Whittlesey 'Straw Man' is burnt symbolically prior to new spring planting and the pilots of a vintage Tiger Moth look down on the Airport where the Cambridge Flying Group have operated Tiger Moths since 1953.

Chapter 5
Evening
6 pm

Any B-17 'stragglers' would be escorted home during WWII by Mustang fighters over the Cambridgeshire countryside. Today, the early evening picnic crowd on the banks of the River Cam relax and enjoy the sight of punters on the river. Opposite, the River Great Ouse runs through Riverside Park in the modern town of St Neots which has absorbed the villages of

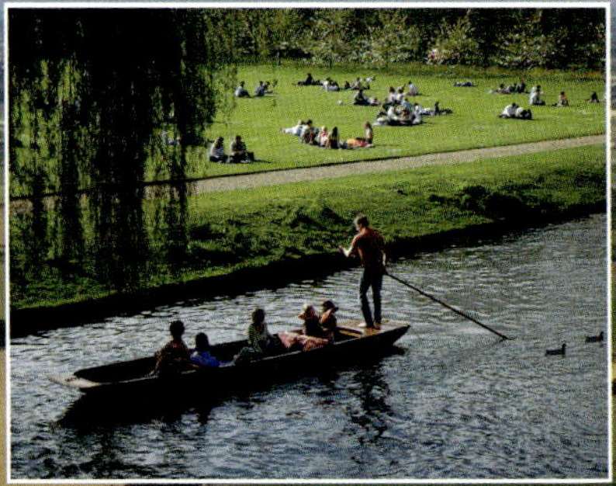

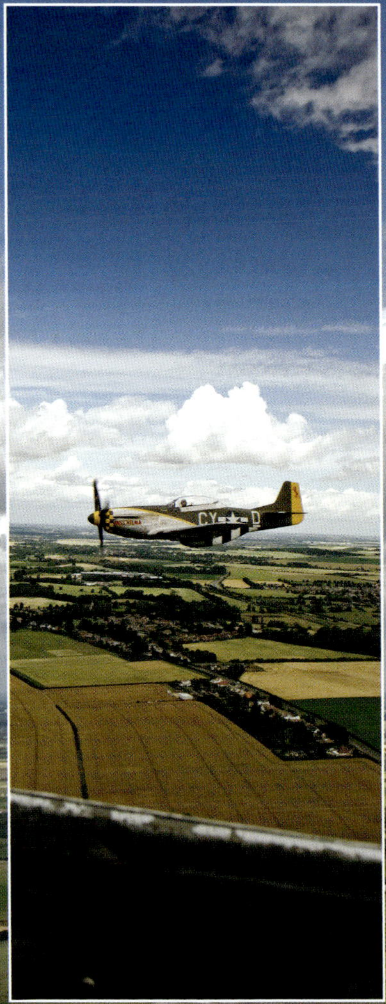

Eynesbury, Little Paxton, Eaton Ford and Eaton Socon to become the largest town in Cambridgeshire. St Neots gained its name from Saint Neot whose bones are buried in St Neot Priory. The town subsequently became a major pilgrim destination and coaching stop on the Great North Road.

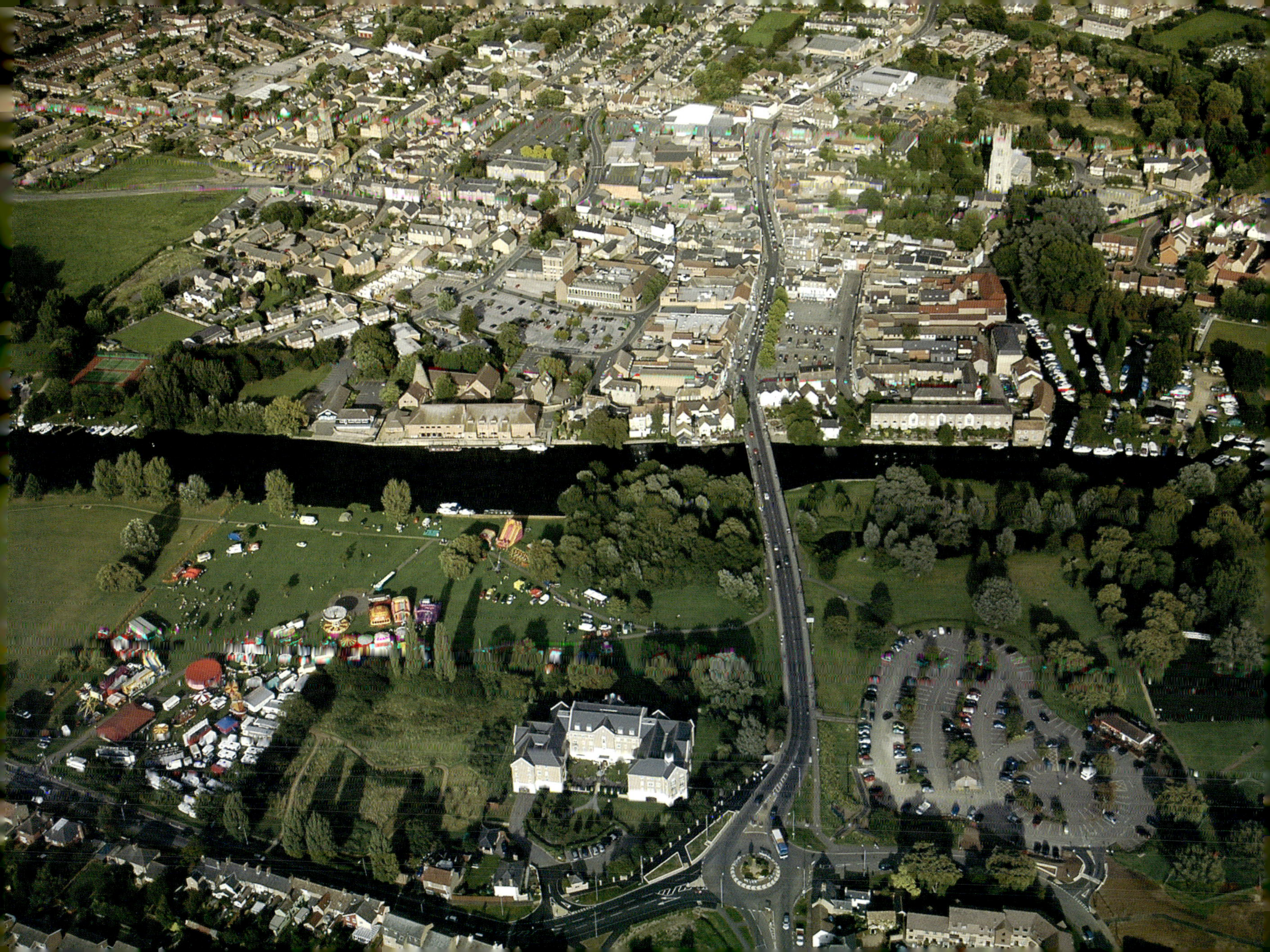

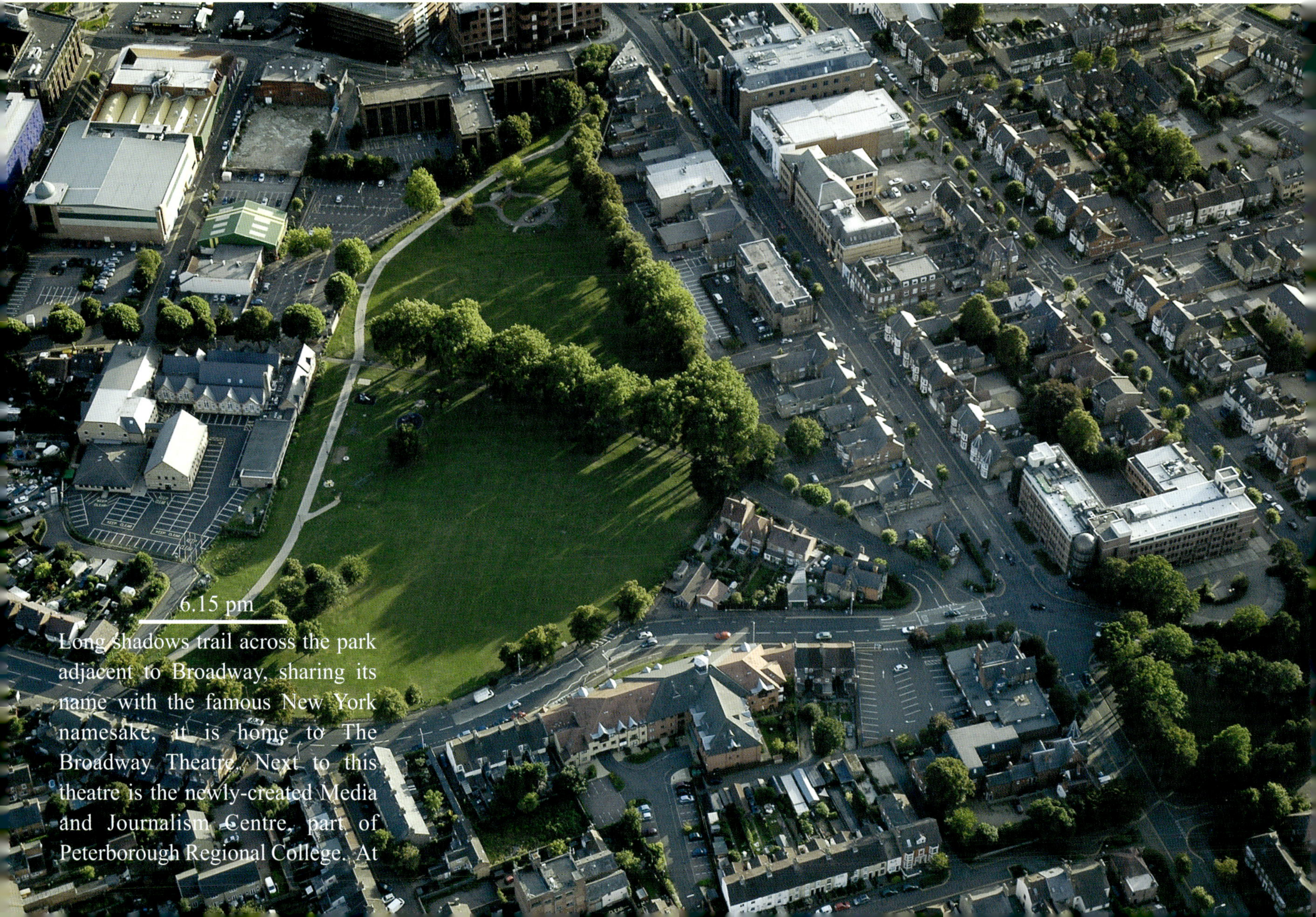

6.15 pm

Long shadows trail across the park adjacent to Broadway, sharing its name with the famous New York namesake, it is home to The Broadway Theatre. Next to this theatre is the newly-created Media and Journalism Centre, part of Peterborough Regional College. At the 'heart' of Peterborough is the Cathedral, the oldest and most architecturally stunning part of the city. The Cathedral was constructed within close proximity to the River Nene, which enabled stone to be transported to the building site. Due south of the Cathedral, sunlight glints

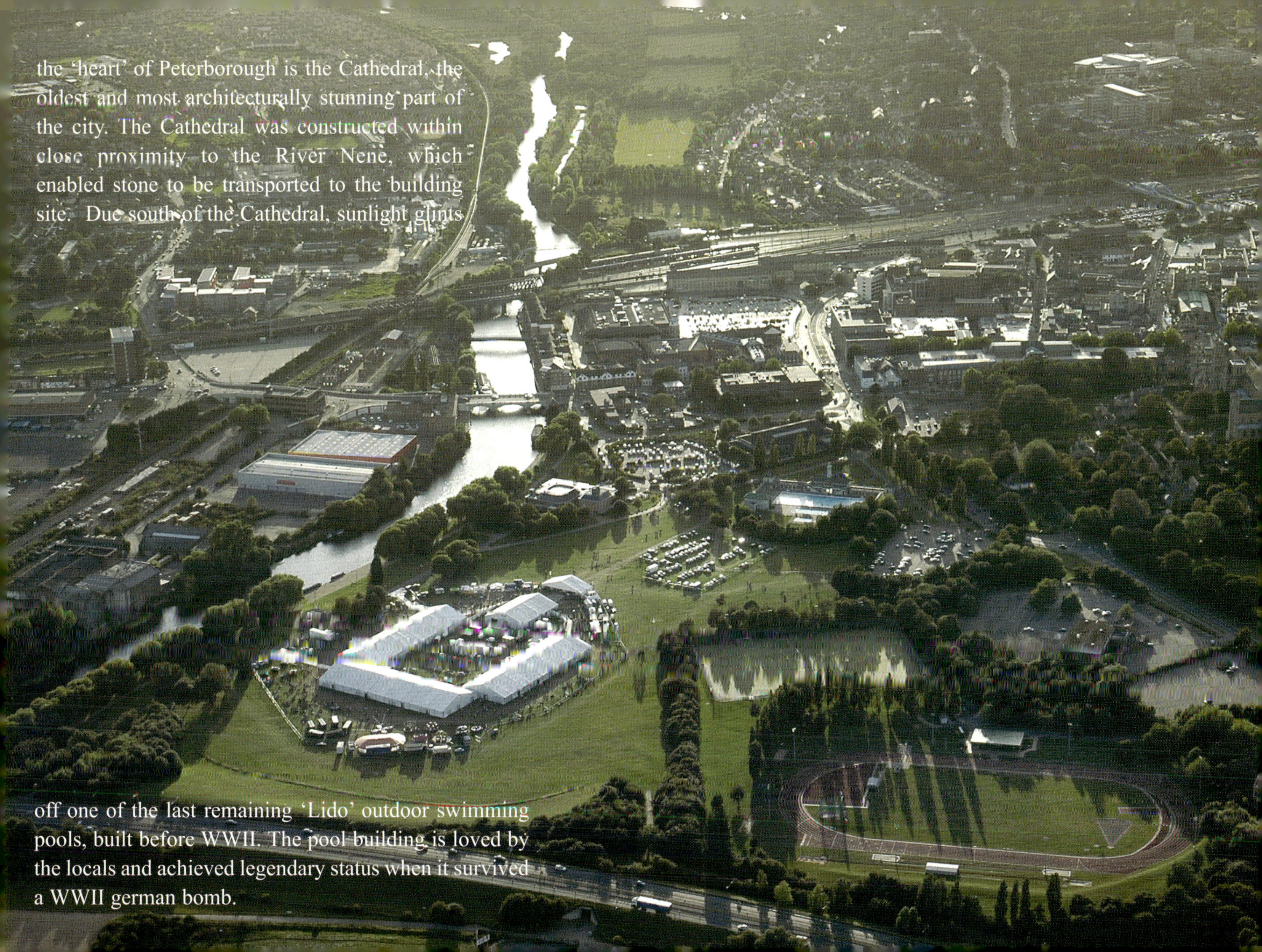

off one of the last remaining 'Lido' outdoor swimming pools, built before WWII. The pool building is loved by the locals and achieved legendary status when it survived a WWII german bomb.

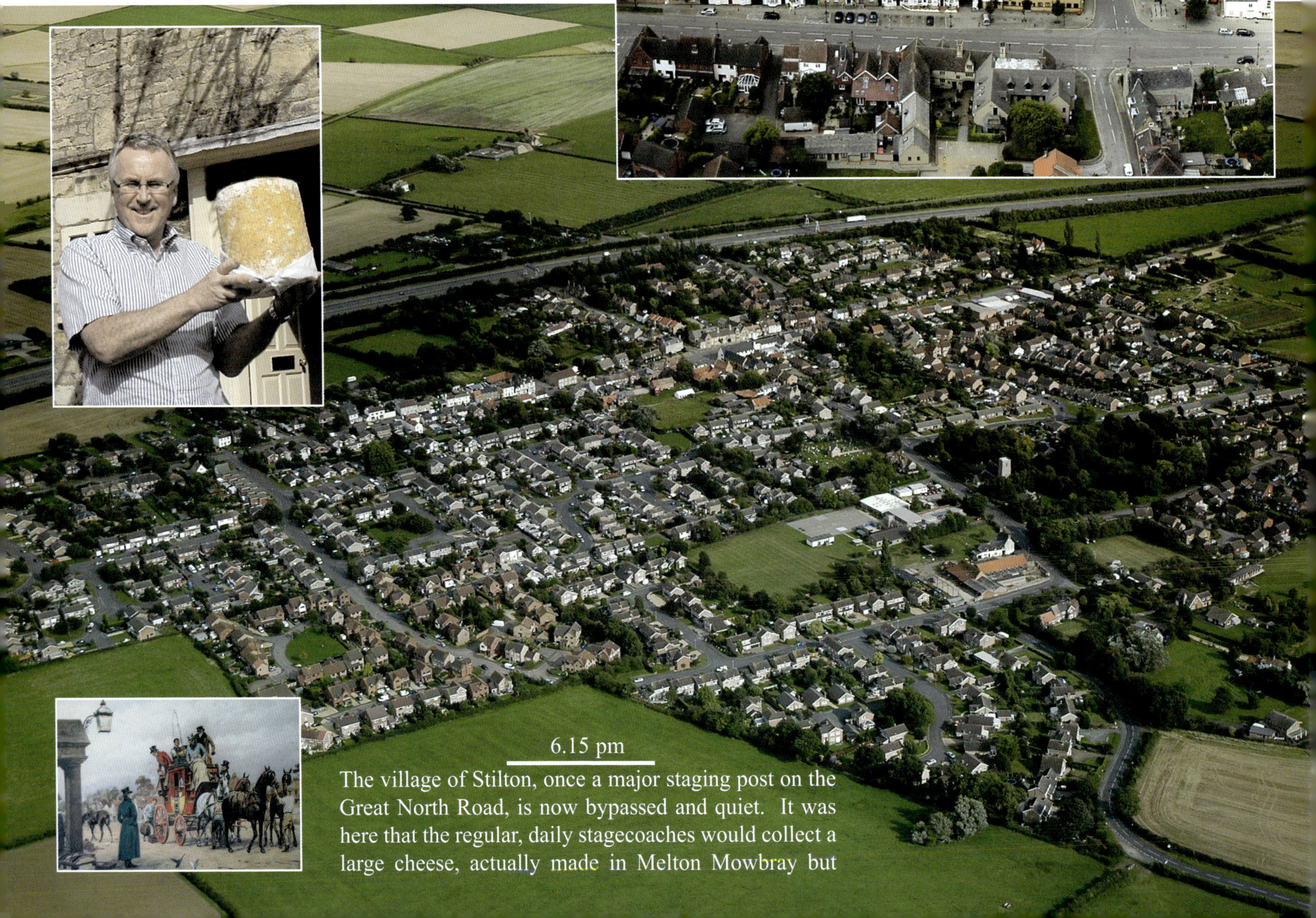

6.15 pm

The village of Stilton, once a major staging post on the Great North Road, is now bypassed and quiet. It was here that the regular, daily stagecoaches would collect a large cheese, actually made in Melton Mowbray but

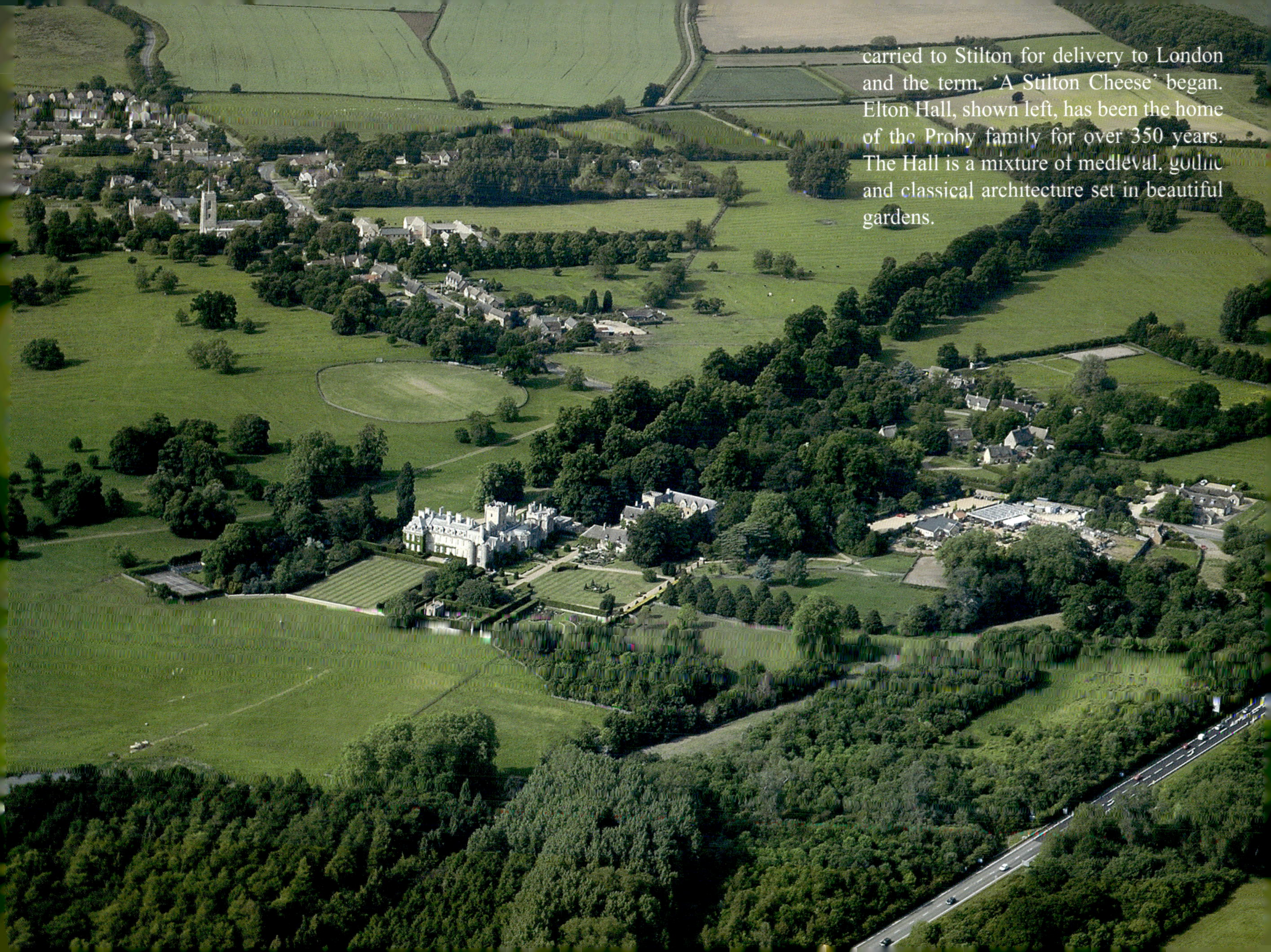

carried to Stilton for delivery to London and the term, 'A Stilton Cheese' began. Elton Hall, shown left, has been the home of the Proby family for over 350 years. The Hall is a mixture of medieval, gothic and classical architecture set in beautiful gardens.

7 pm

In the early evening, formations of 'Eights' pull hard from the motorway bridge back to their various clubhouses. At Cambridge Airport, the bright yellow Tiger Moths of the Cambridge Flying Group enjoy the calm air of the early evening. CFG is the only flying school that still conducts ab-initio, basic flying training on Tiger Moths, an initiative inspired by the late Bill Ison, shown in typical pose lower right. Much lower down the Cam, the punts enjoy the last rays of the sunshine.

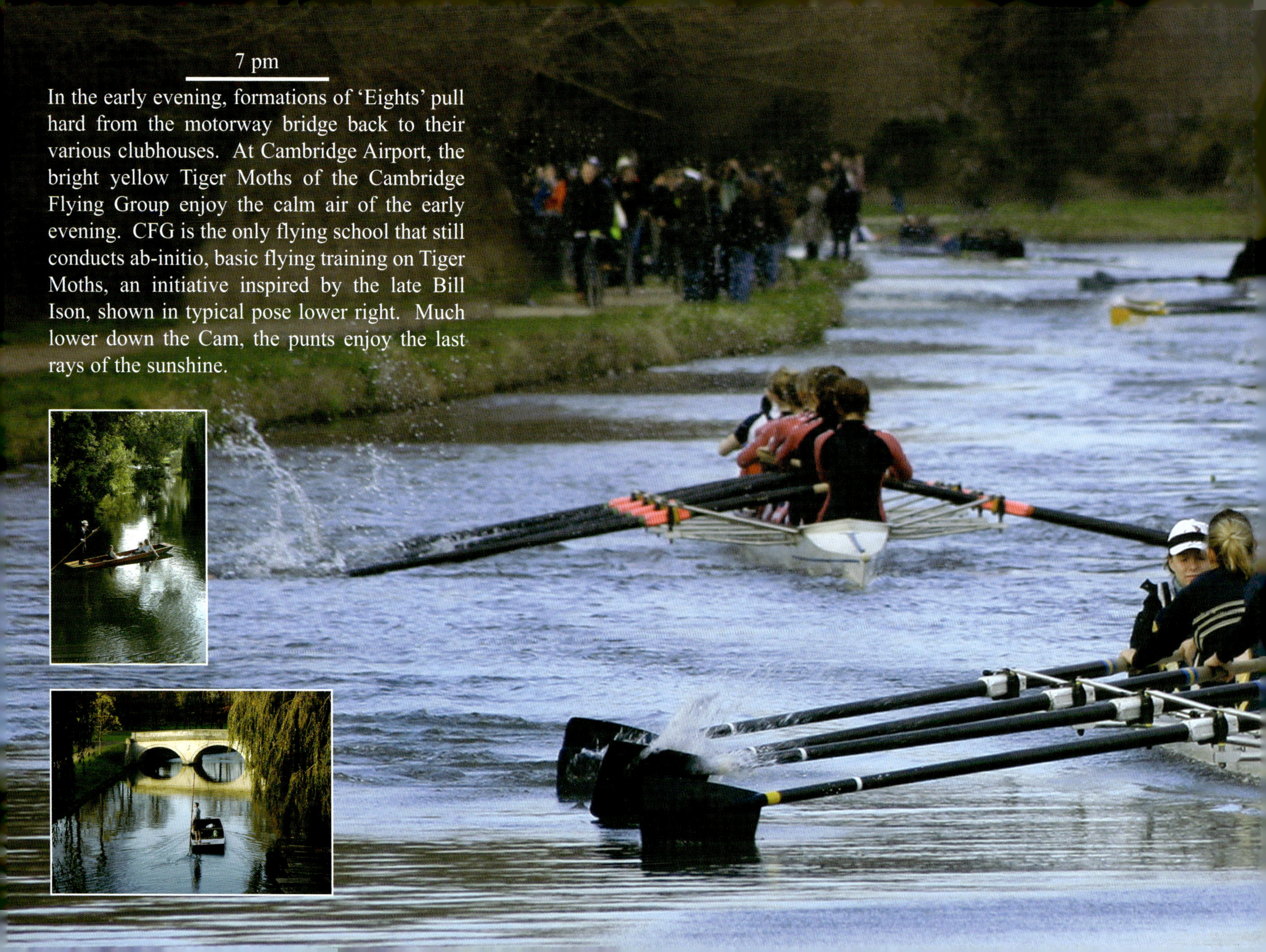

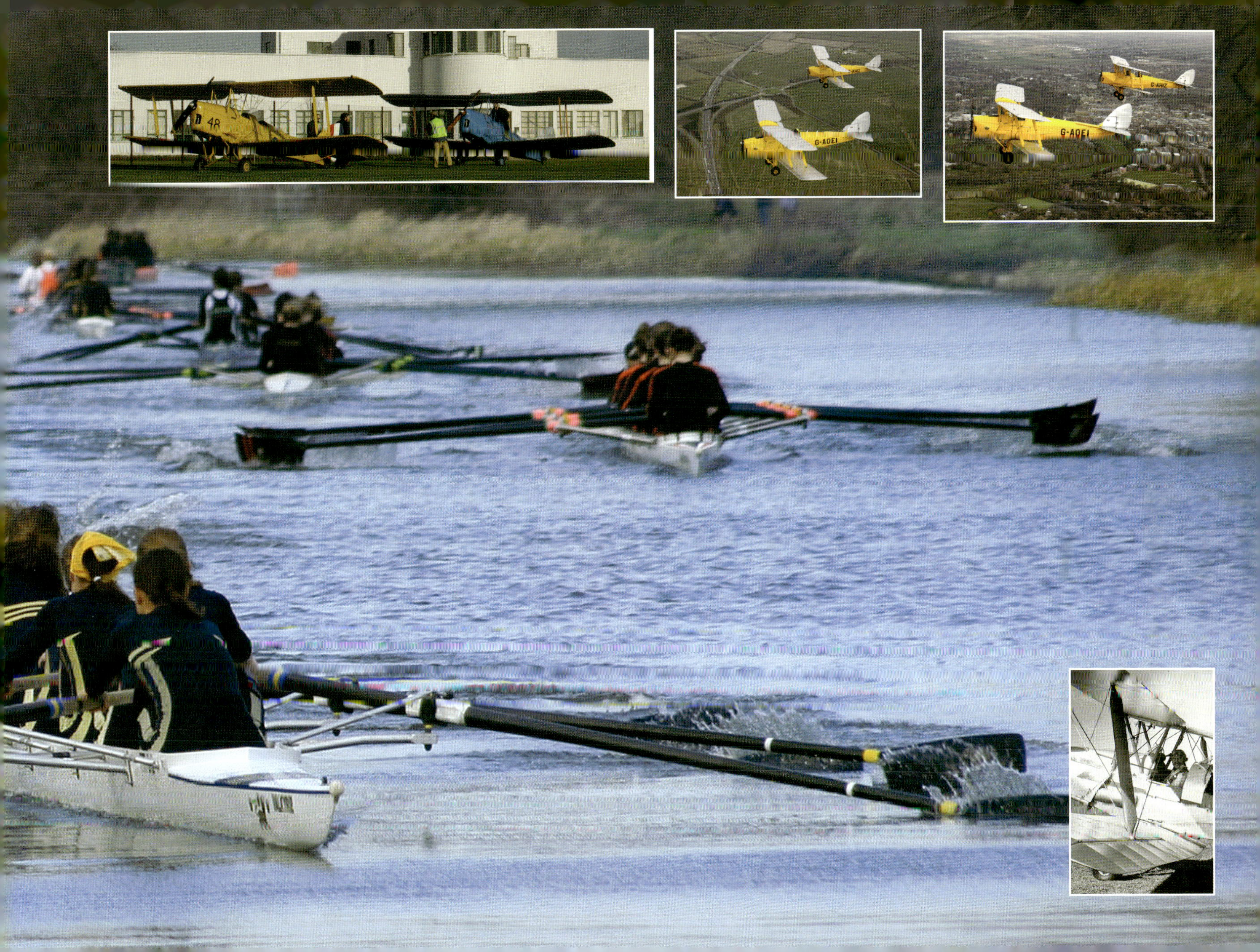

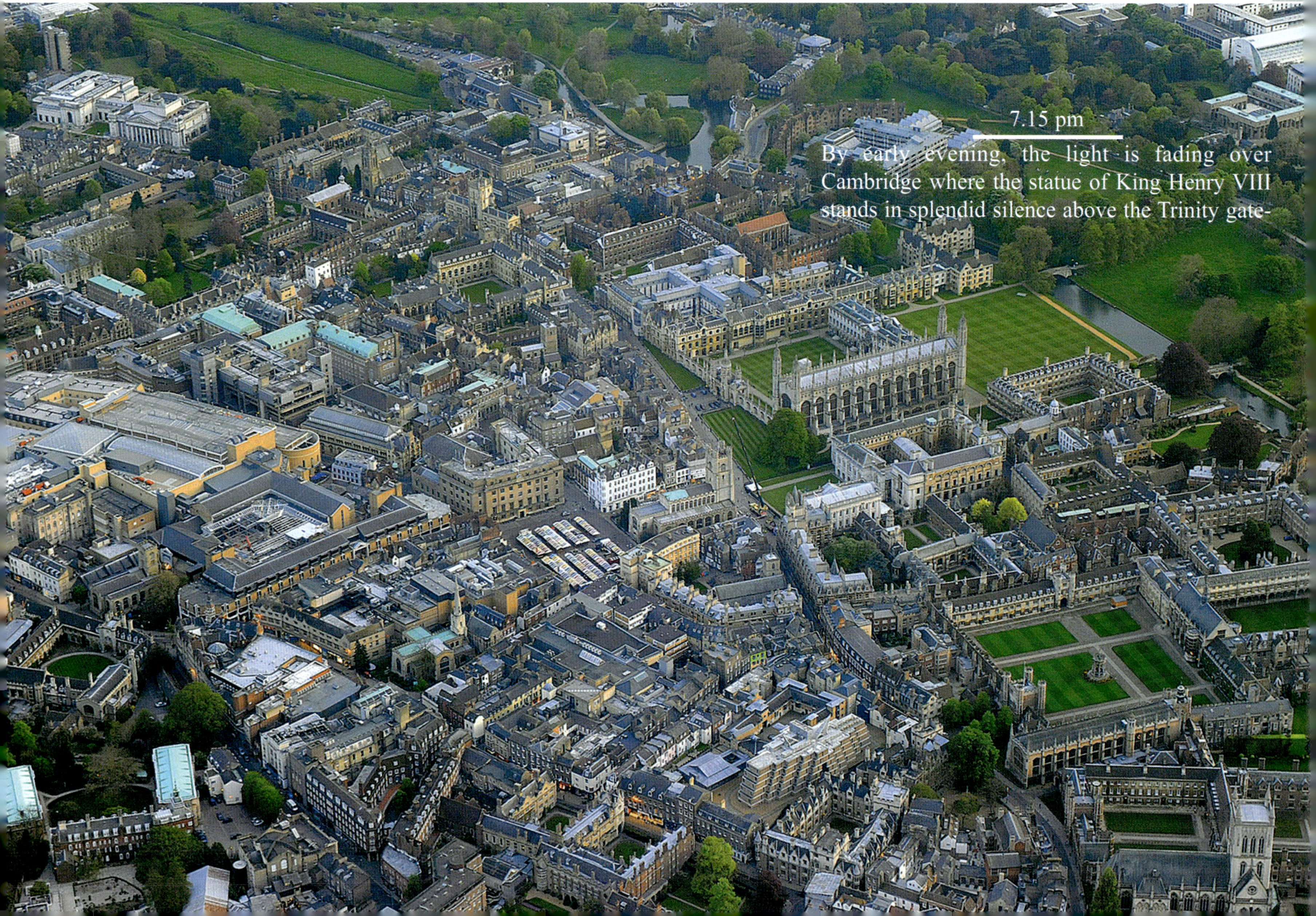

7.15 pm

By early evening, the light is fading over Cambridge where the statue of King Henry VIII stands in splendid silence above the Trinity gate-

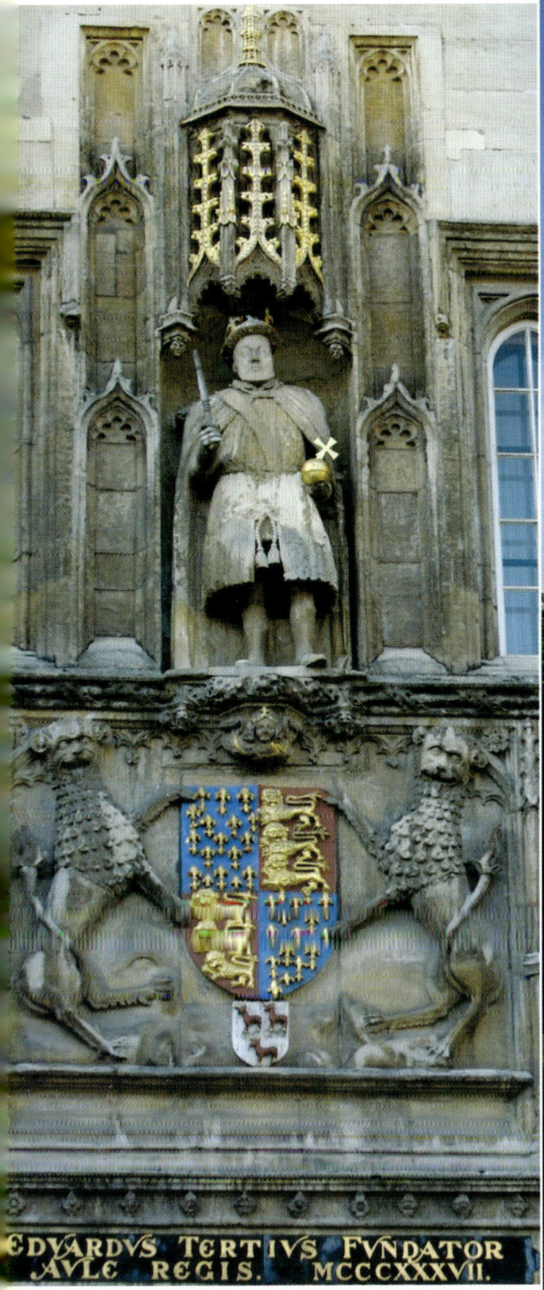

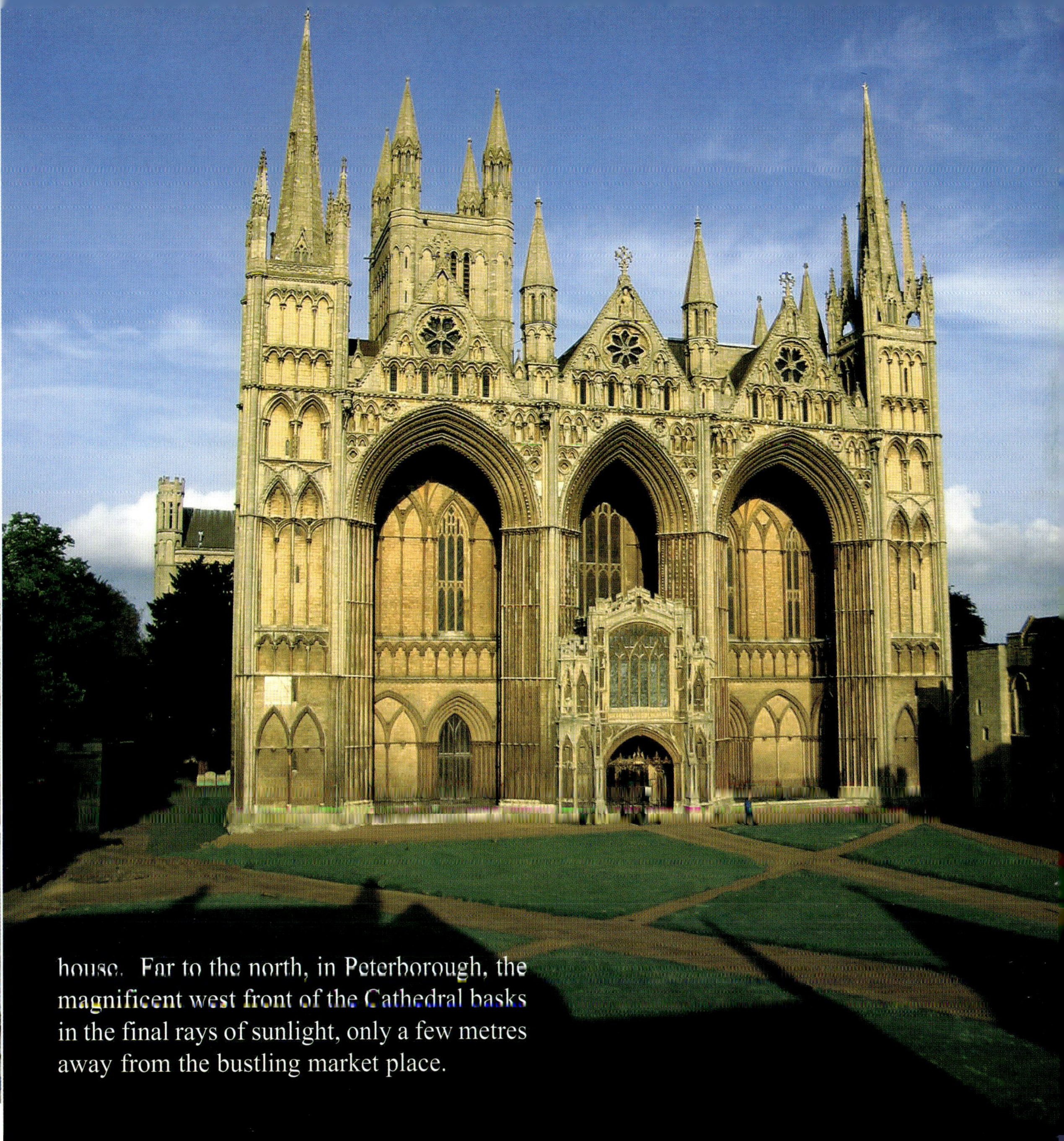

house. Far to the north, in Peterborough, the magnificent west front of the Cathedral basks in the final rays of sunlight, only a few metres away from the bustling market place.

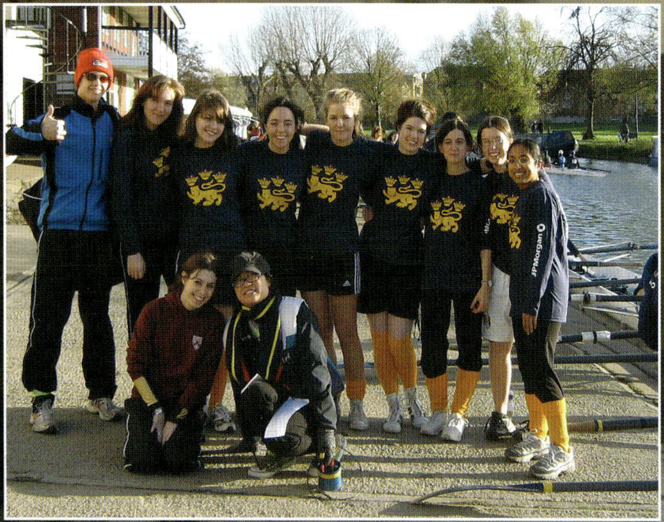

7.30 pm

The measurement term, 'as long as an eight', came directly from the standard length of this classic rowing shell. An 'Eight' is designed for eight rowers, who propel the boat with oars and is steered by a cox. The cox steers the boat using a rudder and sits at the

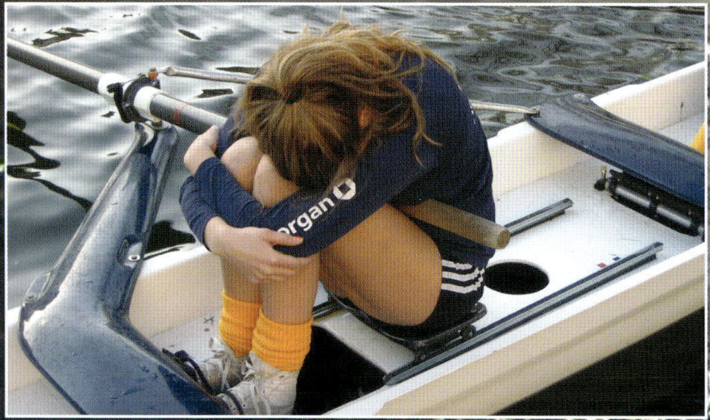

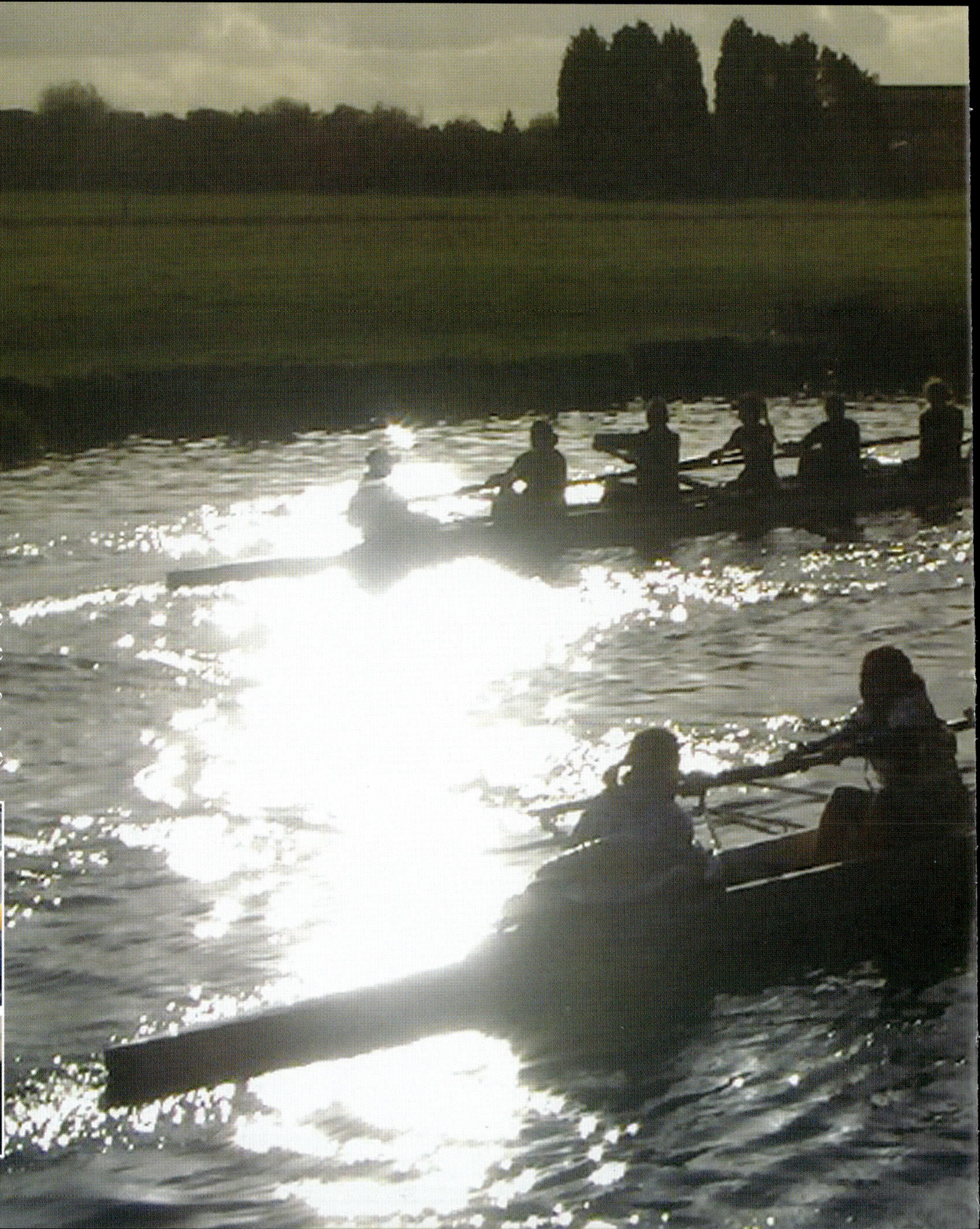

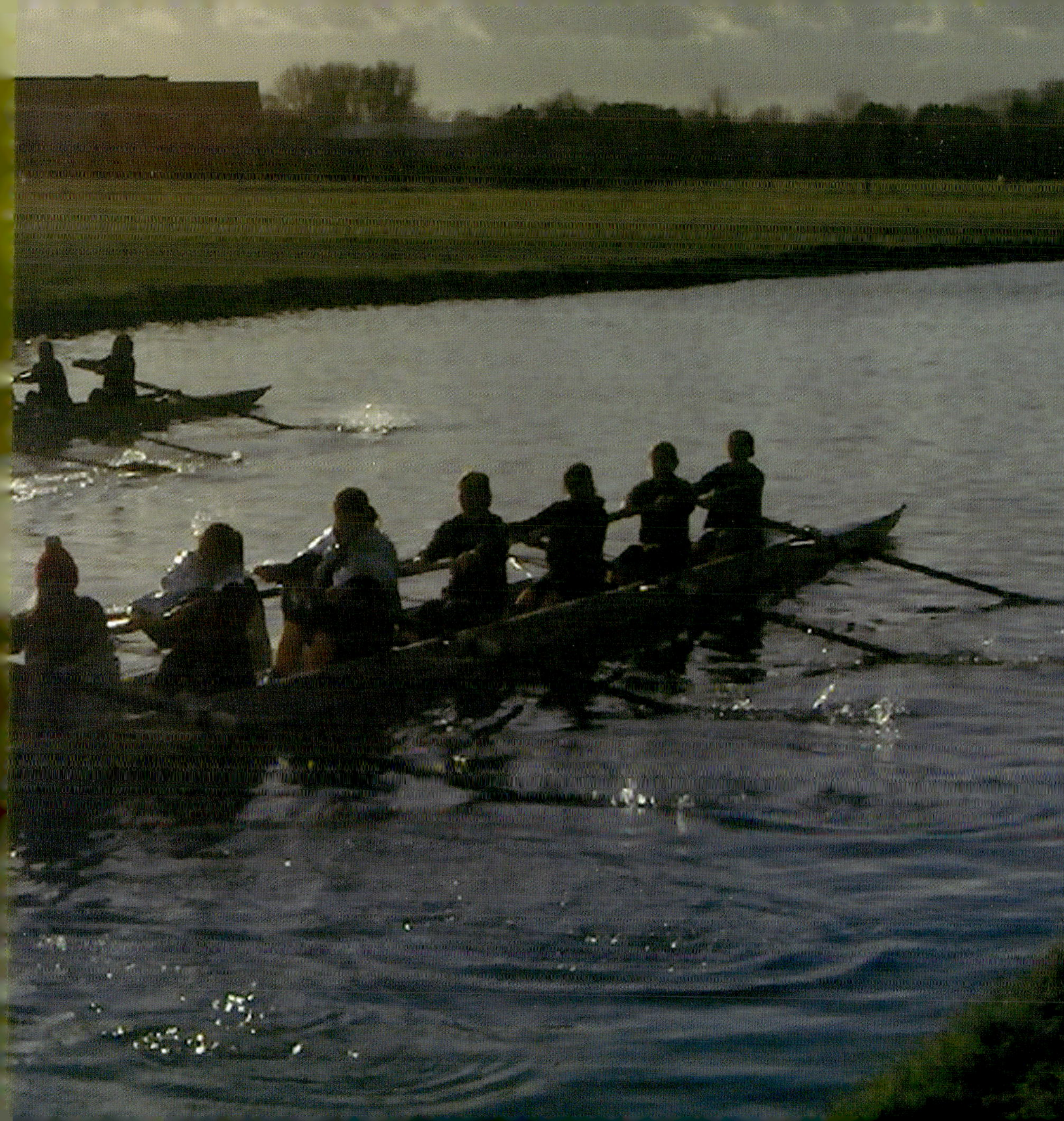

stern of the boat. The 'shells' are long, narrow, and semi-circular in cross-section in order to reduce drag to a minimum. Originally made from wood, shells are now made from fibre glass for strength and weight advantages. Eights have a fin towards the rear, to help prevent roll and yaw and to help the rudder. 'Eight' is one of the classes recognized by the International Rowing Federation and is one of the most exciting events in the Olympics. 'The Boat Race', also know as the University Boat Race, takes place on the River Thames every Spring. The formal title of the event is the Xchanging Boat Race and the members of both teams are traditionally known as 'blues'. Each boat is a 'Blue Boat' with Cambridge in light blue and Oxford in dark blue. An estimated quarter of a million people watch the race from the banks of the River Thames; between seven and nine million viewers see the race live on TV in the UK and an overseas audience of around 120 million watch making this event the most viewed single-day sporting event in the world

7.45 pm

In the fading light, two Hurricanes, bound for North Weald airfield, turn past Ely Cathedral. The final rays of the sun back lights the stained glass window dedicated to the Royal Air Force which clearly shows a Wellington bomber and even a windsock. Ely was built by the Normans on the site of the last Saxon resistance by Hereward the Wake. Here, the magnificent stained glass windows are a tribute not only to the designers but also to the makers of the glass. Colour was vital and a very specialised process. The 'red' glass, in particular, utilised an advanced process whereby the final 'red' coating was applied to clear glass by a process that became know as 'flash-ruby'. By the 15th century, all colours for stained glass windows were being produced by this method.

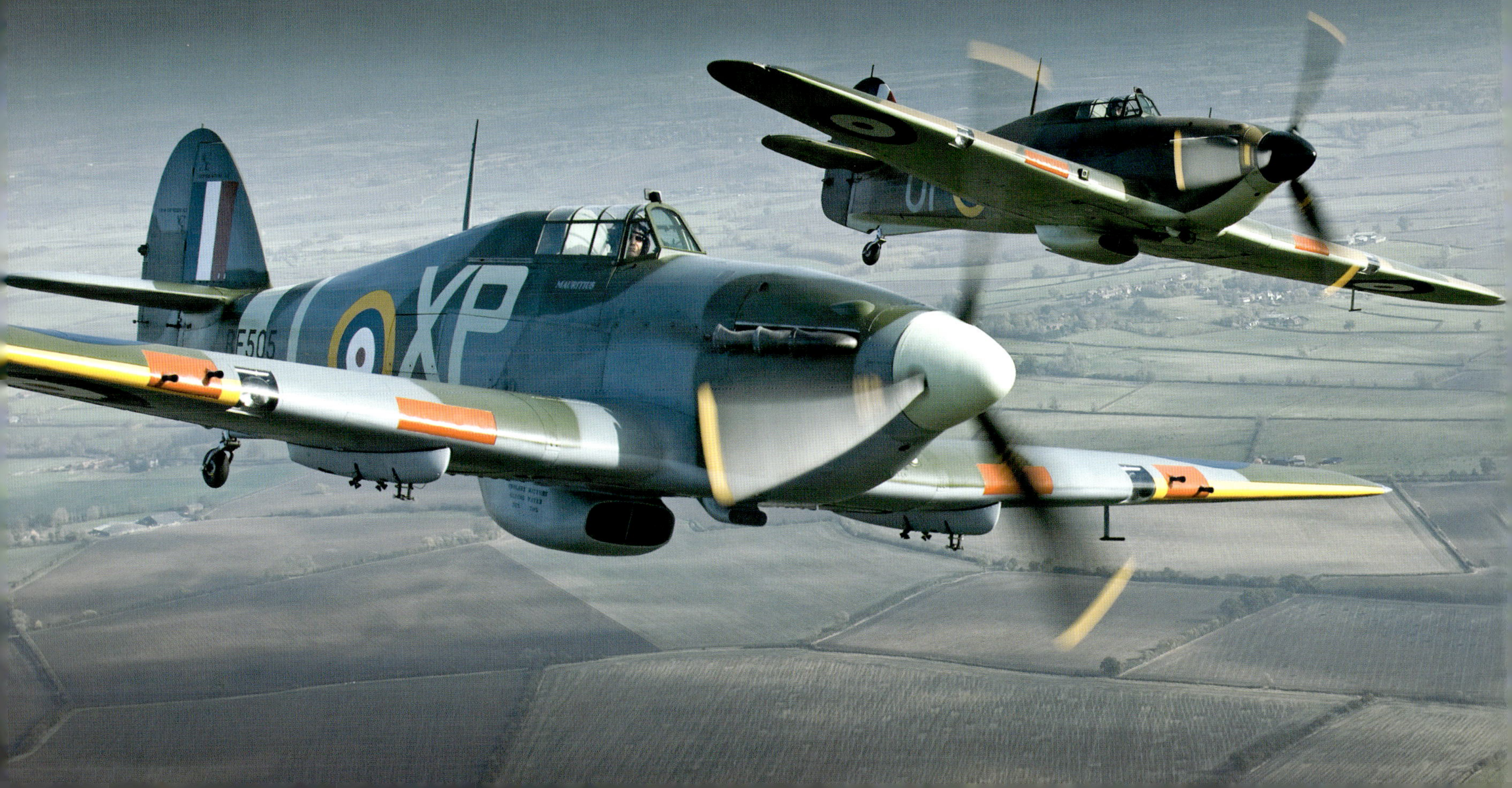

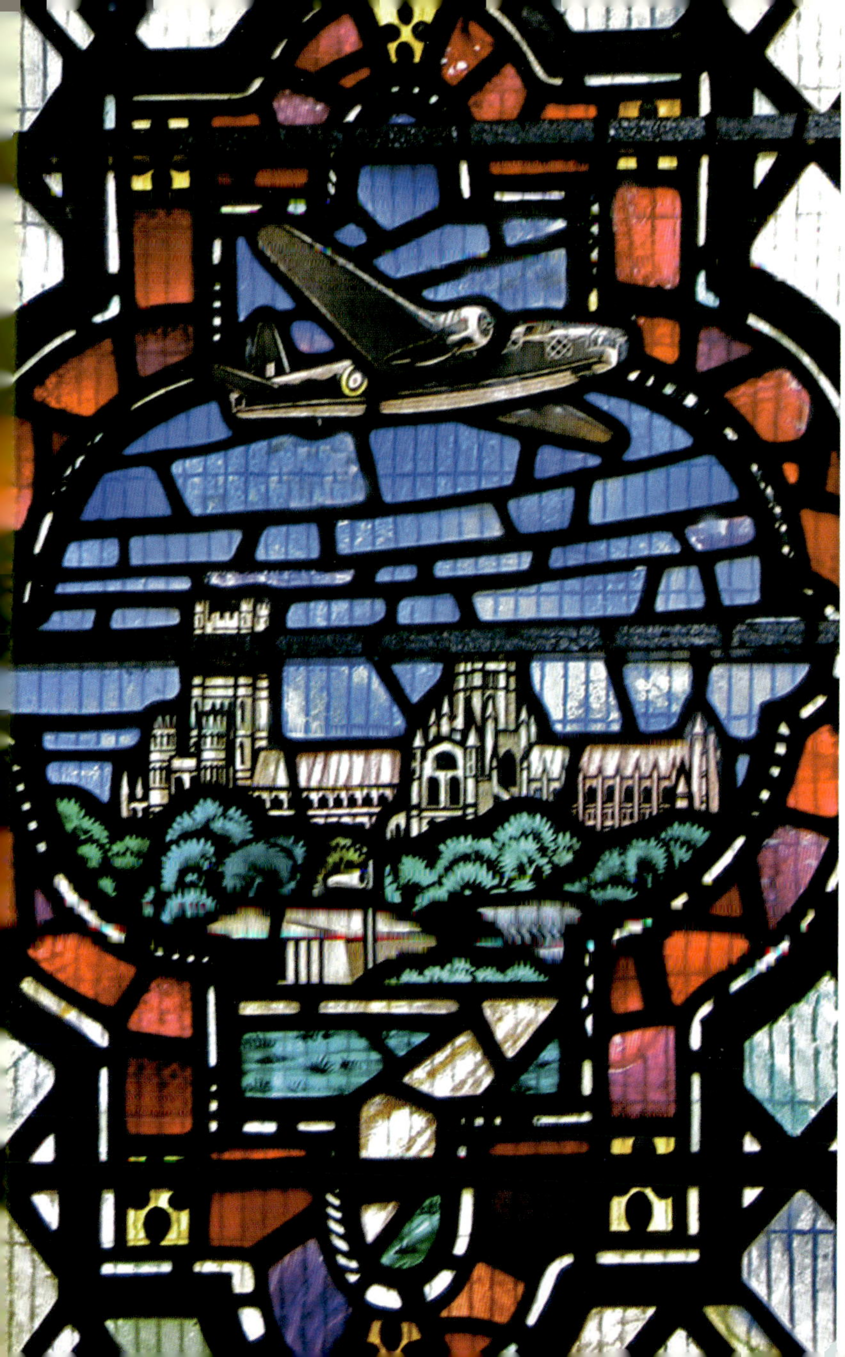

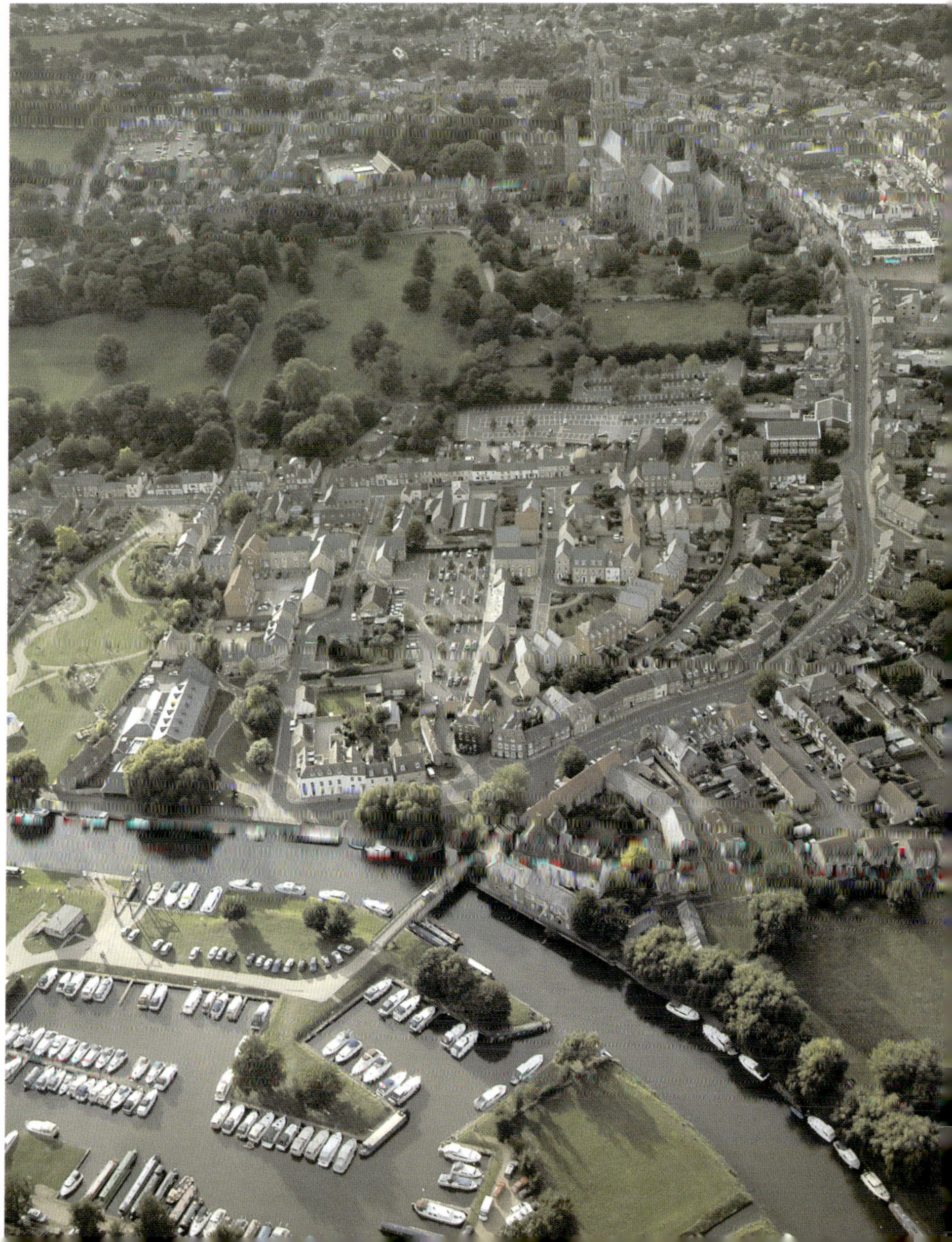

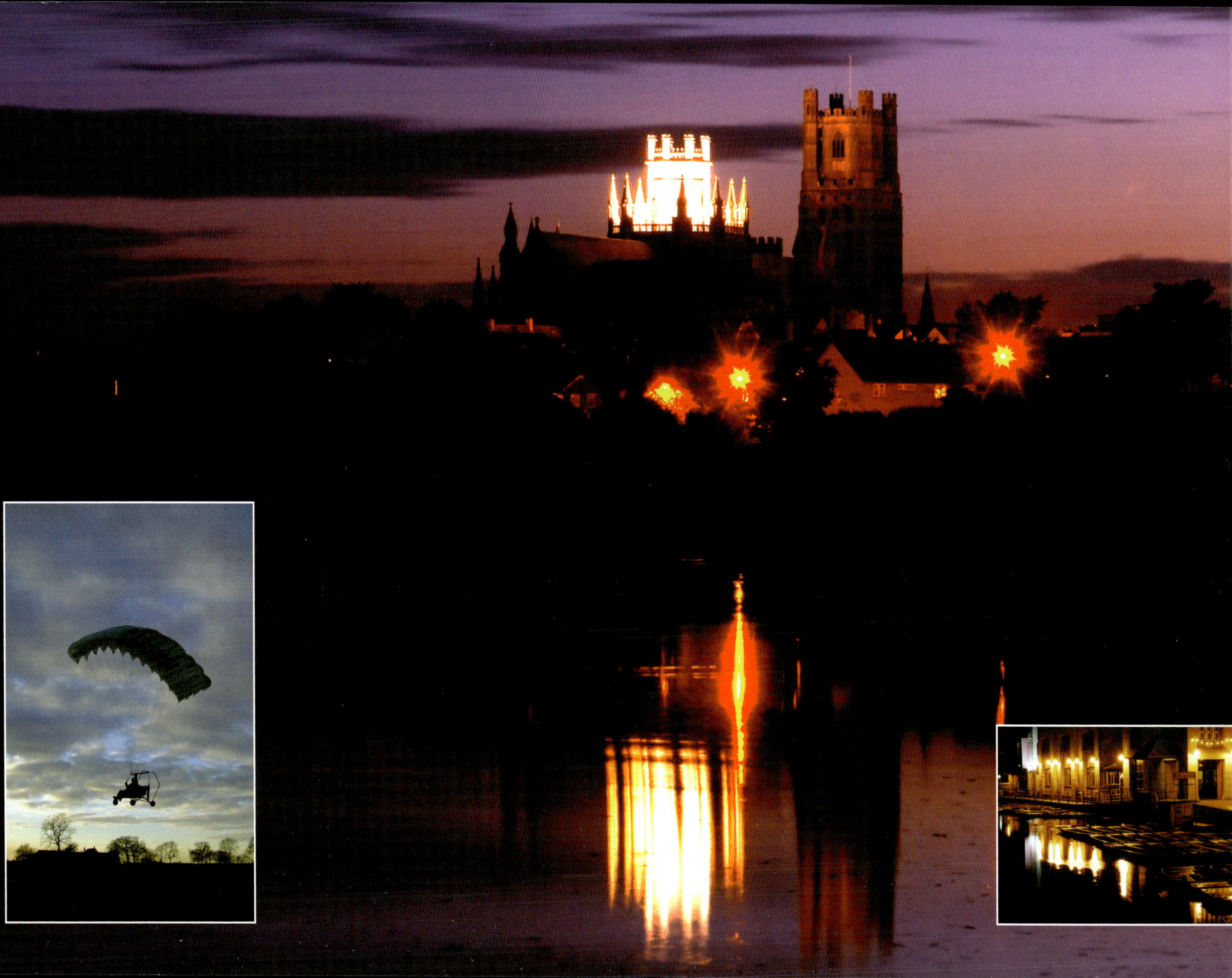

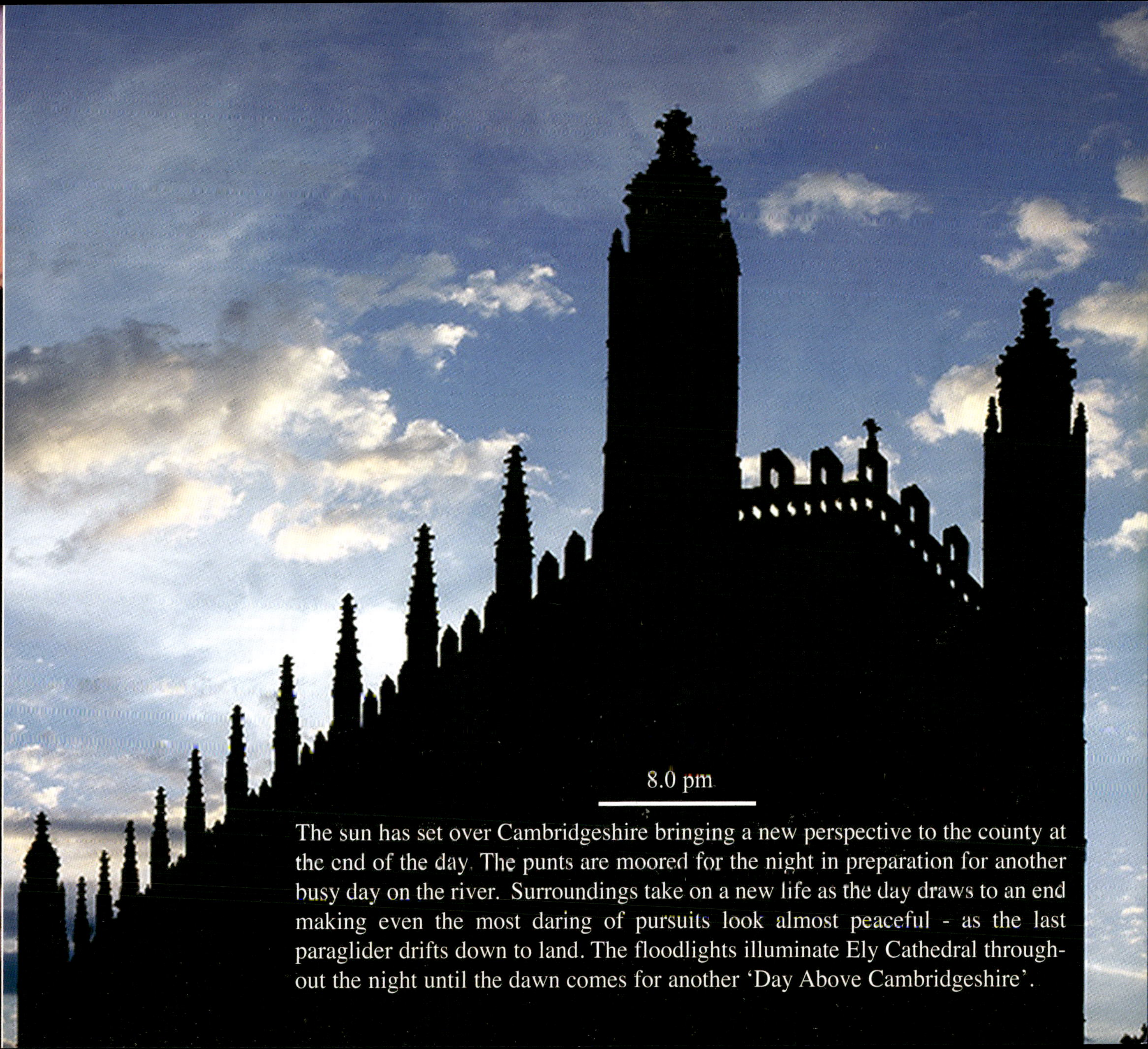

8.0 pm

The sun has set over Cambridgeshire bringing a new perspective to the county at the end of the day. The punts are moored for the night in preparation for another busy day on the river. Surroundings take on a new life as the day draws to an end making even the most daring of pursuits look almost peaceful - as the last paraglider drifts down to land. The floodlights illuminate Ely Cathedral throughout the night until the dawn comes for another 'Day Above Cambridgeshire'.

Many, many people were involved in making a success of this project; first, our thanks to Carolyn Grace who kindly wrote the foreword; Geoff O'Connor, Imperial War Museum (P29, 42, 43, 57, 68, 69) - the RAF photographs are British Crown copyright reproduced by permission of the Controller of Her Britannic Majesty's Stationary Office; thanks to the PR Dept Warner Brothers Inc (P69); thanks to the Oxford University Library (P74) and Studio Editions (P74); thanks to Nene Valley Railway (P31); thanks to Liam McGivern, landlord of the Bell Inn at Stilton who did not hesitate to unwrap a whole stilton; thanks also to Tony Cunnane, Red Arrows and Gordon Bartley of British Aerospace (P28). Thanks to Sarah Attwood, Custodian at King's who not only went the extra mile to help me get my shot of King's but looked after my dog while I did it! Special thanks to members of the First and Third Trinity Boat Club - Charley Bates (P89), Pedro Cunha, Stephen Mertes (P88) and Martin Peck (P84). It was a pleasure to meet and fly with the following aviators; Terry Holloway of Marshalls of Cambridge; the Cambridge Flying Group, Chairman, David Kynaston, Peter Webb & John Gilder (P84 & 85); Mohammed Ali, Patrick Bryan, Jamie Goodwin, Amad Malik, Frank McClurg, Anil Modi & Mike Moore at Peterborough Flying School, Sibson; Aerographics (P76); the balloonist, Alan Lusty; the three ladies, Davina, Hannah & Becky who made a free fall parajump for Cancer Awareness. We enjoyed the company of fellow photographers and artists; Margaret Albaugh (P92); Irene Andrews (P44); Marcus Beard (P17); Nigel Blake (P92 & 94) - see more of his amazing shots at www.nigelblake.co.uk; Robert Bonn (P12); Paul Bury (P39); Tony Crowe; Bruce Darnett (P65); Bob Davis (P47); Mark Edwards (P14); the picture of Paul & Diane Rusher 'flying' down the river on page 38 is courtesy of The Electric Boat Association & Nick Goldring - see www.electric-boats.org.uk; Suzanne Freestone (P82); special thanks to Darren Harbar who went several extra miles (Cover, P2, 12, 18, 24, 26, 32, 36, 64, 75, 77, 79 & 91) see his webpage www.focalplaneimages.co.uk; Mark Heath (P33 & 62); Klaas Heiligenberg (P33); Amy Lloyd (P43); Georgi Mabee (P47); Tony Margiocchi (P22, 57, 86 & 92) - see his website www.bedfordshireimages.co.uk; Tony McGill (P27, 31, 52 & 65) - see more of his photographs on www.flikr.com; John Mulkeen (P23 & 77); Robert Nowell (P29, 51, 45, 93); David Packham (P27); Martin Peck (P84); Robert Phaal (P16); Rob Roy (P93); Dan Smith (P27) - see his website www.ukemergencyaviation.co.uk; Geoff Soden (P52); Andy Taylor (P77); Alan Vaughan (P16); Travis Vinicombe (P55); Ian Wilkinson (P11 & 12); David Wootton (P19, 44, 45, 46, 60 & 66) - see his website www.dw-photography.co.uk. Thanks to Krysia Webb, Mark Butler, Rob Gutteridge, David Hagerty, Lee Holmes, Justin Howell, Alan

Peterborough Flying Club

Helicopter Emergency Landing Pads
County Air Ambulance Trust

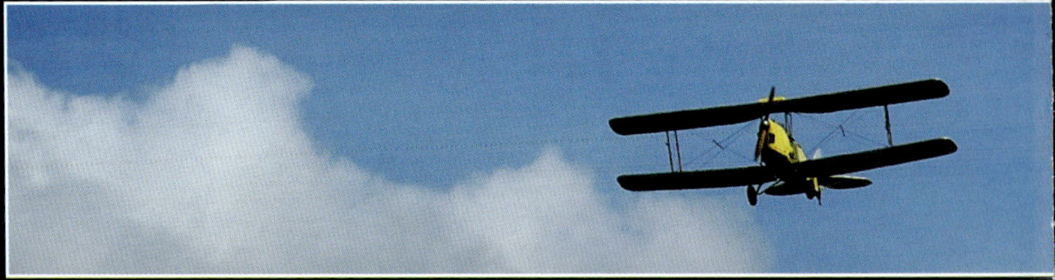

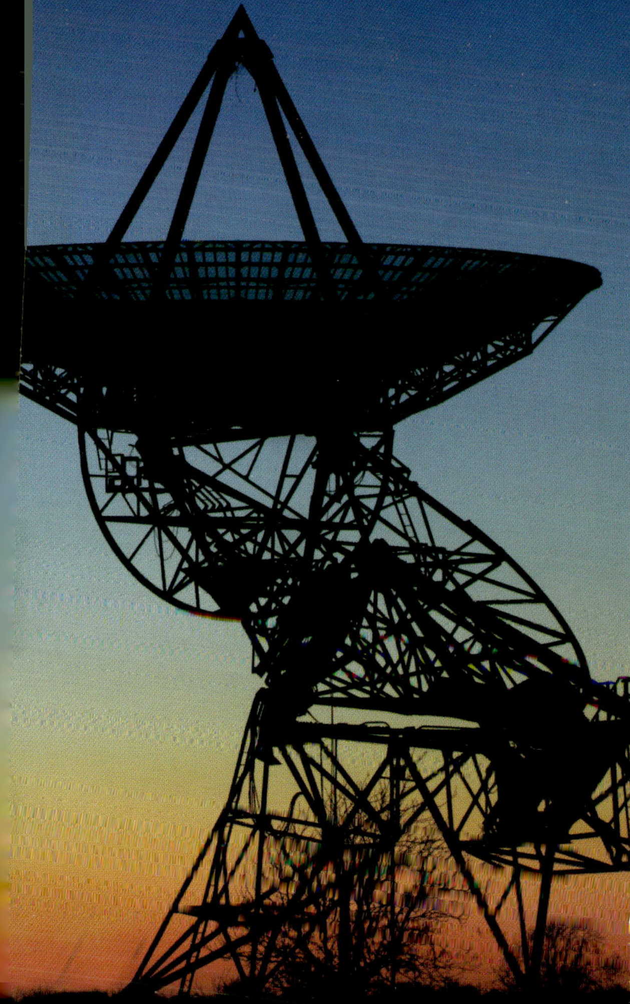

Lever, Kevin Lumb, Michael Marshall, Tom Morse, Martin Reed & Andy Smith, at Gildenburg for their comprehensive support. Thanks to staff at UCP, especially John Bradley, Andy Baxter, Steve Campbell, Adrian Crosnon, Matt Edwards, Michael Fitzpatrick, Rita Gibbard, Liz Knight, Annette Norton, Claire Swales, ever patient security by Derrick Barnes and Jenney Fensome and especially Peter Rook. In turn, it is our pleasure to raise awareness and support the Air Ambulance Service to enable a 24-hour service. The Air Ambulance Services and HELP rely totally on public donations.

Angela Weld, Richard Hall,
Robert Pusey, John J. Nowell,
& William A. Nowell,
University Centre Peterborough,
Broadway Media Centre,

Location Index:

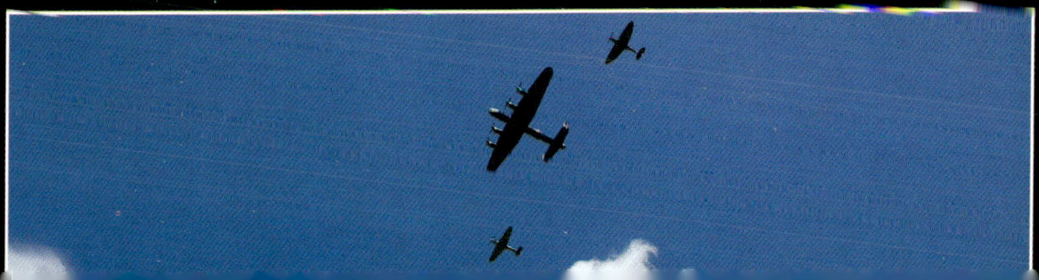

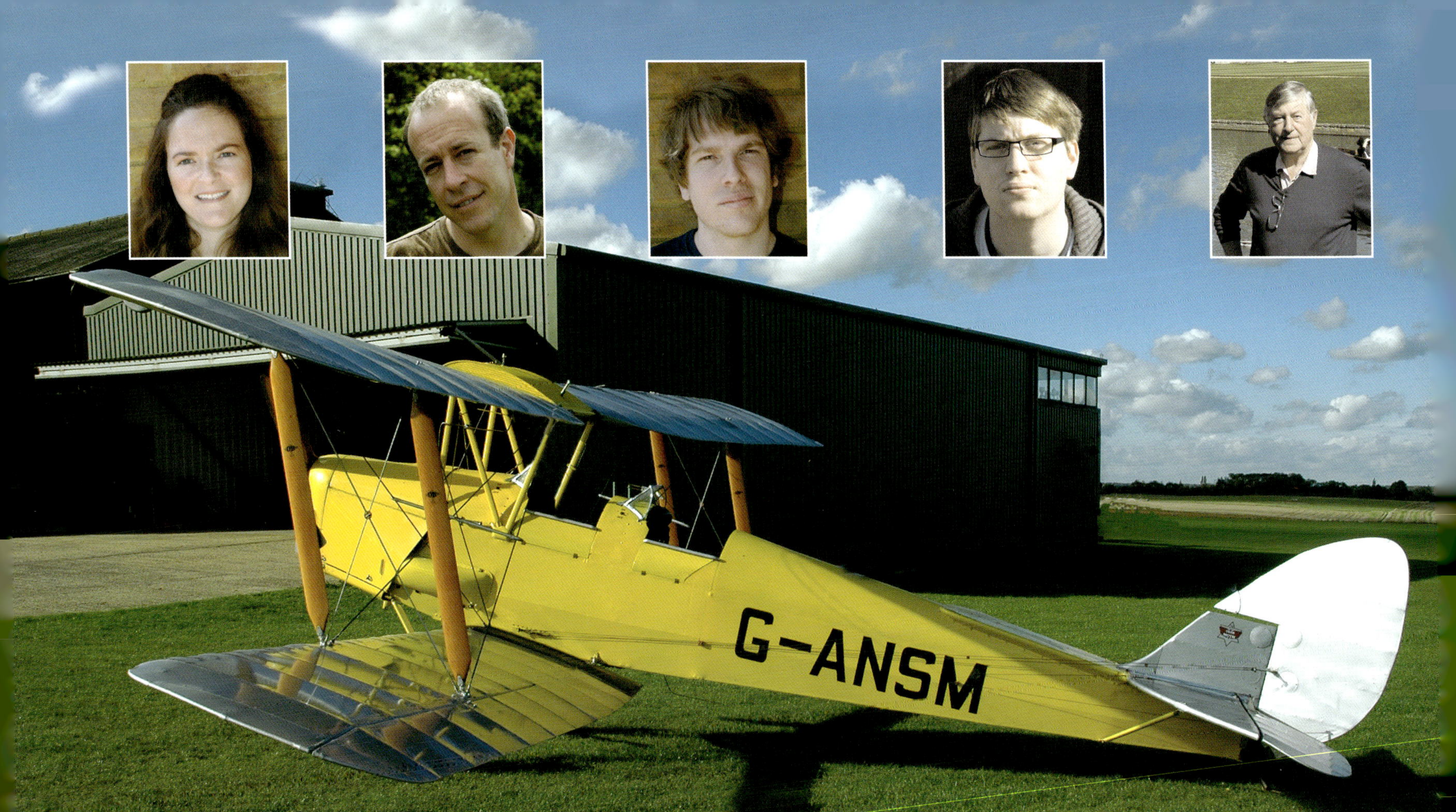

Authors on the wing - shown above an immaculate Tiger Moth, left to right, are Angela Weld, Richard Hall, Robert Pusey, William A. Nowell,& John J. Nowell. All were 3rd year students at the Broadway Media Centre, University Centre Peterborough. This book was produced and published as an assignment of the 'Creative Publishing' part of the course. The students photographed the locations or located suitable photographs from other photographers, researched the text, located sponsors, liaised with many different official bodies, complied the layout using Quark, manipulated the images in Photoshop, made a detailed acknowledgment and location chapter, produced final PDFs which were sent to the printers in Hong Kong. The students then located retail outlets, produced press releases and liaised with newspapers, radio & TV stations - both local, national and international and finally distributed the finished book.